Published by Melbourne Books
Level 9, 100 Collins Street,
Melbourne, VIC 3000
Australia
www.melbournebooks.com.au
info@melbournebooks.com.au

Copyright © Craig Horne 2025

All rights reserved. No part of this publication may be reproduced, stored in a retrieval system, or transmitted in any form or any means electronic, mechanical, photocopying, recording or otherwise without the prior permission of the publishers.

No part of this book may be used or reproduced in any manner for the purpose of training artificial intelligence technologies or systems.

Every attempt has been made to locate the copyright holders for material quoted and images printed in this book. Any person or organisation that may have been overlooked or misattributed may contact the publisher for correction in any future printing.

Title: Full Corset and Stockings: A History of Women's Cricket
Author: Craig Horne
ISBN: 9781922779489
Publisher: David Tenenbaum
Design: Holly Lambert
Editor: Georgia Cooper
Previous Page: Peggy Antonio. Courtesy Bradman Museum Trust collection.

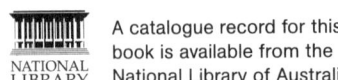

A catalogue record for this book is available from the National Library of Australia

# Full Corset and Stockings
## A History of Women's Cricket

Craig Horne

M
Melbourne Books

We wish to acknowledge the Traditional Custodians of the land on which we write, print and publish, and pay our respects to all Elders past, present and emerging. First Nations peoples should be advised that this publication may contain images and names of people who have passed away.

# Contents

Introduction — 10

01 Nesta Cavill Williams — 14
02 The Origins of Cricket — 25
03 Enclosure and Exclusion — 34
04 Fair Play Old Boy — 42
05 Fashionable Women of Wealth and Taste — 49
06 Rebel Rebel — 59
07 The Marauder Within — 66
08 Australian Class, Misogyny and the Making of a Sporting Colony — 72
09 Bowling Maiden's Over — 81
10 Modernism, Flappers and the Depression — 91
11 1930s, Modernism and the Golden Era of Women's Cricket — 100
12 Women's Cricket and the Media of the 1930s — 108
13 The Dawn of International Women's Cricket — 115
14 Backlash — 132
15 The Cricketing Outliers — 143
16 The Post-War Era in Britain — 157
17 The 1960s and 1970s — 165
18 Women's International Cricket in the 1980s — 176
19 The 1990s — 184
20 The Australian Women's Cricket Team — 195
21 2024/25, An Ashes Clean Sweep — 206

Conclusion — 220

# Foreword

## Belinda Clark, AO.

*Former captain of the Australian national women's cricket team, first woman inducted into the ICC Hall of Fame, Director of the ICC T20 World Cup 2020 Local Organising Committee, founder of the Leadership Playground, and namesake of the Belinda Clark Medal.*

There is something about sporting stories that get beneath your skin. When such stories are told with the intimate perspective that Craig Horne brings to *Full Corset and Stockings*, it soaks deep into your cells.

When I was invited to write a foreword to this book, the title captured my imagination, and I was instantly transported to the beginnings of my cricket career playing in a uniform that was not conducive to athletic feats or the demands of the game. Discovering that Peggy Antonio harboured identical thoughts sixty years earlier brought genuine laughter – and the sobering realisation of how slowly progress can unfold. It was not until 1997 that common sense finally prevailed, and we transitioned to playing in pants.

This book is a fascinating exploration of cricket that extends beyond the field of play. Weaving together the histories of England and Australia, this book examines how societal expectations, progress, wars and political upheavals shaped both the sport and women's lives in both countries. It was fascinating to learn cricket was inclusive, innovative and open to the threat of those wanting to make a quick buck – whether they be entrepreneurs or bookmakers (and that was in the late 1700s!). The parallels to the modern game are evident.

The most compelling aspect of this narrative lies in its celebration of those who dared to challenge convention – including Craig's mum, Nesta Cavill Williams. When underdogs rise, communities unite behind them, and barriers that once seemed insurmountable begin to crumble. There is a long line of women in Australia and England who took it upon themselves to challenge the norms to simply play the game they loved.

The modern game rests on these foundations and these women have become my heroes. Unfortunately, like many of my teammates, I didn't know the full extent of the backstories of our trailblazing sisters. Their names are woven throughout the history of the sport: The Peden-Archdale Medal, The Una Paisley Medal, The Betty Wilson Young Cricketer of the Year, The Ruth Peddey Cup, The Mollie Dive Stand. While their names endure in these honours, their stories of struggle and triumph have remained largely untold.

Thank you Craig for shining a light on these remarkable women and, in doing so, providing a valuable history lesson from the origins of the game to today.

# Foreword

## David Talalla

*Former captain of the Malaysian national cricket team, playing member of the Marylebone Cricket Club, Multicultural Ambassador for Cricket Australia, member of the Women in Sport and Recreation Ministerial Taskforce, and women's cricket coach and mentor.*

I feel privileged to have been asked by Craig to deliver a foreword for this extremely captivating story, inspired by a naturally gifted sports person who was a largely self-taught cricketer ahead of her time. It is not lost on me that Nesta Cavill Williams learnt to play (and came to dominate) cricket in the northwest suburb of Northcote adjacent to Merri Creek – the very creek whose clay has, for many years, been transported to the historical MCG. The very first Test match was played on grounds which, to this day, use Merri Creek clay for its carefully manicured and rolled pitches.

I have coached cricket to young girls and women for many years and am in awesome wonder of how talented they are and their unquenchable thirst to learn this beautiful game. Today, I am one of many coaches tasked with nurturing and developing female talent, whereas the likes of Nesta Williams and Peggy Antonio were afforded limited coaching opportunities. Thankfully, Bert Ironmonger was around in that era to not only coach these gifted women, but also to encourage them to keep playing this beautiful game. Kudos to Nesta's brothers and parents who solidified this encouragement. We still have a long way to go to level the playing field.

I was gobsmacked to read that the first century made by a woman in a cricket match was in 1778! In a match between Maids XI of Surrey v Married Ladies XI of Surrey played at Felley Green on 1 July, Ms S Norcross scored 107 – so much for cricket being a "Gentlemen's Game"! Further, there is record of a ladies' cricket match played in 1747 between the Women of Sussex Hills and Dales in the presence of the Duchess of Richmond and her husband. I read law at the University of Sussex and walked the dales on many an occasion, blissfully unaware of such a momentous event.

Craig has done a sterling job researching the history of women's cricket and capturing the adversity mixed with enjoyment women faced in playing this sport. His book is a fitting tribute to his late mother, is a wonderful and emotional read, and will inspire any budding young cricketer – female or male.

It has given me enormous pleasure to read this story – a mixture encompassing adversity, humility, courage and natural ability. All round, a brilliant read.

# Introduction

# The 2020 T20 Women's World Cup

Enter the Greatest Australian Sporting Team of All Time

I only just made that first ball in Melbourne, early March 2020.

I'm a musician, and had played at a winery that day only to rush back to the Melbourne Cricket Ground once the gig was finished. I was late – I missed Katy Perry's pre-game performance – and only found my seat in the crowd, my wife already waiting there for me, as the first batters walked out.

As I took in the crowd, I nearly burst into tears. The place was packed! The stands were full – a world record of 86,174 smiling, expectant faces – a mixture of home-crowd supporters and Indian families, their young girls proudly wearing the Indian team's blue uniform to watch the T20 World Cup Final – held on International Women's Day, 2020.

Women's cricket had come a long way from its pre-industrial-age origins as an informal pastime, an offshoot of what was a boy's folk game played on village Commons in the southeast of England. Who knew that the game we were about to witness, on this warm March evening, had been shaped by the disparate-though-interrelated forces of the Industrial Revolution, social class and gender politics?

In terms of the latter, up until relatively recently, the very act of women playing "the manly game of cricket" was seen by the enduring patriarchy as an abomination, a burlesque, to be resisted with all prejudice! But there we were – in spite of hundreds of years of gender politics and resistance to seeing women thrive in male-dominant fields – sitting in a stadium packed to the rafters, ready to enjoy what would prove to be a key moment in Australia's sporting history!

And the game could not have been more highly anticipated. The home side had overcome a slow start to the tournament – in fact, the Australian women very nearly didn't make it. The team had lost Ellyse Perry – arguably the greatest all-round cricketer of her generation – to a hamstring injury in a tight match against New Zealand, taking her out of the World Cup. In the "do or die" semi-final clash with South Africa at the Sydney Cricket Ground, it had rained and then rained some more: India and England were due to play their semi earlier in the day at 3pm, but not a ball was bowled. India sailed into the final while England drifted to the airport.

Up next was South Africa and Australia. The first ball was due at 7pm, but it was still raining. Each side needed to face a minimum of 10 overs to constitute a game, and Australia needed to win to progress. It was still raining at 5pm. But then the clouds finally parted, and an inky sun shone on Australia's fortunes.

Thanks to the work of the SCG's ground staff, play finally got underway at 7.25pm – five minutes later, and it would have been game over. Australia achieved a credible 134 off their allotted 20 overs, Meg Lanning's quick-fire 49 a clear highlight. But then dark clouds gathered, and rain began to fall again. There was a breathless hush at the Sydney Cricket Ground that night, with all eyes pointed skyward. Would South Africa bat? Play needed to resume at 9.49pm to allow a minimum of 10 overs to be bowled at the visitors. Miraculously, the rain did stop and play resumed – at 9.41, talk about cutting it fine! – with South Africa needing 98 off their allotted 13 overs. Something to do with the Duckworth-Lewis-Stern formula – I never was any good at maths.

They didn't get there. With rain tumbling down and the visitors needing 19 off the final over, they fell 8 runs short. Australia had beaten both South Africa and the Sydney weather to advance to the T20 World Cup final against India at the MCG.

Three days later and sitting with my wife in the stands, I felt weightless with anticipation. The air went still when Alyssa Healey and Beth Mooney walked out to bat. This was it. Could the Australians overcome their shaky form and defeat the undefeated Indians to retain the T20 World Cup? As Deepti Sharma ran in to bowl the first ball to Alyssa Healy, massed Indian drummers pounded out a Charlie Watts rhythm. An ascending note of expectation accompanied her every stride. Sharma pitched it up, angling the ball into Healy's pads; head over the ball, she drove it hard to the long-on boundary for four. Australia was away. Healy then guided Sharma's fourth ball of the opening over through gully for another four. The roar from Australia's supporters was like Dylan's rolling thunder! But those roars soon tuned to groans when Healy was dropped in the covers in the same over. Beth Mooney was also dropped – a catchable caught and bowled – soon after. Those dropped catches were the moments when the World Cup was both lost by India and won by Australia. I must confess I high-fived my wife at that point. I knew it was Australia's day.

By the end of the power play, Australia were 0 for 49 after the first 6 overs. In the eighth, Healy belted two towering consecutive sixes on her way to a wild 50 in just 30 balls, marking the fastest T20 50 in ICC history – male or female. It was a masterful display of power, courage and elegance mixed with a dollop of good luck. Three more sixes followed before she was caught on 75 off 39 balls. Australia finished their 20 overs at 4/184 with Mooney unbeaten on 78. Cricket is a serious business, but it's also fun – and watching Australia's innings was a great time.

It was now India's turn at the crease. But they were never in it. Megan Schutt's 4/18 and Jess Jonassen's 3/21 were the destroyers. When Ash Gardiner caught a skied slog from Yadav off Schutt on the boundary in the nineteenth it was all over. Pandemonium followed. The dancing was maniacal, the music thumping and the team's singing wildly off-key. Sunday night was turned into a raging Saturday. The Aussie women partied long into the night while my wife and I retired to the bar!

It was Alyssa Healy's master-blaster 75 and Beth Mooney's masterful 78-not-out that delivered the goods. The Australian women's cricket team didn't just claim the T20 World title that night, but also the crown as the greatest sporting team, male or female, in the country's history.

And who would contradict them? The Australian women had won five World T20 Cups, more 50 Over World Cups than all other teams combined, and won all but one of the Ashes series (the 17/18 series was drawn, Australia retained the Ashes courtesy of their 2015 win in England) since 2000.

Melbourne's 2020 T20 World Cup final – the first women's T20 staged as a stand-alone event rather than an accompaniment to the men's game – was a triumph for both the Australian women's cricket team and women's cricket in general. More than 1.2 million Australians tuned in to watched Australia's women cricketers claim the crown, and what those viewers experienced was electric.

But within just a few days, a dark cloud rolled over the MCG, and all fell silent. Melbourne was locked down, first for days, then weeks, then months. Streetlamps illuminated empty waterfront roads while neon signs buzzed unseen messages into a dismantled city. Melbourne retreated to a ghostly stillness as the COVID pandemic covered the globe. There was no jazz or blues, or rhythmical rowdy bars: just Netflix and vivid, electric memories of our victory that night to keep us warm.

# 01

## Nesta Cavill Williams

I remember the day I discovered my mother's secret past quite clearly: I was a child, maybe seven or eight years old. It was 1960, and I was sat on the floor of the laundry in our family's Northcote home. It was the end of the summer school holidays, and a burgeoning quietude had engulfed the suburb and its residents.

Summer is hot in Melbourne, and it was especially hot and wind-blown that day. A scorching breeze scudded across the volcanic basalt plain to the city's northwest, turning the once-green cricket and football ovals in McDonell Park, a block to our south, into a crispy brown wasteland. The park's soil, so sticky and adhesive in winter, had shrivelled and fissured – like a road in an earthquake.

There was not a lot to do in Northcote when temperatures climbed above 100 Fahrenheit. On that particular morning, most sensible families huddled indoors in a state of siege, the hot streets abandoned to those insane enough to venture out. But in our house, it was washing day – no matter that it was stinking hot and the

*Nesta Cavill Williams wearing full corset and stockings at the Sydney Cricket Ground.*

north-westerly brought with it a miasma of yellow dust kicked up from one of the nearby quarries that pockmarked the suburb in those far-off days. It was Monday, and Monday was *always* washing day.

    From the cool of the laundry floor, I watched my mother's brow drip sweat as she plunged a wooden dolly into a steaming copper cauldron and heave hot white sheets from the boiling water. She then fed the sheets into a mangle or ringer – a handle-cranked rolling press that squeezed water from the washed cotton bedlinen. While Mum turned the handle, she asked me to find some of her "blue bags" from the cupboard. These blue bags were marvellous little bundles of powdered ultramarine alkaline. They could ease the sting of a bee or a bull ant – or, when added to the rinse water on washing day, disguise any hint of embarrassing yellow stain on the household linen, making them look whiter than white. On my search through the cupboards, I found the blue bags. But I also found something else.

Something more profound.
I found my mother.

There, in the two cupboards under the cold-water sinks, were cricket trophies; lots of them. Maybe they had been put there recently? Surely, I had opened these cupboards before? But they had my mum's name written on them...

*Why hadn't I seen these before?*

Nesta Williams: batting average Northcote, 37/38. Multiple Nesta Williams bowling trophies for outstanding performances including one for a 4 for 15 in a final against Clarendon. Cups for winning Northcote women's bowling averages for particular seasons, and two mounted cricket balls with shields attached ... Nesta Williams: hat-trick Brunswick, February 5, 1938, and Nesta Williams: hat-trick Collingwood, December 13, 1941. Baseball trophies, mounted baseballs, swimming shields. I was dumbfounded.

I knew my mother was a sportsperson. My uncles talked of her being barred from playing football in the street with their mates – they'd said she could kick like a Carlton fullback and outrun a greyhound. But this was evidence of something more profound, more authoritative than vague stories about a pre-teen tomboy outperforming street kids playing kick-to-kick in St David Street. Mum was an athlete, but this was at a whole other level.

In the full spatial silence of our house, my mother only displayed one trophy on the loungeroom mantlepiece: it was for winning an all-comers swimming contest in the Yarra in 1934. The race splashed off at Deep Rocks swimming hole in Kew, contestants swam a half mile up-stream, turned, and swam back to the swimming hole's bluestone steps. She was sixteen years old, and beat a field of fifty-plus men, women, boys and girls by 100 yards or more.

My uncle Doug always shimmered with amazement when he related that story. From my place at the cupboard, I looked back at my mum – the constant, essential figure of my life – as she stood at the ringer, winding out the bedlinen into cool, blue water. Could this be the same person who swam the Yarra all those years ago? I'd never seen her swim, even on those rare summer occasions when we were at the beach.

*Who was this Nesta Williams?*

"You played cricket, mum!" I exclaimed. "Where ... where are these from?"

"Oh, the trophies!" She replied. "Yes, well, Pop had them at his place, but he

*Northcote Women's Cricket Club, c1934.*

was cleaning out a cupboard, so I took them."

My mother plunged the last of the sheets into the blue rinse water and slowly stirred the whitening linen with the wooden dolly.

"Can we put them in the loungeroom with that other one?" I asked as I placed the trophies around the laundry floor.

"No, no leave them in the cupboard. They'll just be dust gatherers in the loungeroom. Put them all back now, and you can help me hang out these sheets in a minute. I'll call when I need you. Off you go!"

I had so many questions. Why was the 1934 swimming trophy okay to display on the mantel and not the cricket trophies? I had no idea. Did it have something to do with Dawn Fraser – or, as mum called her, "our Dawn"?

Fraser had won the Olympic gold medal for the 100-metre freestyle at the Melbourne Olympic Games in 1956, and was hot favourite to repeat that performance later that year at the Rome Games. Fraser was a national hero, a working-class girl from Balmain who smashed records every time she entered the pool.

Perhaps mum identified with Fraser's success because, in some ways, beating a bunch of men at their own game in a swimming race in 1934 had, like Fraser, sent a ripple of moral disturbance into the conservative, patriarchal pool she inhabited in Melbourne at that time. Fraser broke all the rules and still won. Perhaps Mum wanted to display to the world that she had, in her own way, done the same.

I, of course, knew none of this in 1960: the day-to-day decisions and revisions of a government that spoke for women and not with them, the implications of the dead hand of the patriarchy or the effect of conservatism's rigid, grinding formulations on everyday women, everywhere. I simply wanted to find out more about my mother's sporting life, and knew her trophies and memorabilia would help me unravel the mystery.

I couldn't leave it alone, and within minutes I was back in the hallway in search of the mystery woman who both was and wasn't my mother – Nesta Williams. I knew there was a box of memories in the depths of the closet. To paraphrase TS Eliot, did I dare disturb that universe? I cautiously opened the lid to that box of evenings, mornings, and afternoons long past.

I found photographs. My three uncles wearing their wartime uniforms, my grandfather standing on the front seat of a convertible, one foot on the dash, aiming a rifle. There was a staged portrait of the whole family, mum, her three brothers, Pop and my mother's mother, the grandmother I never knew, Elsie. Then I found chocolate boxes full of letters, more photos of people I didn't recognise, piles of forgotten memorabilia, postcards, souvenirs and tarnished teaspoons. I discovered a clutch of yellowing newspapers, tied with string and stuffed into a large paper bag. I'd unwrap them later.

Then there was a photograph, taken in the studios of H Pullan Cook of High Street, Northcote. The mounted image was of twelve women cricketers, posing with two older women, a very young girl and a handsome bloke sitting in the middle of the second row. My youthful mother wore a cap and cricket whites, and sat on the floor to the left of the fashionably dressed young man, his arms crossed, tie straight, shirt and suit impeccable. The young girl sat cross-legged at the man's feet. I soon found out that the young girl was Una Paisley, destined to play twelve Test matches for her country from the late 1940s into the 1950s, including captaining the women's side against New Zealand in 1956/57.

I looked closer at the mysterious man in the photo, and I realised it was my father! My father, whom I had only ever known as a bald man always dressed in overalls topped off with an old suit coat and a beaten-up Stetson hat. But this was my father alright. The photograph had transformed him into a suavely handsome, fashionable, suit-collar-and-tie-wearing youngish man – with hair!

Full Corset and Stockings   19

*Victorian team 1938/39 (photo Gwen Wilson)*
*Back – Jean Frith, Winnie George, Ruth Tucker, Nester Moon, Myrtle Barnett, Gwen Wilson, Erma Newbecker. Centre Row – Dot Debham (Manageress), Lily Johnson, Peggy Antonio, Ann Palmer, Nell McLarty, Nesta Williams. Front Row – Betty Wilson and Joan Schmidt.*

I found more mounted photographs, and with them more revelations. My mother, perhaps a little younger, sitting second from the left in the front row of a whole new gathering of women cricketers, my father standing in the centre of the back row this time, flanked by four other august men in collars and ties.

I then found the mother lode: a mounted and framed photo of the Victorian Ladies Cricket Team 1938/39 Season. There was my mother, standing extreme right wearing a blazer with a V on her breast pocket. I read some of the names: Peggy Antonio (Captain), Betty Wilson (Vice Captain), Ruth Tucker, Ann Palmer, Jean Frith, Nesta Moon. It was too much to take in. I had to find out more.

I took one of the photos and ran into the laundry, half expecting to be clipped over the ear for snooping in Mum's cupboards. But when I showed her the photograph, she just glanced at it, smiled, and told me it was of the Northcote Women's A Grade cricket team:

"I was sixteen then, so it was at the end of the 1933/34. Your father was the coach."

"Did you win any trophies that year?" I asked.

"No, darling. All that came later."

"So why was Dad your coach?"

"Well, he was the volunteer team coach for a number of years; he was good too, we learned a lot from him. It was your father who encouraged me to go and get some coaching from a fellow named Bert Ironmonger. He was a champion Victorian and Australian slow, left-arm bowler who taught me how to grip the ball for an off break ... twist the ball so the pointer finger is bent at the seam then ... flick it! I found after a while I could get the ball to drift and then, if I could land it right, turn the ball into the pads. I got a lot of LBWs and bowled that way."

Mum had loaded the whitened sheets into the washing basket, and we walked out the back door past the shed to the Hills Hoist in the middle of the back lawn. As she pulled the sheets out of the washing basket and draped them over the hoist's wire, she said:

"Dad wasn't always our coach. You see, the Depression really hit, and your father couldn't coach regularly. He needed to travel for six months of the year so his widowed mum could get a pension."

"What was the Depression?" I asked.

"Oh," she answered. "It was when a lot of people didn't have jobs, thousands of people, like your father. We were so lucky. Your pop, my father, was a postman, so he had a government job and was always in work. But a lot of families relied on charity in Northcote in those days. Better put that photo away now, Craig; come back in a minute and help me hang out the rest of the washing. With this wind, they'll be dry in no time."

It wasn't until I was much older that I finally understood just what a depression meant for poor Melbourne families. The Depression had a horrifying impact on families, particularly in our area:

> *"A headline in the local Leader Newspaper of May 1930 read: Starved, Weak, Haggard and Drawn with a Dying Baby in her Arms, Pitiful Plight of Preston Woman. The journalist wrote: Women in the flower of youth, pinched and drawn through cold, want and hunger, with equally poor and undernourished children, can be seen in these suburbs daily. Too proud to ask, too honest to steal, and yet unable to find work themselves, with husbands unable to find employment..."*[1]

Back in 1960, understanding the ravages of the Depression could wait – I was much more intent on formulating more questions I could drop onto my mother's plate. There were so many things to try and understand.

*Why keep cricket trophies dark and secret in a cupboard? Why keep photos in a box? Why not display them like the trophies and photos Mr Fothergill displayed in the loungeroom of their home two doors down in Swift Street?*

Des Fothergill Senior was the former champion Victorian Football League, Collingwood footballer of the 1930s and 40s. He played in grand finals, was three-time club Best and Fairest winner and jointly voted, with Herb Matthews of South Melbourne, as the Victorian Football League's (VFL) 1940 Brownlow Medallist. Every team had their legend, and for a few years Des Fothergill was Collingwood's – the most feared and successful team in the VFL competition.

When I visited the Fothergill house to play with Des Junior, I loved to look at the photos of those old Collingwood teams, the cups and pennants. Although Mr Fothergill never talked about his playing days, he didn't have to. His trophies were there on display like a Saturday morning movie at the Westgarth Theatre and, like the movies, they told an epic story.

By 1960 Des Fothergill wasn't so heroic. He was a little overweight, drank a bit, loved a punt on the horses, and walked slowly with a limp. His less-than-epic life consisted of loading the *Herald* newspaper onto delivery trucks every afternoon at the *Herald's* Flinders Street offices. But that didn't matter. His life had not been trivial or inconsequential; he had the trophies and the photos to prove it.

But Mum's life wasn't trivial or inconsequential either. She *also* had the trophies that acknowledged her talent, so why hide them away? Why was it okay for Des Fothergill, and not Nesta Horne, to have tangible reminders of recognised past achievements on display?

The answer to that question, as I found out, is complicated.


Over the next few weeks, I asked Mum a lot of those questions. I wanted to know about her cricketing career, how the game was played and organised at that time, and why.

"When did you first play?" I asked.

She told me she started playing at her local club when she was twelve in 1930. She walked into the club just as the Depression hit Australia. But her father was a government man, walking the streets of Collingwood delivering letters, meaning the family was, if not comfortable, then at least reasonably secure. There was no financial barrier holding Mum back from playing cricket, a game she loved.

Her brothers encouraged her. So did my grandma, Elsie: Mum's parents held no objection. Her brothers, their friends and Mum started belting a ball around St David Street, as young kids did in those days. Mum was as good as any of them, even at twelve, so why not play more seriously? A magic lantern was lit.

The Northcote Women's Cricket Club played at a local park a few blocks away from Mum's family home in Clarke Street. With Elsie in tow, Mum precociously arrived at the first practice session of the 1930/31 season ready to play. She was twelve years old.

"When I say 'play'," she told me, "I only practised for that first year or so, I never actually got a game. I was, after all, up against grown women. It was only in my second season that I broke into the team, bowling slow straight breaks. I could land the ball on a spot, but I couldn't spin it at all – that came when I perfected Bert Ironmonger's flick."

My mother's sometime-rival and sometime-Victorian teammate, the great Peggy Antonio, would later confirm to Gideon Haigh in 1992 that she, too, was taught to bowl by the boys around her Port Melbourne home and she was also inspired by the cricketing zeitgeist of the 30s. Peggy – the over-the-wrist, leg-spin slow-bowler that would one day come to be known as "the Girl Grimmett" – a bowler that Haigh declared was so brilliant that male critics debated the possibility of unisex Test matches. But I would learn this much later. Right now, I wanted to tell my school friends what I now knew about my mum.

In the lead-up to the start of the school year, I asked Mum if I could take a trophy or two to school for show and tell on the first day, and she reluctantly agreed. The big day arrived, and I slung a carefully packed bag containing the trophies and a few books across my back and walked with Mum to school. I'd been steeling myself for show and tell, but there was a problem.

I stuttered; I could hardly string two words together. How could I get across to my classmates that my mother was, just like Mr Fothergill, a champion sportsperson?

Mum had nothing to prove to me. She was always a heroic figure in my life, determined to help me overcome my disability. She took me to doctors, to speech therapists, even elocution lessons. Night after night, I would recite my poetic exercises to her. The poetic meter, she was told, would help with my speech.

*Northcote Women's Cricket Team, 1934. Nest Williams second left, front row. Alexander Horne (coach) middle, back row.*

"RRRRobert RRRRRolly rrrrrolled a round rrrrroll, rrrrround!"
And:
"Theophilus Thistle the successful thistle sifter
In sifting a sieve full of unsifted thistles,
Thrust three thousand thistles through the thick of his thumb..."

Mum's persistence on my behalf had little effect – I've never quite overcome the horror of public speaking; the pain of watching faces flush with embarrassment, eyes turned down and the shuffling of chairs.

But on this day, in 1961, I proudly stood in front of the class and, with the help of my teacher, managed to convey the importance of my mother's trophies. Expecting a sudden burst of reflected boyhood notoriety, I was met with disbelief. My classmates simply didn't believe me.

"Girls don't play cricket!" They exclaimed.
"Yyyes!" I retorted. "Look! A hat-trick!"
The teacher read the words etched on the shield attached to the ball.
"Nesta Williams, hat-trick Brunswick—"
The class cut her off.
"Nah! Nah, girls don't play cricket!"
I packed the ball and the trophies away and went back to my desk. I was

humiliated by my classmates, but not shattered. My teacher understood what I was trying to explain to the class. Women *did* play cricket, and my mother was a champion.

My teacher said to me as I sat silently at the back of the room, "You must be very proud of your mother, Craig." And I was. Hugely.

Over the course of my childhood, my mother gave me permission to relinquish that which was beyond my reach. In so doing, she gave me the space and the confidence to excel at that which I could. I didn't need to prove anything to her, and Mum didn't need to display trophies to prove anything to me. But it would have been gratifying if the world knew what I knew: that she was special.

Perhaps they still can.

# 02

# The Origins of Cricket
## A Game You Can Punt On

A document in the Bodleian Library, dated 1344, depicts a grey-habited nun holding a ball while a monk waits a little way off, ready to strike it with what looks like some kind of old-fashion cricket bat. In the background are four fielders. Two are monks, seemingly on leave from their primary duties of contemplation and dispensing political and spiritual advice to secular rulers. The other two fielders are nuns, who are not for the moment distributing alms to the poor, but rather standing with their hands raised waiting for a catch. Alternatively, the nun's raised hands may have been a form of salutation to Edward III, begging him for release from their vows. I jest – there's no question as to their participation in the game. The question we do need to ask is, is this medieval image unique?

There is strong evidence that cricket had its origins as a folk game played in the south-east counties of England from as early as the fifteenth century. It was

*Ladies' Cricket Match, at the Association Ground, Sydney by Edward M Grosse, depicting the second match between the Siroccos (batting) and the Fernleas played on 5 April 1886. Source: Clearing the Boundaries: The Rise of Australian Women's Cricket by Fiona Bollen with Matt Bonser. Bradman Museum, 2020.*

an informal child's pastime, probably derived from bowls and played by boys on village Commons where a "batsman" tried to stop a ball rolling at speed from hitting its target, usually a tree stump. There is also evidence that more formal "cricket matches" were played infrequently between teams of boy cricketers representing rural parishes.

According to the International Cricket Council (ICC), the first reference to cricket being played as an adult sport between delineated teams was in 1611, a year when other important references to the sport were made. However, cricket was still very much in its infancy. There was not a set number of players, no pads and no standard dress code. Players used curved bats, tree stumps acted as wickets, and the bowler released the ball underarm.

By the middle of the seventeenth century, village cricket had become an important adult pastime in the south-east counties, remaining an inclusive, knock-about village game where rules remained erratically localised. Most of us today, as children, have played similar games with localised rules: a ball caught on the full off a wall is out, over the fence is six and out, break a window – well you're just out and gone! But the question is, in the seventeenth century, did both women and men participate in the village game from its beginnings?

It's difficult to know. Putting aside the bowling and fielding nuns of the Bodleian Library painting, women in England (and most other parts of the world) at the time were the legal property of men. Women's lives were governed by work and sacrifice. They would have found it difficult to both negotiate the time and the mandate to play the game. But then again, who knows? That women cooked and cleaned and raised children is no surprise – but it has recently come to light that most village women from the fifteenth century followed the harvest as gleaners and reapers. In addition, they planted vegetables, weeded, threshed, winnowed and thatched. Village women were the first beer brewers; they were sheep shearers and spinners of yarn – and I'm sure that, away from prying male eyes on an isolated moorland, village women loosened their hair and ran in the wind. Some may have emulated their sons and hurled a sphere at another holding a stick who, in turn, tried to hit it.

In those far away times, there were no artists at the ready to record such plebeian activities. But fundamental changes were not too far away – and some of those changes would eventually involve women regularly playing the game.

In the meantime, between 1611 and 1725, fewer than thirty men's cricket matches were played between recognised teams made up of village boys and young men. At these games, booze flowed freely; fighting was common and heavy betting on the outcome almost compulsory. The unsavoury origins of the game may explain its relative obscurity over such a long period. The wider public was only alerted to its existence when it was signalled out for encouraging unseemly behaviours such as Sabbath-breaking, drunkenness and "riotous spectators".

A Puritan pamphlet in 1712 gives a fake-news account of death at the hands of the Devil when four young men at Maiden Head thicket broke the Sabbath by playing a game of wicked cricket! Suddenly, in mid-over, the earth shook and:

> "There arose out of the ground a man in black with a cloven foot ... the devil flew up into the air, in a dark cloud with flashes of fire, and in his room left a very beautiful woman. Robert Yates and Richard Moors hastily stepping up to her ... went to kiss her ... but instantly fell down dead ... The other two, Simon Jackson and George Grantham seeing this tragical sight, ran home to Maiden-Head, where they now lie distracted."[2]

Seems odd that the church would come down so hard on cricket. After all, the favoured spectator sports of the time were bearbaiting, cock-fighting, bareknuckle-fighting and the most popular of all – public hangings. Yes, the grotesque horror of hangings, where the spectacle of thieves, poachers and political reformers "dancing on nothing" drew tens of thousands of eager spectators to watch their fellow citizens die. Cricket as a pastime seems positively benign in comparison.

Away from the prying eyes of the church, men, boys and even women certainly enjoyed a game of bat and ball played on the village Common. But then, in 1745, a year after the publication of the *First Code of Rules* in 1744, two opposing village teams of women cricketers entered a playing field to contest a game – and, in doing so, changed the game forever.

## *The Laws of the Game*

As mentioned, cricket's origins were as a village folk game played with localised, variable rules often in front of a juiced-up, riotous crowd huddled around a betting ring. But such variable rules coupled with wagering could only lead to one thing – violent disagreements between warring spectators. Consequently, many disputes found their way into the courts, especially when the nobility became involved in the sport.

One example of this is in 1719, when a trial was launched at Guildhall before Lord Chief Justice Pratt. The case was between two cricket teams: the Men of Kent – the plaintiffs, and the Men of London – the defendants. The dispute was over a £60 wager on the outcome of a game:

> "*After a long hearing and near 200 pounds expended in the cause, my Lord not understanding the game ordered them to play it again. The outcome of the trial meant it became common for contests to become governed by written contractual agreements ... in order to prevent disputes by clarifying various aspects of play and setting the terms of the wager.*"[3]

It was from such contractual agreements that the generally accepted laws of cricket evolved.

At a gathering of "noblemen and gentlemen" at the Artillery Ground in London in 1744, the first known Laws of Cricket were decided: laws that determined a wicket was made up of two uprights on which sat a crossbar and not a tree stump (a third stump was added in 1788). They also determined that a cricket pitch would be twenty-two yards long, a ball would weigh approximately 5.6 ounces, and an over would consist of four balls.

The 1744 laws decreed that a bowler could be "no-balled" for overstepping the bowling crease and the batter was out if:

> "*If ye wicket is bowled, it's out*
> *If he strikes, treads down, or falls upon, but not over running in striking the wicket, it's out!*
> *A stroke or nip over, or under his bat, or upon his hands, but not arms, if ye ball is held before it hits the ground, though it be hugged to the body, it's out!*
> *If in striking both his feet are over ye popping crease and his wicket is put down, except his bat is down within, it's out! (Johnny Bairstow and the august members of the Marylebone Cricket Club members please take note)*
> *If he runs out of his ground to hinder a catch, it's out!*
> *If a ball is nipped up and he strikes her again, wilfully, before he comes to ye wicket, it's out*
> *If ye players have crossed each other, he that runs for ye wicket and is put down is out. If they have not crossed, he that returns is out!*"[4]

The purpose of codifying and regulating the game had nothing to do with introducing the notion of "fair play". As we will discuss in more detail in following chapters, around the middle of the eighteenth century in the south-east of England, there emerged a select number of formal cricket clubs presided over by members of the British elite. Mirroring broader changes in professions such as medicine and the law, these elite club members saw the need to both regulate and rationalise the game, for less than respectable reasons – cricket's codification made it suitable to be presided over by the wager.

The laws of cricket as written in 1744 have formed the basis for the game up to and including the present day. Those laws allowed a formulated, understandable cricketing prose to inform the game we now know and love – a love currently tainted by endless Sportsbet advertisements both at the ground and on television. Yes, yes we know, sometimes you lose and sometimes … you lose. However, a lot was lost with the introduction of those laws – not least the messy poetry and joyous fun of the village.

The introduction of high-stakes betting meant cricket was played not so much for the sheer pleasure of the game, but often for more commercial reasons. Cricket became a popular vehicle for both investors and entrepreneurs to turn a profit. But this all came at a price: lost innocence. As Bob Dylan once wrote, "*money doesn't talk, it swears*" and nowhere was this change more profoundly felt than in the women's game.

## *From the Village Common to Lord's*

The first recorded women's cricket match was played between two southern English villages in Guilford on July 26, 1745. The *Reading Mercury* reported enthusiastically:

> "*The greatest cricket match that ever was played in the south part of England was on Friday, the twenty-sixth of last month, on Gosden Common, near Guilford, in Surrey, between eleven maids of Bramely and eleven maids of Hambleton, all dressed in white. The Bramley maids had blue ribbons and the Hambleton maids, red ribbons on their heads. The Bramley girls got 119 notches and the Hambleton girls 127. There was of both sexes the greatest number that ever was seen on such an occasion. The girls bowled, battered [sic], ran and catched [sic] as well as most men could do in that game.*"[5]

Presumably, the twenty-two be-ribboned maids had learned the game playing with local boys on the village common.

By the mid-1700s, village women's cricket matches were now if not regular then at least semi-regular events held especially in the counties of Sussex and Surrey. They were popular occasions, with eager spectators flocking to matches where opposing teams of Marrieds and Maids battled it out on the green and expansive southern village cricket ovals of England.

The women's game proved to be a viable alternative to men's cricket and was watched by hundreds, if not thousands of mainly male spectators. There are extensive newspaper accounts of games played between the villages of Upham, Harting, Rogate, Moulsey, Hurst Felley Green and more, all commenting on the standard of play and the raucous behaviour of the crowd. Enter now a gaggle of shady entrepreneurs eager to monetise the women's game's growing popularity.

In July of 1747, women cricketers from three Sussex villages Westdean, Chilgrove and Charlton were invited to play a Hills verses Dales Charlton match at the Honourable Artillery Company Ground. The invite came from George Smith: publican, groundsman and inveterate gambler who saw a profit in organising "grand" cricket matches for high stakes – frequently for £1000 or more. Gambling was a key factor in the game's development and Smith was able to offer such generous prize money because the game had become a formalised sport courtesy of its official codification in 1744. It was, after that time, a sport of known parameters where a spectator could safely punt on the outcome.

The crowd began to gather at the Artillery Company Ground that July afternoon in 1747. With the game's geographical and cultural irregularities now eliminated by a governing code of written laws, Smith and the crowd clearly felt safe to wager significant amounts on the outcome of the match. Smith was still nervous – but he needn't have been.

Small-scale punting was a big factor in formally organised cricket matches from the outset, because charging "gate money" was difficult in rural areas since cricket was mostly played on open common land. So, teams used the proceeds from gambling to fund travel costs, equipment and the afternoon's refreshments.

Smith's decision to play the game at the enclosed Artillery Company Ground and charge the public an entry fee for the match of sixpence came with some risk. But he knew he could minimise the risk if he could cream profits from more high-stakes gambling and from selling food and alcohol to spectators. He also understood the power of celebrity in attracting a crowd.

The Duchess of Richmond was a proto-cricket tragic and was "firmly behind the ladies of Sussex", and her husband the duke was a patron of the game. She was clearly "the lady" who, according to a newspaper report in the *Whitehall Evening Post*, attended the game: "They played very well ... being encouraged by a lady of high rank in the neighbourhood who likes the diversion."[6]

Added to these inducements, the salacious prospect of witnessing young "maids" with ribbons in their hair "bowling, batting, running and catching" coupled with the presence of a fashionable royal and the prospect of good food, rivers of grog and the thrill of the punt, meant George's instincts were proved correct. The game was a hit; spectators turned up in droves.

But it was the formalisation of the game that allowed high-stakes gambling on the outcome of a match that was the real winner. Entrepreneurs now had a successful blueprint for future matches, but things did get out of hand here and there. As is the case now, massive crowds of spectators drinking copious amounts of alcohol on a warm summer afternoon while eager to bet large sums often led to violence. And that's exactly what happened at this game, played in the presence of the Duchess of Richmond and her husband that July day.

The game between the women of the Sussex Hills and Dales had it all: drinking, barracking, pitch invasions, fights; surprisingly, there were no streakers. Nonetheless, women cricketers fled the field in fear of being hurt. Think of the final session of a scorching hot Boxing Day Test in Bay 13 at the Melbourne Cricket Ground: inelegant, but no doubt enjoyable in a twisted kind of way. The riotous game had to be abandoned due to the crowd's outrageous behaviour:

*The Post* reported that the game "could not be played out ... but" was rescheduled for 9am the following morning on the proviso that "the company (crowd) will be so kind as to indulge them in not walking into the ring, which will not only be a great pleasure (to the players) but a general satisfaction to the whole". The article added helpfully: "the women of the Hills of Sussex will be in orange and those of the Dales in blue".[7]

Despite raucous crowds, by the late 1700s women's cricket was flourishing, especially in the rural parts of Britain's south. In 1775, the *Weekly Register* reported the first six-a-side women's game when a team of Single Women defeated a team of Married Women at the Moulsey Hurst ground in Surrey by 17 runs:

*"The women of the village of Bury (in Cambridgeshire) had the confidence to offer to play against any eleven, not only of their own village, but in their own county, for any sum!"*[8]

It was common for women's games to be played for prize money, but more common to play for inducements: a barrel of ale, dinners, cakes, hats, and as was the case of one match, eleven pairs of gloves and pieces of lace. But always, on the sidelines, the bookies did a roaring trade while village women played on.

In 1778, the first recorded century made by a woman occurred in a game between a Maids XI of Surrey and XI Married Ladies of Surrey at Felley Green on July 1. Miss S Norcross scored 107, an innings described by FS Ashley Cooper in 1902 as among the "curiosities of batting."

Newspapers from the day continually described women's village cricket contests as "robust", "colourful", "boisterous" and "rowdy". Clearly not too far from the barracking at Peggy Antonio's Depression-era women's games while playing for Raymond:

*"And the barracking! We had fights break out. Between the men of course!"*

It seems lusty domestics and farming maids from the villages of southern England were having a lot of fun. But the fun was not to last.

# 03

# Enclosure and Exclusion
The Hostile Takeover of Cricket

Towards the end of the eighteenth and the beginning of the nineteenth centuries, British society – and, by extension, the game of cricket – was turned upside down by two related factors: the Industrial Revolution and the Enclosure Movement – the privatisation of once commonly accessed rural land. Both were founded on notions of scientific application of new technologies to the natural world as a means of unlocking untold wealth for those who owned and controlled it. These new technologies were applied devoid of moral, social or aesthetic concerns, where both nature and society were perceived as mechanisms that could be dismantled and reassembled to service production and profit.

One particular scientific invention had a profound social and environmental impact in Britain – in 1769 James Watt, a Glasgow instrument maker, invented the atmospheric steam engine. Watt's machine was adapted to many uses, such as powering railways and shipping, but this reliable and efficient power source was also adapted to power rotary machinery in factories, mills and mines, as well as the threshing machines of the privatised agricultural sector. These were the engines of the Industrial Revolution: machines that facilitated the shift of British society from feudalism to capitalism and, in so doing, changed the nature of work and societal relations irrevocably.

Almost overnight, the steam mill created a new class of people grown rich on the proceeds of the "new social energies" created by the steam engine and the new form of production. While the steam engine made the owners of this new "means of production" extraordinarily wealthy, it simultaneously created a new underclass of people condemned to live and work in a state of penury. A quote from Marx succinctly described the process: "The hand mill gives you society with the feudal lord: the steam mill, society with the industrial capitalist".

In the space of a few decades, Watt's invention destroyed a centuries-old way of life. It drew working populations together in masses around the factories and mills housing the steam-driven weaving machines, creating what we now know as an industrial working class. And it ultimately drove the lusty domestics and farming maids from the villages and cricket fields of southern England into the manufacturing centres of Britain – and, from there, fed into the belly of the machines of the Industrial Revolution.

Scientific advancement was also used as the justification for the privatisation of once commonly accessed lands and the subsequent gradual yet forced dispossession and relocation by landowners of hundreds and thousands of their tenant farmers and families. It was argued that dispossession and subsequent cultural annihilation were the prices to be paid for machine-driven increases in agricultural yield. But it was the dispossessed and only the dispossessed who paid that price. It was to the machines in Manchester, Bristol, Nottingham and London that the grain sowers, the vegetable growers, the reapers, the free thinkers and village cricketers were now chained.


As the social- and community-based linkages that had made cricket such a special pastime dissolved under the new economic system, a strange revolution took place. By the end of the eighteenth century, as steam engines powered Blake's "dark satanic mills" and whole landscapes of people were subjugated to their service, an aristocratic take-over of cricket was well underway.

It was at this moment that cricket shape-shifted from a localised folk game into an organised sport of aristocratic indulgence, participation and patronage. This was cricket's own revolutionary moment. No longer was cricket an inclusive pastime, it was now an exclusive sport administered by men of privilege and power who determined who played cricket and who did not.

At first, those men of privilege, the landowners and aristocrats, sponsored teams of paid "common cricketers" who had honed their skills playing riotous village games. But as the eighteenth century progressed many fine gentlemen patrons wanted to play the game themselves. Most were washouts. Here, we have a growing demarcation between the "amateur cricketing gentlemen", who played for pleasure and the honour of representing his social class, and the skilled "cricket professional", who played for money. It was the professionals who were tasked with the job of winning cricket matches on behalf of their aristocratic employers.

The most profound example of this phenomenon was the Hambledon Cricket Club, where aristocratic patronage and professional cricketers from the disappearing villages coalesced in their cricket teams.[9] Between 1770 and 1790, the club selected teams with as many elite professional cricketers as was socially and politically acceptable. Such a formulae proved very successful. With a total stake of £32,527 wagered in special "challenge matches" by the club's aristocratic patrons during that time, our aristocratic punters managed to win a total of £22,497 – approximately £2.8 million today, which is AU$6 million – largely due to the skill of cricketing professionals.

These cricketing professionals were the remaining local farmers from the villagers of aristocratic estates. While the villages and parishes of England were depopulated by the twin push-and-pull forces of Enclosure and the Industrial Revolution, the "pride and honour of the parishes" stayed behind to work as retained or indentured professional sportspeople.[10] They were given token jobs on the estates of aristocratic cricket patrons such as grooms or the like, but spent the greater parts of the summer months playing in challenge matches sponsored by their employer.

## *Professionalism Enters the Game*

Possibly the first recorded aristocrat-sponsored match was played as early as 1728, probably in Sussex. Thomas Waymark, a local village cricketer, had come to the attention of cricket patron and inveterate gambler the Duke of Richmond. The good duke offered Waymark a job as a groom on his estate with the idea of him playing as much cricket as humanly possible for Hambledon.

On 6 September 1728, Waymark played for the duke's Sussex, Surrey and Hants side against Kent. Waymark is accredited as the first professional cricketer to turn in a match-winning performance on behalf of his aristocratic employer. Waymark "signalized himself by such extraordinary agility and dexterity to the surprise of the spectators, which were some thousands, and it's reckoned he turned the tide of victory which for some years had been on the Kent side."[11] No doubt the duke cleaned up in the betting ring.

Later in the century in 1789, an advertisement was published in London's *Morning Star* newspaper promoting a match played at a ground owned by Thomas Lord in Dorset Square, the home of the recently formed Marylebone Cricket Club (MCC). It was a game played between two teams, eleven players from Hambledon Club and thirteen All England cricketers, both teams representing various members of the English aristocracy. The *Morning Star* advertisement explained that the odds on the side of the Hambledon club were set at six to five, and the stake to be played was set at 1000 guineas. Once again, the match was to be an amusing diversionary entertainment tricked up to satisfy the gentry's insatiable gambling appetite. But it was the emergence of the cricketing professional that made this match notable.

Hambledon won the match largely due to an inspired innings by a twenty-three-year-old farmer William Bedlam, who scored 94. Bedlam was a product of the folk origins of the game, having learned to play in his North Dorset home village of Farnham in the south of England. In time, Bedlam's proficiency with the bat would see him hailed as the leading batsman of his era.

More and more leading village cricketers defied the rural-urban drift of the eighteenth century by being employed on the estates of aristocratic punting patrons. John Marshall, for example – the man who scored the first recorded century – worked as a gardener on the Duke of Dorset's estate. Marshall, Warwick, Bedlam and their fellow indentured professionals mainly worked in menial roles on the estates, turning out to play in major cricket matches, at m'lord's pleasure. It was a life far preferable to that of their fellow displaced villagers, who now worked in the "hum and whirl and click, click clatter, the steam and dust and flying matter of the cotton mills ... of the Industrial Revolution." Of course, the displaced villagers who had enjoyed common-right tenancy of cottage and land for generations now toiled in appalling factories and mills simply because they had no other choice.

Tenants were, by definition, not the owners of property and therefore not entitled to compensation – it mattered not that they'd laboured for hundreds of years on behalf of the landowner. As such, a new form of capitalist property relations emerged that, with a stroke of a pen, legally obliterated traditional elements of English peasant society.

## *The Common, Where Games were Played*

The village common as an institution dated from a time before the Norman conquest of Saxon Britain in 1066. Unlike the British invaders of Australia in 1788, Norman conquerors recognised the Saxons' traditional connection to land and acknowledged the rights of villagers and peasant farmers to access:

> *"Common land for the purpose of grazing, fishing, hunting, peat collection, hay making and the like ... it was not a concession granted by the lord of the manor, but rather it was integral to the world view in which it was taken for granted that a person belonged to the place they came from."*[11]

The feudal system and the village Common were embedded into the very fabric of the English countryside. However, by the middle of the eighteenth century, the Common began to rapidly disappear via a system of privatisation, commonly referred to as the Enclosures. From the middle of the eighteenth century, a suite of newly imposed property laws was passed by land-owning parliamentarians and backed by the full military power of the state. Between 1760 and 1870, one sixth of the area of Britain – some 6.8 million acres – was privatised. The result of this process was a massive redistribution of land from traditional village farmers to the British landowning aristocracy.

Enclosure was justified on the basis of increased yield of farming land through new cultivation methods such as broadacre farming and the application of newly invented mechanised farming machinery. But really it was a giant land grab. Come the mid-nineteenth century, just 363 individuals owned 25% of all British property.[12] These laws effectively destroyed traditional English peasant society, the Common, and with it village cricket.

Deforestation soon followed this redistribution of land. In the first decades of the nineteenth century, forests of mighty oak and elm were being felled and burned across Britain at pace. In the middle of the eighteenth century, around 15% of Britain was covered by woodland – but by the end of the nineteenth century, just 5.2% remained.[13] Poet and political activist Mary Botham Howitt was witness to the destruction on Christmas Day 1801; I paraphrase what she saw and felt:

> *As the last flake of an evening snow storm melted on her windowsill, the house stirred. The morning peace was broken by the call of harness bells shaken by the tramp of horses' hooves. Outside Mary's bedroom window, the foresters were marching through the narrow, winding cold streets of Uttoxeter in Staffordshire to do battle – not with a marauding army, but a wild wood. The battlefield was the nearby sylvan relic of Needwood Chase, a place of snow and mighty oak, lime and hollies, a forest that had emerged from the once frozen tundra and moorland of the British Midlands some twelve thousand years before. On that cold winter's morning, forest shadows seemed to hold their breath knowing the axe brought only death to these ancient trees.*

The process of deforestation of Needwood Chase began in 1800 when a parliamentary act for the enclosure of the woodland was passed. The forest was divided into five wards. As the Christmas morning became the afternoon, an army of foresters swung their axes, which bit deep into the oak trees and unleashed their terrible cries of agony. Those terrible forest screams were heard all over Britain for the next century or more.

In the weeks that followed there was, according to Howitt, "a scene of the most melancholy spoilation. There was a wholesale devastation of small creatures that had lived amongst the forest's broadly growing trees, its thickets and underwood. Birds flew bewildered from their nests as the ancient timber fell before the axe; fires destroyed the luxuriant growth of plants and shrubs."

Apart from the destruction of a remnant Ice Age masterpiece, a way of life was also destroyed for hundreds of villagers – men and women whose families had for centuries relied on accessing the resources of Needwood Chase for their very survival. But now in 1801, all that was washed away by a king-tide of economic rationalism.

Villagers across Britain were faced with the same dilemma: stay in their rural villages as their parents and grandparent had done and eke out a diminished living, or leave their traditional home for the emerging industrial centre of nearby Nottingham.[14]

The case of the first Duke of Southland is also illustrative. Devoid of any moral concerns, the duke at the turn of the nineteenth century assessed his peasant workforce – whole families who for generations had made him wealthy – as impediments to further wealth creation. What came next was brutal. The duke, known as "a leviathan of wealth" by diarist Charles Greville, became Britain's biggest landowner with more than a million acres held in Scotland's Northern Highlands. His million-acre holding had traditionally been portioned into small, mixed farming lots by his thousands of tenants; but much higher rents could be extracted from new tenants who engaged in highly profitable sheep grazing. The new farming method required his traditional tenants to be evicted: Betsy Mackay was the daughter of one of those tenants, and she and her family were evicted from their home in approximately 1807:

> *"Our family was very reluctant to leave and stayed for some time, but the burning party came round and set fire to our house at both ends, reducing to ashes whatever remained within the walls. The people had to escape for their lives, some of them losing all their clothes except what they had on their back. The people were told they could go where they liked, provided they did not encumber the land that was by rights their own. The people were driven away like dogs."*[15]

Betsy and her family, along with thousands of other traditional village tenant families, were stripped of any legal or even moral rights of continued occupation of their homes and their way of life, including access to their life-sustaining common lands now hidden behind hedges and private fencing. Behind those hedges and fences were the fields where once they rolled a ball at speed along the ground towards a boy, man or woman who tried to hit it with a stick.

Betsy joined the army of displaced rural villagers and cricketers on the hard road to find an alternate source of income. She found it in Manchester, tending a steam-driven loom in a newly built factory.

In this period of British history, the foundations of a fundamentally rigid and hugely inequitable class system were made impenetrable.[16] It was the reality of the British class system that Australians saw many decades later: in both the Bodyline series of 1932/33, and the first tour of an English women's cricket team of Australia in 1934/35.

# 04

# Fair Play Old Boy
## Cricket, Cultural Hegemony and the Ruling Class

Those who benefitted most from the Enclosures, the British nobility, were known to embrace *idiosyncratic leisure habits*. Did they not love the thrill of polo; a game played on horseback, a game born from the evolution of a sabre-training drill carried out by the cavalry? Polo was played on the sumptuous private estates of the British elites, where spectators indulged in a cheeky drink, lounged on avant-garde garden furniture and enjoyed a little side wager with friends. So too, for this reason, did the elite love cricket – precisely because it lent itself to lounging, drinking, betting and scheming!

But perhaps there were other, somewhat-more-subtle motives for the aristocracy's embrace of the game.

The phrase "it's just not cricket" came to exemplify "common British notions" of "sportsmanship, healthy exercise and fair play." Such tropes acted as the ideological mortar that fixed the aristocracy to the apex of British society and as the moral leaders of the world. In the words of Dr Thomas Fletcher from Leeds University, cricket was:

> "*offered as an instrumental form of socialisation ... presented as a means to a civilised world, promoting teamwork, obedience to the rules, and respect for 'fair play'... Within the British Empire, cricket was an important national symbol of 'Englishness' and, it was widely believed, cricket helped inculcate many of the qualities fundamental to Victorian gentility which the English perceived as being essential to building strong English character ... it was cricket that emerged, not only as the most prominent sport within the British Empire, but also, as 'the symbol par excellence of imperial solidarity and superiority epitomising a set of consolidatory moral imperatives that both exemplified and explained imperial ambition and achievement' ... Within the colonies cricket's elites, they quite consciously sought to maintain and promote a specific moral code which revolved around white hegemonic masculinity.*"[17]

Cricket became a tool to reinforce a hegemonic social order that gave legitimacy to the aristocracy as the natural, moral leaders of Britain and its Empire. The process began in the eighteenth century and evolved in the face of world-shattering events.

## *Let Them Eat Cake*

In the mid-1700s, a game "between a set of Gamesters headed by his Grace the [Duke] of Richmond on one side and a set headed by Sir William Gage, Bart and Knight of the Bath" on the other, was played at Berry Hill near Arundel in Sussex. The game served as a brilliant propaganda exercise for His Grace and his friend the Bart.

The game was watched by a "vast concourse of people" and once stumps were drawn, "His Grace the Duke of Norfolk gave a splendid ball and entertainment that night at the castle." What the "vast concourse of people" were exposed to was not only a splendid afternoon's entertainment, but also a display of largesse by a pre-eminent noble in a subtle boast of his social status and wealth. Who could resist the subtle PR spin, especially when the game was used as a vehicle for a health promotion?

A report of the sporting activities of His Grace and his friends from the time reinforces the leadership role played by the aristocracy in promoting cricket as a "social good". The *British Journal* explained:

> "His Grace the Duke of Richmond, and several other young Noblemen and Gentlemen, have begun to divert themselves each Morning, at the Play of Cricket in Hyde Park and design to pursue that wholesome Exercise every fair Morning during Spring [sic]."[18]

With cricket's endorsement by the very influential Duke of Richmond, the game became not only fashionable with the British elite – it was now accepted as a healthy, wholesome pastime by the wider British public. Consequently, it's no surprise that the game's popularity skyrocketed. All over London, noblemen could be seen belting a ball around Regency and Hyde Park, while an impromptu cricket game with noble friends on estate grounds with servants as fielders fitted that idiosyncratic bill perfectly. Others chose to sit back, relax and make profits off the players. This, by implication, reinforced deference to their exalted position at the head of British society – or, as Calvinists attest, the noble's wealth and status was clear evidence that God had chosen these men to receive grace, salvation and the right to assert their authority over inferior souls destined for damnation.

Of course, the aristocratic ruling class of Britain had every reason to use every tool available to assert their natural, God-given authority over British society at this time. They were scared to death because just across the channel, thick, blue aristocratic blood ran deep in the gutters of Paris.

## *You Say You Want a Revolution*

"*Liberty or Death!*" was the catchcry of French revolutionaries in 1789. It was a cry for democratic freedom by starved and powerless French commoners against a bloated absolutist monarchy led by Louis XVI.

In January 1793, Louis was executed while his wife, the last Queen of France Marie Antoinette, lost her head later in the same year. Their executions were not just an act of bitter revenge against a hated aristocracy by the new Republic. They were an action by radicals fearing a counterrevolution attempt by French nobles and their bourgeois supporters to restore the nobility to power. It proved just a foretaste of the bloodbath to come. La Terreurr (The Terror) was unleashed by the Revolutionary Council against the former French aristocracy, an action that sent the ruling classes of Europe into a blue funk. Three hundred thousand royalist and their sympathisers were swept up by the new regime and thrown into prison. Of that number, over 17,000 were executed and a further 10,000 died of starvation and disease in prison.[19]

The British aristocracy's fear of a similar revolutionary fever erupting in England was profound, especially given all the recent unrest caused by the Enclosures Act and the Industrial Revolution. At the highest level of British society, decisions were urgently needed to stave-off a French-style British bloodbath. They needed especially to persuade the *hoi polloi* that a hierarchical society, with the aristocracy firmly and unassailably at the top, was the natural order of things ... even to suggest otherwise, they implied, was to shake the very foundations of morality. Cricket, shockingly, played a very big role in that process.[20]

## *Professionalism and Cricket*

In the mid-to-late eighteenth century, professionalism had entered men's cricket – and this change wasn't just about scooping up mountains of money from the bookmakers. It was also about imposing a class hegemony on British society.

In the late 1700s, a game was sponsored by the Earl of Winchelsea and the Hon. Colonel Charles Lennox – both men were instrumental in providing Thomas Lord with the financial backing to acquire his Dorset venue, the first site of the "Home of Cricket" Lord's. The competing teams included aristocrats such as Lord Dunkellin and Viscount Palmerston, father of the Victorian statesman, as well as the renowned patrons of eighteenth-century cricket, the Earl of Tankerville and the Duke of Dorset. Similarly, both teams included talented professional cricketers recruited from across the southern counties to play beside their aristocratic betters.

These were clearly transitional times in the game. With the inclusion of lower-class professionals into competitive competitions, it allowed the belief that classes could play side-by-side on the cricket field – that, somehow, the playing of cricket had ushered in a new form of class consolidation in Britain.

But, of course, the opposite was the case.

To accommodate lower-class professionals into the sport, there needed to be a new form of player etiquette devised by cricket's noble administrators. Without such strict social guidelines, a coarse cricketer from the village may offend, or worse *undermine*, the authority of his aristocratic teammates:

> "The integration (of amateur and professional) was highly structured within the confines of a deferential master-servant relationship. Amateurs were the leaders, the dashing officers of cricket, while the professionals were the foot-soldiers of the game. Consequently ... cricket revealed the way in which the dominant class viewed the social structure. One is presented with an idealised picture of class relations and how the dominant class believed the subordinate class should behave. The cricket authorities of England produced what can only be described as social apartheid."[21]

The mixing of amateur aristocratic players with working-class professionals in English cricket teams was a social experiment that was played out over the next 150 years. The nobility, as in the wider society, always maintained their primacy in all things cricket. As Raghu Bakkapatnam writes:

> "It isn't a surprise that the amateurs were the law-making authority. They held all the key positions on and off the field. Only an amateur would captain the national team or administer the game in governance roles. Further, the amateurs had the luxury of just having to bat and field in convenient positions. They only ever bowled if they 'wanted to'.
> The professionals were relegated to the more tedious aspects of the game. They had to bowl all day, field in difficult positions, coach and practice fielding and even umpire. The only batting they got to do was 'if needed'. The next best chance was if the professional happened to be an exceptionally good bat, he would follow after the weakest amateur in the batting order ..."[22]

## *Class in Cricket: A Persistent Reminder of British Society's 'Natural Social Order'*

Such class distinction within British cricket persisted well into the middle decades of the twentieth century and was most evident in the lead-up to the famous Bodyline series played in Australia in 1932/33.

As Abhishek Mukherjee writes, in the year before the tour Errol Holmes, the amateur captain of Surrey was embarrassed and no doubt offended when Wally Hammond, Britain's leading professional batsman at the time, addressed him by his Christian name. Holmes wondered whether he should report Hammond to the cricket authorities for such an insult! It was the convention of British cricket in Hammond's era that professionals were to refer to their amateur teammates only as 'Sir' or 'Mister.'

Hammond had broken a convention that ran deep in the British psyche.

According to writers such as Srdjan Vucetic, it was an inter-subjective culturally accepted fact that members of the upper class were by definition "exceptional". For most British, the superiority of the British elite was a common-sense notion discursively formulated not only amongst elites, but also vertically between elites and the masses. The basis of British exceptionalism and the rigidity of the British class system can be traced to the philosophies of Herbert Spencer and Charles Darwin. Spencer applied Darwin's theory of evolution to society in a concept we now understand as "Social Darwinism." This is where humanity evolves as part of a natural process of evolutionary progress informed by Darwin's concept of the "survival of the fittest." His theory, when applied to human societies and "races", inevitably led to a natural hierarchy of human beings, with the "fittest" at the apex of human development and the less fit "savage" at the base.[23]

When Hammond referred to his captain by his first name, he broke a deeply held national convention that he must, as an inferior member of Britain's lower orders, offer due deference and respect to those of the superior upper classes. By breaking that convention, Hammond challenged the very basis, not only of Holmes' natural "god-given" authority over him – as expressed by the British class system – but also challenged the very foundations of the natural world.

Such a challenge could not be tolerated. *Well, maybe if you happen to be the greatest opening bat in the country ... But don't do it again!*

Aside from Wally Hammond, most members of the British cricket team at this time understood that amateurs and lower-order professionals never travelled together, did not share a changeroom, bedroom or even eat together – and they always entered the field of play from different gates!

Of course, the captaincy must be in the hands of a "gentleman," because noble birth bestowed leadership. That "gentleman" in 1932 was Douglas Jardine. The aristocratic Jardine wore not his MCC cap out onto the field, but the colourful harlequin cap of his university. The cap was a symbol of his exulted rank in British society; it reminded both his inferior opponents and his amateur and professional teammates of his superiority as both a player and human being. The tens of thousands of English, Indian, South African and Australian spectators also understood that message perfectly.

A "gentleman" visitor to the Oval described society's "natural order" ten years earlier when he wrote in 1924 of his discomfort at witnessing a violation of what amounted to be the laws of nature:

> *"On Monday we had several bad shocks to our sense of the solemnities of cricket ... we saw (Percy) Fender, the Surrey captain lead the 'gentlemen' members of his team to the 'professional's' quarters and bring them out into the field in a body, just for all the world as though they were all flesh and blood. It was a painful site (sic), and many of us closed our eyes rather than look upon it. We felt Bolshevism had invaded our sanctuary at last!"*[24]

It goes without saying, Bolshevism was very much in absence in the English touring team of 1932/33.[25]

It's unsurprising that these rigid class distinctions were also evident in the women's game from the eighteenth century and beyond.

# 05

# Fashionable Women of Wealth and Taste
Pad Up!

Women's cricket in Britain, at least from the eighteenth century until relatively recently, has almost solely been the preserve of wealthy, if not upper-class women. The reason for this is simple – it was only women of wealth and status who had the leisure time, the financial resources and the social licence to play the game. But who were these women, these ladies of fashion and taste, and how did they appropriate women's cricket for themselves?

We know via ballads and pamphlets that in 1677, the Earl of Sussex's wife reported she was growing tired of cricket, one of the amusements she encountered at Dicker, near Herstmonceux. Perhaps her ennui was the result of her status as a spectator rather than as a participant. If so, who could blame her? Perhaps her tedium inspired her to ask an overwhelming question: *why not me? Why should I – a woman of high rank – be dissuaded from playing the game myself?*

In fact, by the mid-1700s, many other upper-class women asked themselves the same question and arrived at the same answer – they would indeed play cricket. But they would not replicate the "gentlemen's game", theirs was a more serene and proper form. It was cricket played as a womanly art.[26]

In 1777 at The Oaks in Surrey, the "enchanting rural retreat" of the Countess of Derby, a game was played between a team of women chosen by the countess and eleven other ladies of "quality and fashion". Popular with Britain's *beau monde*, the countess and her cricket match no doubt had the effect of publicising the game to other members of her rank and standing within the community.

The game was a notable event firstly because it was reported in the *Morning Post* and secondly because of one of its players, Elizabeth Ann Burrell. Besides being a fine cricketer, Miss Burrell, then aged twenty, happened to be stunningly beautiful. The *Post* reported:

> "She got more notches in the first and second innings than any lady in the game and 'Diana-like', created an irresistible impression[27]... specifically on the eighth Duke of Hamilton."

Elizabeth and the duke were married in under six months, transforming Elizabeth Burrell into the Dowager Duchess of Hamilton. Extraordinarily for the time, the marriage didn't last, and Elizabeth divorced the duke, marrying Henry, tenth Earl and first Marquees of Exeter soon after! Apparently, the Diana-like Dowager continued to play cricket well into her forties, no doubt notching up more than her fair share of "runs" along the way.

By the time the Right Honourable Elizabeth Burrell had retired to her draughty country estate to contemplate her distracting cricketing career, the game had undergone significant change in terms of how it was played and the social background of its players.

Perhaps it was the Kardashian-like celebrity of Her Ladyship that encouraged more "ladies of fashion" to arrange regular, structured cricket contests in the enchanting rural retreats of Britain's aristocracy. No doubt many of the "ladies" also hoped to snare an earl or duke for themselves in the process! But whatever the reason, women's cricket thrived amongst the young, female aristocracy, and they had the unbridled support of the third Duke of Dorset.

Writing in the *Ladies & Gentlemen's Magazine* in 1777, he encouraged all his lady friends to ignore those "trifling apologies of men who exclaim with the greatest vehemence ... 'How can the ladies hurt their delicate hands and even bring themselves to blisters, with holding a filthy bat?'" Rather, the third Duke equated the athleticism of women cricketers with British patriotism! He wrote:

> "What is human life but a game of cricket? And if so, why should not the ladies play it as well? ...Let your sex go on and assert their right to every pursuit that does not debase the mind. Go on, and attach yourselves to the athletic, and by that convince your neighbours the French that you despise their washes, their paint and their pomatons – you are determined to convince all of Europe how worthy you are of being considered the wives of plain, generous, and native Englishmen."[28]

With such august endorsement from the fashionable quarters of the British aristocracy, cricket became quite the thing within smart Georgian circles. Whereas once most elite Georgian women spent their time strolling along the serpentine pathways of their Capability Brown designed gardens, now, for some, their downtime had taken an unexpected and no doubt welcome athletic turn.

Rather than a life dominated by menu suggestions for their husband's dinner parties – menus that inevitably consisted of veal, turkey or beef garnished with artichokes and French beans, prepared by their discrete maids and served on Wedgewood plates made by six-year-old children at Charles Darwin's uncle's great pottery in Staffordshire – they practised their bowling action on their rolling green lawns.

Topics of conversation between some women friends also changed. Rather than talk of the weather or their travel plans, they discussed the difficulty of bowling underarm while wearing a hooped skirt and pondered the pros and cons of a more round-arm action.

That dilemma was finally put to bed by Christiana Willes, the daughter of Sarah Snelling and William Willes, wealthy landowners from the manor of Tonford near Canterbury. The story goes that in 1807, twenty-one-year-old Christiana bowled to her brother John, who played for Kent, in the barn of their parents Tonford pile. But bowling the accepted underarm delivery was difficult wearing the full skirt of the period. Legend has it that, in a brilliant piece of lateral thinking, Christiana adopted a more round-arm action to literally get around the problem. Over time and with practise, she eventually delivered the ball with the high-handed overarm action we all know today.

Her brother John immediately saw the potential of his sister's bowling innovation and adopted the round-arm style himself. But legend has it that when he bowled overarm in a game playing for Kent, he was immediately no-balled ... at which point he stormed from the ground, jumped on his horse and rode off into the sunset, never to play for Kent again

However, in a classic case of cultural, or perhaps gendered appropriation, John Willes' tombstone reads "John Willes, Kentish squire and sports patron, the first to introduce round-arm bowling in cricket".[29]

And so, some thirty to forty years after Elizabeth Ann Burrell made such an impression on the eighth Duke of Hamilton, women's cricket was now a respectable and highly saleable pastime to a certain fashionable, moneyed element of British public. Shady entrepreneurs such as George Smith continued to organise the occasional representative exhibition match at whatever venue could accommodate the cricketers and their eager spectators – and, just as men became professional cricketers under these circumstances of patronage and profit, so too did women.

## *The Professionals*

As with the men's game, in the latter part of the eighteenth century into the early nineteenth, one or two talented local village women were frequently recruited to play alongside "ladies of high rank" at cricket matches in order to inject a certain amount of professionalism into the games. But they entered such teams knowing they needed to follow all the class conventions – as we have discussed in the men's game. They were to play blue-blooded matches on the beautiful grounds of some of the statelier homes of England – but their *entre* into the halls of privilege came at a cost. As "village rustics", they were to bat, field and bowl at the pleasure of their noble lady teammates.

In 1811, an inter-county women's cricket match was played between the women of Surrey "wearing colours of blue surrounded by orange", and Hampshire "wearing colours of true blue pinned to their bonnets". The game, played for 500 guineas in prize money, was a three-day fixture at the back of Newington Green near Bell's Pond in Middlesex. Judging by newspaper reports, the standard of play was excellent despite the match being played late in the season – possibly because of the familiar reason that men used the ground throughout the summer – and punctuated with multiple rain interruptions.

The match was particularly notable because it was a civil affair "watched by an assembly of elegant persons." Clearly the boozy rowdies and the bookie spivs were no longer welcome – but their absence didn't dissuade the crowd from a "triumphant march to the Angel at Islington for a 'handsome entertainment'." Women's cricket, just like the men's, had evolved.[30] The game was now a welcome addition to the social calendars of most fashionable women of standing. Perhaps it was a little daring – young women bouncing around a field, an arousing flash of ankle. But most of all, cricket was a perfect vehicle for a distinctive social and cultural exchange between women of an independent mind.

And there was much to discuss.

Following the bloodbath of the French Revolution, Napoleon Bonaparte was eventually installed to power. His driving passion was the military expansion of the French dominion. As he swept through Italy, Austria and Egypt – the latter a tactic to strike at a primary source of British wealth by controlling the shipping route to India – the British panicked. The Quaker poet Mary Botham Howitt was not immune.

In the leadup to the decisive battle of Waterloo in 1815, Mary remembered in her autobiography her parents talking "together of the war, of fearful battles, the increasing price of food, the distress of the poor, the increase of the army, of the jails being filled with young men – Friends (Quakers) who were resolutely determined not to serve in the army. The hatred and bitterness against the French that rose up in our young hearts I cannot describe. We were frightened out of our wits at the prospect of an invasion."[31] Perhaps cricket served as a distraction to the rising fear of French invasion amongst the British establishment.

Formal women's cricket matches were becoming more frequent. When they were staged, they were well attended, especially by ladies eager to forget the ruin that was France and the dry, sterile thunder that rolled across the British countryside courtesy of Enclosure and the Industrial Revolution, and simply relax and have some fun. It's no surprise that, especially in the affluent southern counties of England, women's cricket was hugely popular.

The *British Newspaper Archive* reported a match described by the *Sherborne Mercury* where "nine married ladies" and "nine single ladies" played at Pickle Post, in the New Forest – a game the married ladies won by 1 run. The paper reported that: "The single ladies played with a great deal of spirit, but the matrons were one too many for them. One of the young ladies with a sigh said, 'Ah, I wish I were married, for then I should have won.'"[32]

As the *Archive* reported, the custom of married women versus single women cricket matches was widespread in Britain at this time. A July 1860 report in the *Morning Advertiser* reports the annual cricket match "between eleven single and eleven married ladies of Littlehampton," Sussex:

> "The annual cricket match, between 11 single and 11 married ladies of Littlehampton, was played on Monday last, in a field adjoining Mr Henly's Hotel on the beach, and attracted a large concourse of persons. On the present occasion the game was in favour of the married, as last year it was won by the single ladies. Miss Glover, of the above hotel, provided tea, &c. for the party, and after the match, the lads and lasses danced on the green to an excellent quadrille band provided for the occasion, and the remainder of the evening was spent right merrily."[33]

Inevitably, in the tight, patriarchal world of elite Victorian British society, women of means and an independence of mind were eager to search out a more formalised island of social relief. This came with the establishment of women's-only cricket clubs, where they could relax and play a game they loved away from the male gaze.

The first women's cricket club was the White Heather Club formed in 1887 by an assembly of cricket-loving aristocratic women from Yorkshire. The club proved to be a turning point in the evolution of the women's game.

> "The club flourished, in three years its membership had risen to fifty. Its players were all of independent means and most were of aristocratic birth.

*Founding members Lady Idina Nevill and her sister Lady Henry Nevill, of Eridge, became respectively Countess Brassey and Lady Abergavenny.*[34]

One of White Heather's most notable players was Lucy Risdale, a fine batter and wife of the wealthy industrialist, British statesman and conservative Prime Minister Stanley Baldwin. Lucy said of her engagement and subsequent marriage to Baldwin that she overcame a crippling apprehension when going out to bat: "When I became engaged to Mr Baldwin, I lost all my nervousness and it was in the year I was married that I made my best batting average, 62 runs for the season."[35]

Apparently, her devotion to cricket never wavered, and she did not miss a varsity match between Eton and Harrow for forty years: "She always occupied the same seat in the stand at Lord's immediately under the figure of Father Time."[36]

At this time, the exclusivity of ladies' cricket remained largely intact. But, towards the end of the nineteenth century, the aristocratic administers of the game saw the need to increase the size of the player pool – enter the nouveau riche!

In the latter years of the nineteenth century, an attempt was made to reach out to middle-class, private-school-educated women cricketers to broaden the appeal of the game. Adventurous ladies from the families of the emerging industrial class were invited to ignore "the impertinent interrogatories of silly cox-combs, or the dreadful apprehensions of demi-men and join other sporting ladies of high rank on the cricket field of dreams ... and engage" – to again quote the third Duke of Dorset – "in an athletic that gave every right to pursue that which does not debase the mind."

"Girls from wealthy families ... had the chance to play at the new girls' public schools like Roedean and St Leonards." However, cricket's bawdy village origins still hung like a putrid miasma around the game: "other schools banned the sport for being 'unladylike'."[37]

In the final decade of the nineteenth century, women's cricket had become so popular it was further professionalised via a scheme dreamed up by a gaggle of shonky entrepreneurs. Netta Rheinberg reports that a prospectus was issued and published in the leading periodicals of the day. It read:

*"With the object of providing the suitability of the National Game as a pastime for the fair sex in preference to lawn Tennis and other less scientific games, the English Cricket and Athletic Association Ltd. have organised two complete elevens of female players under the title The*

*Original English Lady Cricketers (OELC)."*³⁸

The OELC was formed as a commercial enterprise. The promoters recruited talented women cricketers from the middle classes. They were to be players "elegantly and appropriately attired", trained by professional male county cricketers and well paid. They were to be chaperoned at all times while they toured up and down the country. Almost from the very first game, the idea of an all-women's professional cricket proved to be a success.

The two teams – Red XI and Blue XI – played in front of enthusiastic crowds of 15,000 and more at any one time. But crowd numbers alone don't explain the success of the enterprise – they were, in their own way, groundbreaking.

> *"Exhibition matches were played on almost every county ground in England ... and OELC were (possibly) the first cricketers to play cricket at Headingly ... as the turf was still being laid when the two teams entered the ground."*³⁹

A press report of an OELC game about to be played in London commented:

> *London will have the opportunity during the next few days of seeing how the much discussed professional lady cricketers play the game into which, up to the present year, the sex only entered on a kind of sufferance ... apparently the cricket played was of a fair standard, decorous and dignified ... the women were well coached, bowled overarm and although the press, came to scoff they remained to praise ..."*⁴⁰

The professional lady tours lasted for two years, with the promise of an exhibition series played in Australia. But the parents of players refused to give permission for their young ladies to embark on such an arduous journey, despite the promised presence of a matron or manager.

Of course, the good times couldn't last. During the second year of the OELC enterprise it was suddenly disbanded – apparently the managers had absconded with the profits! Perhaps the whole enterprise was a stunt set up to extract a quick profit from a curious public. Whatever the motivation of the OELC, it managed to expose to the British public a brand of women's cricket that was both skilful and entertaining.

Throughout the nineteenth century in Britain, a minority of independent, middle-class and upper-class women with leisure time and financial means at their disposal came to share in the male Victorian "sporting revolution" by playing cricket as well as hockey, lacrosse, lawn tennis and golf. This came about largely because of the enlightened policies of a select number of elite private girls' schools.

Raf Nicholson quotes Kathleen McCrone's seminal work *Sport and the Physical Emancipation of English Women*, a work that examined Britain's elite private education system and highlighted the activities of the minority of girls who participated in cricket at girls' public schools and the new women's Oxbridge colleges. She quotes McCrone:

> "The Victorian pioneers of women's education strongly believed that sporting activities should be part of female education as well as male. Following the Schools Enquiry Commission of 1867-8, schools for middle-class girls rapidly increased in number; these included public boarding and day schools modelled on their male predecessors, which offered a wide variety of games and gymnastics, aiming to provide the same opportunities for academic and physical development as were available at the male public schools. The schools of the Girls Public Day School Trust (GPDST), founded in 1872 to provide daughters of professional men with a reasonably priced education, also introduced games."[41]

There was one proviso in all of this: yes, girls at some schools may have been encouraged to participate in sports such as gymnastics, but largely because other sports such as cricket or football were seen as an encroachment on the manly domain. More importantly, vigorous sports such as cricket were seen as detrimental to a woman's reproductive health and harmful to the maintenance of a delicate appearance.

Of course, no sporting and athletic advantages were available to working-class girls of the nineteenth century, simply because schools did not exist for them to attend. Nicholson writes:

> "Meantime working-class girls didn't go to school, worked in factories or farms from the time they could walk and had neither the time, the resources or the opportunity to play sports of any kind, especially cricket!"[42]

In nineteenth-century Britain, some young women were groomed for reflected greatness as consorts of powerful, wealthy men, while a larger cohort were destined for the factory or the street. It was simply a matter of birth – intelligence and ability had nothing to do with it. Nineteenth-century Britain was the antithesis of a meritocracy, and an accident of birth dictated a girl's "life chances" – their ability to not only reach her full potential as a woman, but also gain agency over her life. If, for a century and a half in Britain, women's cricket was offered exclusively at a select number of elite private girls' schools, it stands to reason that the talent pool was very limited. This meant the development of the women's game was positively glacial as it moved into the twentieth century.

Of course, another factor in the game's arrested development was the social violence throughout Britain in the late eighteenth and early nineteenth centuries which not only destroyed self-governing, traditional village life, but upended hundreds of years of British tradition and indirectly led to the founding of Australia.

## 06

## Rebel Rebel

Any man walking through the British Midlands at the dawn of the industrial age, historian EP Thompson wrote, might have come across a flaring, steam-driven mill spewing smoke and effluent onto what was once a rolling pastoral Common where, for generations, the livestock of local peasant villagers grazed undisturbed. In his wanderings, our tourist might have encountered a new class of man arising out of this changed landscape – the nouveau wealthy mill owner – whose riches were made from that which despoils "Nature." Stopping for rest in the moorland town of Uppermill north of Manchester, our traveller might have picked up a book of poems by William Wordsworth and read his sonnet *The World is Too Much With*, a poem lamenting the era's absorption in materialism and isolation from the natural, creative world. This may have caused our traveller to reflect on what he had seen and caused him concern. Entering the recent manufacturing centre of Manchester, our traveller may have come upon another totally unfamiliar class of men and women within whose aggregate contained something portentous and fearful – the world's first proletarians.[43]

These new proletarians were, just a few years before, occupiers of common-right cottages, gathered together in villages scattered across a rural landscape. But now, these massed human novelties were transformed by the steam mill into a manufacturing population living on starvation wages in overcrowded hovels on streets deep in sewerage. There was now little opportunity or inclination in these broken places to do anything other than go to work and then blow their brains out on gin.

Some resisted the new world order, inspired by political writers – such as Thomas Paine, a Quaker corset maker, excise officer and political philosopher from Thetford in Norfolk. Others from the newly formed working class looked to the French Revolution of 1787–99 across the Channel for inspiration. Both responses led directly to the founding and the character of Britain's new colony, the island continent of Australia – where political and half-starved resisters were exiled. Did Britain's once-village cricketers play according to the rules of the new age once transported Down Under?

Thomas Paine's most famous and influential book, *The Rights of Man*,[44] inspired a whole suite of radical agitation in the late eighteenth and early nineteenth centuries, especially the Chartists – a radical working-class movement dedicated to breaking the hold of "the corrupt models of the old world." They campaigned for parliamentary democracy and supported universal male suffrage as a way to break the aristocracy's control of parliament. Paine's work also inspired Irish rebels to fight for independence, and rioters to agitate across Britain in the cause of parliamentary reform – and it was Paine's incendiary polemic that galvanised the guerrilla weaver collectives of machine breakers and mill burners – the Luddites – to become the most radical working-class movement the country had ever seen.

Luddites were a violent reaction to the giant "satanic" machines of the Industrial Revolution and were a precursor to the formation of the trade union movement across the industrialised world. Luddite bands armed themselves with muskets, pistols and axes, and targeted those businesses harbouring the hated new wide-frame machines. A correspondent for the *Leeds Mercury* wrote: "the insurrection state which the country has been reduced for the last month has no parallel in history", adding, however, that they "broke only the frames of such as have reduced the price of men's wages, those who have not lowered their price, have their frames untouched."[45]

What did the authorities do in the face of what seemed to be a rising tide of radical resistance flooding through Britain? They responded with the two weapons the state had at its disposal: military force and draconic law designed to avenge a sense of disturbed social order. For example, the military, under the direction of parliament, was employed to brutally suppress any squeak of dissent by the masses. One brutal example occurred at Peterloo in Manchester.

Following the defeat of Napoleon at Waterloo by Wellington in 1814, England was plunged into a severe economic depression. The war had been good for business – armies needed uniforms and ordinance, while the navy needed ships. Wages were high and so were food prices. But with Napoleon's defeat, demand for military material dried up, unemployment exploded, wages were slashed, and people were desperate.

Subsequently, parliament passed legislation known as the Corn Laws – legislation designed by the property-owning parliamentarians to maintain the price of corn, wheat, barley and oats and therefore farming profits. For the starving people of Britain's north, the Corn Laws were the last straw – all hell broke loose. It all culminated at Peterloo in central Manchester when tens of thousands of desperate men, women and children marched in protest in 1819.

Fearing a Jacobean uprising, the protestors were met by an armed militia made up of manufacturers, merchants, publicans and shopkeepers supported by a regiment of mounted Hussars. It was a simple case of class warfare, a bloody repressive gesture to keep down the lower orders. Protesters were cut down with swords or run through with sabres while women and children were trampled under horses. In all, eleven people died and over 500 men, women and children were injured – many severely. But this was just one of many famous incidents at this time as working-class unrest swept across Britain.

## *Cricket, Riot and the New Industrial Age*

EP Thompson refers to this era as the Apollyon time – referencing a figure in Christian apocalyptic theory associated with destruction. The forces of unfettered enclosure and industrial capitalism unleashed events of riotous dissent throughout the country. Even the green and pleasant cricket fields of the nobility were not immune to the violence of the age.[46]

A number of years before the Peterloo uprising, at a cricket match sponsored by the Duke of Richmond, his team was "greatly insulted by the mob, some of the men having the shirts tore off their backs" while at a match between Kent. At an All-England side some years later "there was great disorder throughout the contest ... it was with difficulty the match was played out."[47]

It was as though "the thieves and rioters of working-class England" had infected the behaviour of gentlemen cricket spectators – a disease compounded by the scourge of commercialism.

The George Smith model of "Great Matches" played in London a century before – often in front of large crowds and for high stakes – was becoming the norm. In fact, by the 1820s, cricket had emerged from its heartland in England's south-eastern counties to convert the denizens of "Satan's strongholds" – the harlots, thieves, Luddites and rioters of the expanding urban industrial regions of Britain's north and Midlands. Well, perhaps not the rioting Luddites ... maybe more the nouveau riche, the industrialists, the petit bourgeois shopkeepers and the engineers, all of whom loved a punt.

Rob Light writes that an estimated crowd of 20,000 watched Sheffield play Nottingham for 200 guineas in prize money at Darnall Sheffield in 1824. The Nottingham team was assembled by entrepreneur George Clarke, who recognised the financial opportunity presented by the popularity of cricket amongst the emerging industrial middle class. Not only could Clarke turn a profit by charging an entry fee to games, he also reaped a large take from the proceeds of gambling. Like their aristocratic betters, the emerging industrial capital class loved a punt. But attending the cricket also presented an opportunity to network.

As the gentry and new industrial elites poured into the grounds at Darnell for the All-England game, they no doubt muttered to each other about the heinous threat posed by the activities of political reformers, "illegal" unionists, the thousands of unemployed miners and demonstrators fouling the streets of Nottingham and nearby Manchester. The Sheffield capitalist model of "professional-centred commercial cricket" greatly appealed to the emerging industrial leviathans of the British Midlands. Capitalism and sport were a potent societal force making Clarke a wealthy man.

He was now able to open a commercial cricket ground at Trent Bridge in Nottingham in 1843, where he took the commercial model for cricket one step further. Tapping into the commercial zeitgeist of the age, he assembled an elite, All-England Eleven and toured the team throughout the British Isles in 1846.

*"It's Clarke's All England team that is widely recognised to have played a pivotal role as cricket became a sport of truly national dimensions ... which (later) stimulated the game's growth overseas..."*[48]

Clarke's challenge matches and his professional-centred commercial model transported cricket's popular traditions, forged in the villages of rural England over centuries, into new urban industrial centres of Britain.

It is this commercial model that later found expression with the development of league cricket; traditionally a semi-professional form of the game centred on local clubs mainly drawn from small-to-medium-sized mill towns of the Midlands. It could also be argued that Clarke's commercial model has re-emerged in the various Indian professional competitions such as the Indian Premier League (IPL) and other professional cricketing franchises that currently exist throughout the cricketing world. But as in George Clarke's time, the commercial model for staging competitive cricket matches is challenged today by many cricket traditionalists.

Light writes that by the 1820s, the growth and vitality of the game had shifted north to Yorkshire, Lancashire, and Nottinghamshire; but for all of its progress, the game continued to revolve around "the distinctive social, economic, and cultural relations of pre-modern society."[49] Of course, that pre-modern society was being blown apart by the turbulence swirling around the new industrial age.

The aristocratic gentlemen of the Marylebone Cricket Club – scared to death of the violent protests sweeping Britain at the time – held back the game's social and economic development because of their reluctance to relinquish cricket's control to a grasping bunch of nouveau riche industrialists, profiteers and coarse lower-class cricketing professionals. Most MCC members associated such "coarse gentlemen", either directly or indirectly, with the rampaging mobs storming across Britain. As Rob Light writes:

> "The changing structure of agriculture in rural south-east England resulted in significant reduction in work and wages which began to undermine many of the region's communities. Their decline was met by an increase in social unrest that exacerbated the general withdrawal from public life by the aristocracy ... aristocratic involvement (in the game) became centred on London and especially the MCC at the expense of the rural heartland."[50]

Fearing a repeat of the French Revolution, the aristocracy of the mid-nineteenth century retreated to the safety of the leather couches of the Marylebone Cricket Club, Lord's and St John's Wood. Once safely ensconced in the Member's Pavilion, they were comfortable directing the games development to suit themselves. At the same time, over a well-stirred gin and tonic, they discussed with their fellow landowning parliamentarians the range of legislation required to make the heathen rioters go away.

It was clear military force alone was not enough to stem the "violent revolutions" and intemperate harangues spreading throughout Britain. A series of destructive riots erupted in cities such as London, Leicester, Derby, Bristol, Worcester, Birmingham and Nottingham – those very same cities in which George Clarke's commercial challenge matches proved hugely popular with the British public. Perhaps it was because they incorporated many of the popular cricketing traditions forged in the villages of rural England over centuries: gambling, drinking and barracking.[51]

While the remarkable crowd at the Nottingham vs Sheffield match grew fat and dangerous on ale and mutton, a few blocks away from Clarke's future commercial cricket venue at Trent Bridge, the locals were rioting. They were in a blind fury at the Lords' rejection of the Reform Bill, legislation designed to remove a gerrymander in the House of Commons favouring the interests of large farmers by the aristocratic, estate-owning members of the House of Lords. If successful, the bill would have eliminated constituencies that elected one or two landowning representatives to the Commons with very few voters – and would, for the first time, increase representation in the booming Midland cities of Manchester and Nottingham.

Poet Mary Botham Howitt wrote that the Reform Bill's rejection:

> *"Ignited an incendiary spirit amongst the poor ... No wonder, therefore, at attempted revolution; more especially as the toilers heard of the country's money being lavished by millions. I, who never in my life had been a politician, and whose prejudices from childhood had been in opposition to democracy, now most cordially allied myself in spirit with the party who cried out for radical reform."*[52]

After three days of rioting, the mob stormed Nottingham Castle, owned by the Duke of Newcastle, and set it ablaze:

> *"Frequently parts of the roof or beams within fell with a louder thunder, and sent up fresh volumes of smoke, dust, and coruscating sparks. The rioters had torn down the wainscotings of cedar, piled them up in the*

*different rooms and fired them, and the whole air was consequently filled with a peculiar aroma from the old cedar thus burning. In the morning the great fabric stood a skeleton of hollow doorways and windows, blackened walls, and heaps of still smouldering and smoking materials within."*[53]

The Nottingham rioters were an alliance of displaced rural workers, starving labourers, artisan socialists and shopkeepers; an alliance that terrified British authority, be it progressive Whig or conservative Tory. The alliance needed to be broken or the feared "British Revolution" must surely come.

Something had to be done, and that something was the arrest of as many Jacobeans, Chartists and political dissenters from the lower orders as the authorities could put their hands on and either hang them, or exile them to Australia.

By the early nineteenth century, some 3600 Chartists, Tolpuddle Martyrs and Swing Rioters, together with 2000 Irish rebels and a smattering of Canadian dissidents, were all shipped to the far-off mutant shores of the Great Southern Land, most never to return. It is argued that executing or exiling the radical leadership of Britain's working-class reform movements of the eighteenth and nineteenth centuries averted British revolution and largely maintained – after granting minor social reforms – their existing social class structure. But in doing so, Britain may have just planted the seed of liberty in Australian soils so fundamental in creating the early "Australian character" – which included how sport was played in this country, and who played it.

But the ruling aristocracy and emerging industrial capitalist class of England were not safe yet. A new frightening marauder had emerged from the city slums to threaten the very edifice of Britain's social class system.

# 07

## The Marauder Within

> "In their most sanguine moments, (British) authorities hoped that (Australia) would eventually swallow a whole class – the criminal class – whose existence was one of the prime sociological beliefs of late Georgian and early Victorian England ... British lawmakers wished not only to get rid of the 'criminal class' but if possible to forget about it."

—Robert Hughes, Fatal Shore

In late Georgian and early Victorian times, there emerged a tale of two Britains. On the one hand, there was the Britain of the pre-modern age, where the aristocracy remained firmly at the apex of British society, directing the operations of parliament and ensuring legislation and government policy maintained and enhanced their power and privilege. This was the Britain of the Marylebone Cricket Club, where the aristocracy steered the game towards their own enthusiasms as a game played for the pleasure of noblemen and county gentlemen. It was the Britain of the Hambledon Cricket Club in Hampshire, where likeminded Royal Naval officers and country gentlemen met and discussed the issues of the day while watching professional cricketers play games for their pleasure.

Both London's MCC and the more rural Hambledon were safe spaces where the aristocracy could relax, have a drink and a punt, and reinforce their collective social and economic interests. This was old Britain – the Britain of the Duke of Richmond, the Duke of Dorset and the first Duke of Sutherland. It was the Britain of an expanding, veracious Empire!

But then there was the other Britain. The Britain of "lumpen workers" who lived in stinking, rat-infested shacks amongst the tanneries and slaughterhouses of London, Manchester, Liverpool and Nottingham. They were 'the mob,' as the gentlemen of the MCC called the urban proletariat. To them, they were an object of terror and contempt: "a malign fluid, a sort of magma that would burst through any law or custom, quick to riot and easily inflamed to crime by rabble-rousers".[54]

Something had to be done about them! We can imagine a bunch of cricketing spectators and British lawmakers sipping a gin and tonic in the MCC's Members' Pavilion while hatching a plan. As balls were glided to the Lord's boundary, they decided to launch a massive, rapid legal assault that was so outrageous in scope it could only be compared to that of the 2003 American tactic of shock and awe in Iraq ... and it was just about as effective.

They devised a plan capable of annihilating "the Georgian mob", or what the Victorians would come to call "the criminal class" – the shallow and pallid thieving pickpockets, muggers, bear baiters, "immoral women," scavengers and forgers. That weapon of mass destruction was a form of state-sponsored terrorism – hundreds of new statues that made crimes of poverty such as theft punishable by hanging or transportation – that, by the very nature of its solemn and fatal consequences, was designed to terrify Britain's lower orders.

But who were these people who sent deep chills down the spines of the aristocracy and emerging middle class?

They were all part of a kind of slum version of "the Sicilian omerta, contemptuous to everyone and everything outside the group".[55] The sub-political wanton mob:

> "Were Georgian society's id – the sump of forbidden thoughts and proscribed actions, the locus of the raging will to survive. Amid the general fear of Jacobinism that swept England after the French Revolution it would seem they were an even greater menace."[56]

Mary Botham Howitt described her distaste for the riotous mob when she wrote to her sister Anna in a letter railing against the dangerous Nottingham mob:

> "A few years earlier the lowest class in the town, elated with prosperity, had become a perfect nuisance to society by braving all order and defying all authority, and had taught us that, if once inflamed by rage, these roughs would make Nottingham a dangerous place."[57]

Mary's pathological fear of "the lower orders" was an interesting contrast to her sympathy for the Reform Bill rioters of 1831. Perhaps in the minds of the progressive middle class there were, respectively, the deserving political agitators versus the undeserving roughs full of violence, dirt and gin; but whatever the source of Mary's fears, they were replicated throughout Britain's genteel classes.

Such fears may explain why, between the enthronement of Charles XI in 1660 to the middle of George IV's reign in 1819, 187 new capital statues became law. An extraordinary 63 capital offences were added to the statues between the years 1760 and 1810 alone. Petty theft, destroying weaving looms, wrecking the fences of the enclosed privatised Common, poaching a rabbit, cutting down a shrub, appearing on the high road with a blackened face, or firing corn stacks, were all punishable by death. You could even be hung for impersonating an Egyptian![58]

For some time in Britain, public hangings were treated by the public either as a deterrence; mothers for example brought their children to the scaffold so that they might remember the example they had seen. But more usually they were an entertainment, a kind of spectator sport, accompanied by a cheering, jeering and heckling crowd:

> "The procession to (the gallows) outside Tyburn (gaol) ... was a central ceremonial of eighteenth-century London. The condemned in the carts – the men in gaudy attire, the women in white, with baskets of flowers and oranges which they threw to the crowds – the ballad singers and hawkers, with their last speeches (which were sold even before the victims had given the sign of the dropped handkerchief to the hangman to do his work): all the symbolism of the Tyburn Fair was a ritual at the heart of London popular culture."[59]

This "patrimony of brigands" was largely forced to thievery and sabotage through pitiable necessity. They were mere drops in the swollen torrent of eighteenth- and nineteenth-century crime,[60] the victims of the stresses of industrialisation and laissez-fare economics. They were born of slums and disease and too many babies.

What to do?

Introduce a suite of social and economic reforms that addressed the atrocious conditions confronted by the impoverished, urban poor? Of course not! It was preferable to invent a form of propaganda we all recognise today – they embarked on a campaign of victim blaming.

Authorities decided to propagate the notion that the lower orders were incorrigible; they were simply a sub-human class of "roughs" born to crime. They were labelled a "criminal class," a descriptor that quickly entered the lexicon of the British language and consciousness.

Crime, in most cases, was not wanton; it was not so much the "wild work" of a "lawless, furious rabble" as one nineteenth-century commentator described it. And not all of the 115,000 Londoners who lived off the proceeds of crime at the time of King George III[61] were career criminals. Many people were simply called to crime as a desperate act of survival, just like the starved, ragged women who spent their days scooping up bucket loads of dog shit to sell to tanneries. As Hughes observed, the helpless begged, while those of more art and courage stole.[62]

The swelling wave of misery (coupled with the Georgian fear of the mob) shaped the laws of the British realm and sent hundreds of thousands into "houses of correction" – those evil, disease-ridden places managed by corrupt overlords. In the minds of the Georgian legislators, harsh punishment was carried out in the name of deterrence! But authoritarian cruelty deterred nothing. It was like trying to halt a flooding tide.

The gaols of Newgate, Marshalsea and Ludgate became full to overflowing and, as such, new forms of imprisonment were needed – the prison hulks of the Thames were those new forms. As the years passed, these decrepit holding pens received more and more victims of the British new order: Hughes estimates about 1000 per year. Thieving peasant children; "ruined" women driven to prostitution, or "taken up as a disorderly girl," were joined by the desperate, destitute and degraded. They were all huddled together on longboats and rowed out to those floating oak ruins to await their fate.

Over time, even the hulks became stuffed full of "drag sneaks" (stealers of luggage from coaches or carts), skinners (women who enticed sailors or children to go with them and then strip them of their clothes), till friskers (who emptied tills when the shopkeeper wasn't looking), dead lurkers (stealers of coats and umbrella) and bluey-hunters (stealers of roof leading).

It didn't take long before rumblings for action emanated from polite society. When typhus became endemic on the prison hulks, those rumblings were heard loud and clear in the halls of British Parliament. Even aristocratic MPs were at risk if the dreaded disease spread from the Thames' hell-ships to the free citizens of London.

But, again, what to do?

With Britain's defeat at the American War of Independence, authorities could no longer transport their "robust and rowdy" criminals to work as one of the 52,000 white slaves on the plantations of Maryland and Virginia. But then Cook sailed into Botany Bay in 1770 and "discovered" an ideal place to make Britain's penal overcrowding problem disappear.

This criminal waste disposal system, as Hughes described it, was a toxic failure. That's because poverty begets theft, monotonously and predictably.[63]

> "The final aim of the transportation system ... was less to punish individual crimes than to uproot an enemy class from the British social fabric. Here lay its peculiar modernity; its prediction of the vaster, more efficient techniques of class destruction that would be perfected, a century later, in Russia. However, it failed. Transportation did not stop crime in England or even slow it down. The 'criminal class' was not eliminated by transportation, and could not be, because transportation did not deal with the causes of crime."[64]

While tens of thousands of convicts were stuffed into the putrid hulls of heaving transport ships and sailed out to New South Wales, thousands more took their place in the prison hulks anchored on the Thames off Portsmouth, Woolwich and Deptford. It was the criminal class of Britain exported to Australia, along with thousands of radical political reformers, that laid the foundation for a new society in the Southern Ocean.

Between 1787 and when the last convict ship sailed from Britain in 1868,[65] over 160,000 destitute, pauper criminals and thousands of political prisoners sailed to Australia, making Britain relatively safe for the Earl of Winchelsea and the Hon. Colonel Charles Lennox to provide Thomas Lord with the finances to establish a new cricket ground and venue for the new MCC in London's Dorset Square (before moving it to its current location in St John's Wood in 1814).

Secure in the knowledge that a system had been put in place to shield the aristocracy from revolution and wanton crime, the earl and the colonel and many more felt safe to raise teams of professional cricketers to play the Hambledon Club at their new home of cricket in Dorset. As leather hit willow, the earl and colonel were now free to share a Pimm's with those renowned patrons of eighteenth-and early-nineteenth-century cricket, the Earl of Tankerville and the Duke of Dorset.

A system of state repression now firmly in place, coupled with cricket's administration resting firmly in the grip of the gentlemen of the MCC, resulted in the multiplying of gentleman's cricket clubs throughout the country. They sprung up in Datford, Bromley in Kent, Croydon in Surrey, as well at Coxheath, Bridge Hill Sudbury and the Sudbury Cricket Society in Suffolk.

Safe from the villainy of the criminal classes, even the gentle noblewomen of the southern counties felt secure to take up the bat and ball and play some cricket at the back of Newington Green in Middlesex. It was a game played in front of a collection of eager "elegant persons" between the women of Hampshire and the Surrey Heroines. By accounts, in was an event full of virtue and leaping maids that induced renewed desire for the game amongst the nobles.

But what happened to all of those transported political prisoners, the harlots and the thieves? How did they fare in the Great Southern Land?

And did they play cricket?

# 08

# Australian Class, Misogyny and the Making of a Sporting Colony

On 26 January 1788, eleven British transport ships carrying 775 convicted criminals and a collection of marines, sailors, civil officers and a spattering of free settlers, sailed into Botany Bay in what we now know to be Sydney Harbour. Moving up the wide bay, they slid past the pink sandstone cliffs of Vaucluse, topped by rough, bronzed, vermilion-leaved trees alive with an exuberance of multicoloured birds. On and on they sailed towards the headlands now hosting the Opera House and Harbour Bridge.

The commander of the First Fleet, Captain Arthur Phillip RN, came with secret instructions to find an empty continent. The British colonisers wanted to avoid entering treaties and paying compensation to the traditional custodians of the land, as they had done in America and Canada. They wanted to find a *Terra Nullius*, an empty land that could receive the first batch of "excrementitious mass" extracted from the British criminal class.

Inconveniently, Australia was not as empty as Phillip hoped. As he hoisted a British Flag at Sydney Cove, he saw a people who had lived on this continent for millennia, a people who had thrived and developed a complex, intricate spirituality that had sustained them on this, the harshest continent on earth, for 65,000 years.

As Phillip's ships began the unloading of their human cargo, one thing was obvious – overwhelmingly, the new arrivals were men. Men outnumbered women convicts by a ratio of six to one.

Phillip founded what was effectively a male-dominated gulag: a place where thieves, poachers, political agitators, forgers and, yes, prostitutes, could be made invisible and forgotten by English lawmakers and polite British society alike. But a colony of men inevitably became a place full of trouble, especially if you happened to be Aboriginal, a woman or a combination of the two. How did Australia's male dominance translate to playing cricket?

It's unsurprising that the first recorded cricket match in Australia – in Sydney, 1803 – was played by men. But perhaps cricket had been played on a less-formal basis for many years before then. It's difficult to judge, although according to an article published in the newly established *Sydney Gazette* in January 1804, it appears informal recreational games of cricket were well-established in Sydney and beyond. By 1826, the sound of bat on ball could be heard throughout Sydney. Regular cricket matches were now played between newly established clubs for most of the subtropical summer. Women had to wait over a half a century to enjoy the same privilege.

Mirroring their English cricketing counterparts, the administrators of cricket clubs were drawn from the colony's elites. Unlike Britain however, the players were mainly military men. An article published in the *Sydney Mail* March 5, 1898, headed *Seventy Years of Cricket 1826–1898*, reports that the early competition consisted of three clubs: the Currency, Military and Australian, made up variously of military officers, government officials, bankers and landowners.[66]

Like the Marylebone Cricket Club, it was the elite members of the three clubs that controlled the administration and running of the game. Nowhere was the elite nature of the early Australian game more evident than in the colony's southern capital of Melbourne. The Melbourne Cricket Club, universally recognised as Australia's most prestigious and influential cricket establishment, was founded November 15, 1838, by five men: Frederick Powlett, Robert Russell, George B Smyth and brothers Alfred and Charles Mundy. Three of the five were neighbouring pastoralists on the Kilmore Plains.

The Kilmore's grassy plains were part of the Goulburn River district, the traditional lands of the Taungurung or Daung Wurrung peoples of the Kulin Nation. But by 1838, the traditional custodians had been dispossessed of their homeland by invading squatters such as Powlett, Smyth and Mundy – and their 700,000 sheep. James Boyce writes that this land-grab was part of "one of the fastest land occupations in the history of empires".[67] which devastated the area's First Nations Peoples through massacre, disease and alienation of traditional food sources. The hard hooves of sheep trampled the Taungurung's murrnong vegetable gardens and fouled their water supply. With traditional food sources in decline, Aboriginal hunters speared sheep but were in turn murdered by the British trespassers. With nothing to eat, the First Peoples starved. Some drifted to Melbourne – the city of the occupier.

Boyce writes that as early as 1839 (only four years after settlement), the missionary Joseph Orton commented that the Indigenous people in the Melbourne area "were almost in a state of starvation and can only obtain food day by day, by begging". How did this happen in an area so naturally rich?[68] The answer to that question is simple; it was a case of administrative genocide. Within 20 years of settlement, the population of the Kulin Nation had plummeted by 90%.[69]

I wonder if the august gentlemen of the Melbourne Cricket Club expressed concern at the plight of their grazing property's traditional owners. I suspect not. They had money to make and deals to be done. Alf Batchelder writes in *The First 50 Years of the MCC*, the club was established not only as a cricket club, but also as a male-only vehicle for elite networking:

> "The first members were pastoralists, government officials, bankers, insurance men and merchants. In the main, their presence in the colony was a direct result of the opportunities generated by the wool industry. For men in their late twenties or their thirties, the Club offered a means of recreation and of socialising with one another. The concept of playing matches against any other group was very low on their priorities. Most sporting teams formed in Melbourne before 1860 played most of their games among themselves."[70]

## *Men Only*

It was the formation of the Melbourne Cricket Club, along with other "men's-only clubs" such as the Melbourne, Savage and Athenaeum, that helped consolidate the hegemony of a colony-wide, patriarchal ruling class. This was a particular brand of ruling class defined by notions of exclusivity and manliness mixed with an innate personal exceptionalism born of their British heritage. These men were part of the 200,000 free settlers who came to Australia between 1793 and 1850, many of whom had grown wealthy on the backs of slavery – men such as the prominent founder of the Bright Brothers and Co steamship company, Charles Bright. Bright was president of the Melbourne Chamber of Commerce, trustee of the Public Library, Victorian Museum and National Gallery, and a Union Bank of Australia director. He came to the colony already a wealthy man: his family had benefited from the £8384 compensation paid by the British government for the loss of 404 slaves from their Barbados estate.

Compensation for loss of slaves?

Britain abolished slavery in the British Empire in 1833 with the passing of the Abolition Act of the same year. But to get the Act through parliament, the government had to agree to pay compensation to British slave owners – many of whom were both parliamentarians and plantation owners in the West Indies and Virginia – for their loss of "property". The compensation paid by the British taxpayer was enormous – in 1835, the British government spent £20 million to compensate slave owners, and it took until 2015 for the debt to be fully paid.

Edward Eyre Williams was another to benefit from slave compensation. He arrived in Melbourne in 1842 and ten years later became a Supreme Court judge. Williams also arrived in Port Phillip already a wealthy man: the future judge carried with him the proceeds he, along with his Trinidad planter father and brother, had received for their loss of "human property" – some £210,000 – paid to them by the British taxpayer. The forfeited "property" consisted of the 514 enslaved people from their estates in Trinidad and the Bahamas.

Then there were the graziers.[71]

Barry Golding gives the example of Alexander Mollison and Charles Ebden, who established large grazing properties in central Victoria in the late 1830s and early 40s, close to the runs of Frederick Powlett, George B Smyth and brothers Alfred and Charles Mundy. Both Mollison and Ebden:

> "Inherited and brought with them huge family wealth from colonial enterprises involving large scale slavery in the Caribbean and southern Africa. This capital was essential to help set up their (vast) pastoral enterprises on the Coliban and Campaspe Rivers from 1837. In addition, Mollison was effectively the beneficiary of the state subsidized slave labour of forty-nine servants (including twenty-two ex-convicts) and Ebden."[72]

Men grown rich – either directly or indirectly – from slavery were the backbone of the Australian establishment. They possessed the racial prejudices and class exceptionalism born in the clubs and elite social circles of Britain. They could be seen in the Long Room in the Members' Pavilion at the MCG, or the Members' Reserve at the Sydney Cricket Ground alongside other colonial men of influence and prestige enjoying a game of cricket while discussing matters of business and social importance. This same class of men sat on the governing councils of the game and, as with their English counterparts, determined how and who played the game in Australia and – in the case of women's cricket – if, when and where it was played, and how it was perceived.

As Clare Wright writes in her book *The Forgotten Rebels of Eureka*, by the mid-nineteenth century, Australia was unequivocally portrayed by opinion leaders as a country exclusively the preserve of men. Muscular, brave men who bore "a free and manly gait ... and possessed, an aspect of self-reliance, begotten of their untrammelled life and independent habits."[73] Women at this time were not only thin on the ground; they were virtually invisible in Australia.

In the mid-nineteenth century, in all sectors of Australian society, women's voices were drowned out by dominant, loud, confident and often very wrong male pronouncement. Consequently, it is of little surprise that it took a further thirty-six years from the founding of the MCC before women took to the cricket field for the first time in Bendigo in 1874. Not only did women have to fight to get their wishes to play cricket heard at this time, they also had to fight to overcome the perception that cricket was totally unsuitable for "the fairer sex" to play. This from the captain writing in the English publication *The Old Fag* and quoted by James Bradley:

> *"Cricket is not a girl's game, and so I do not feel disposed to give you any advice about how to bowl over-arm. I don't believe in much gymnasium work for girl's games. Nature never intended that a woman's body should be wrenched about and made muscular."*[74]

A nineteenth-century quote by McCrone may explain the captain's thinking. Nineteenth-century Britain, and by extension Australia, was a very conservative place for independent women of mind and wealth, especially those possessed of athletic enthusiasms. As discussed, this class of women were encouraged to engage in healthy sporting activities: tennis, or perhaps gymnastics, but certainly not sports like cricket that were seen as strictly the preserve of men. This was especially the case in the elite private girls' school system, both in Australia and in England, where:

> *"The promotion of games, and cricket in particular, within the school environment was ... part of the 'double conformity' that the founders of female public schools subscribed to: an education for girls in alignment with male academic standards ... while at the same time submitting to the constraints of ladylike behaviour. In Victorian and Edwardian England (and Australia), girls' games at school reflected these constraints, both in terms of dress and the lack of especially strenuous, contact sports."*[75]

The captain was writing at the butt end of the nineteenth century when a new definition of femininity had permeated the middle class; a definition that excluded women from many sports both in Australia and Britain. Consequently, women only hesitantly and intermittently entered the sporting arena late in the nineteenth century – and when they did, they were largely from non-conformist families of independent economic means. But there may be another reason for women's late arrival to the cricket field in Australia. It goes to the social circumstances of transported female prisoners and free-settler women and the circumstances they confronted on arrival.

When convict women disembarked in Sydney or Hobart in the late eighteenth or early nineteenth centuries, they were displayed in a kind of slave market, where a helter-skelter of aroused colonialists salivated over the newly bathed and preened female transportees. The colonists entered a kind of lottery, where their prize would be an allocation of a desirable "female servant." But there was a strict protocol to it all. Hughes points out that Military Officers got the first pick, then non-commissioned officers, followed by privates. Having carried off the most "desirable women", it was now the turn of the ex-convicts deemed "respectable enough" to be allocated a female domestic. Of course, many women were taken as sex slaves rather than servants to be driven down by "jealousy, vexation and want." It was the same across most of the country.

Victoria, or Port Phillip as it was then known, was founded in 1835 and in its first decade the colony's population grew at a startling rate as women were encouraged to venture out. It's no surprise, as men outnumbered women at this time to a ratio of seven to one. According to the State Library of Victoria:

> *"The majority of Port Phillip's women were initially unmarried free settlers. Single women were in demand as house servants, and the government paid for them to travel to Victoria safely, with married couples or families: £19 would be allowed for every unmarried female domestic or farm servant, not below fifteen, nor above thirty years, coming out under the protection of a married couple, or forming part of a family."*[76]

Unsurprisingly, the single women who arrived in the colony were very vulnerable to exploitation in all of its forms. Domestic servants were safe as long as they were of use to the free settlers. If they fell pregnant or lost their job, they were out on the street or forced to rely on charitable organisations. The situation for female *convict* arrivals to Port Phillip was even worse. Many were prostituted on the voyage to Australia, soldiers and military officers having selected their "companions" for the voyage. Then, on arrival, the women were handed over to settlers as domestic servants where they were at their mercy. It's little wonder that many convict women absconded to Melbourne's seedy criminal underbelly.[77]

Even as more free women came to take up the opportunities offered by the new colony, especially those who came after the 1851 Victorian Gold Rush, the circumstances for some women may have improved – but not to the extent that they could fully engage in all aspects of colonial life, including fully participating in independent leisure activities such as cricket.

Initially, the diggers were young and wifeless, but as Clare Wright points out, with the passing of time, Victoria's goldfields were not so much rough and ready outposts of bachelors but a heterogeneous and largely orderly community of working families. By 1854, the Ballarat goldfields "rattled with industry and hummed with domesticity ... 45% of Ballarat's inhabitants were women and children."[78] In Sandhurst (Bendigo) by comparison, that figure was 31%. Women were a crucial presence on the Victorian goldfields, but did they achieve anything like a position of emancipation?

Overwhelmingly, the dominant social norms of the time emphasised the primacy of maleness in Australian and specifically Victorian society. Women were expected to be kept in their place; peeling the potatoes as they stared out on creek-facing hills from a flapping tent opening on the goldfields. Women served their men, nurtured their children and kept away from any public display of individuality or unique personal capability. Women were cast to society's shadows, where they remained largely invisible.

## *Australia's Egalitarianism*

Given this proviso, it must be said that the establishment of a thief colony in the Southern Ocean did result in some progressive reforms to its democratic institutions. Accompanying the criminals on board the transport ships were exiled leaders of political movements such as Chartists, Luddites and more, and these new arrivals helped transform what was a gulag into a democracy. But it didn't come without a struggle.

Australia's political prisoners brought with them radical proposals for universal suffrage and working-class inclusion born of the political reform movement of Britain. As Monash University historian Dr Tony Moore points out,

> *"Australia is often called a Chartist's democracy because by 1856 and the decade following, many of the key six points of the Chartists had been realised in Victoria and New South Wales ..."*[79]

... including universal manhood suffrage (for white men), which was introduced 60 years before Britain, and secret ballots, which were legislated in 1856.

Universal manhood suffrage (women would have to wait until 1902 to cast a ballot) was achieved through the leadership of Chartists at the Eureka Stockade: that explosive moment in the Ballarat goldfields of Victoria where the concepts of universal suffrage born of Eureka's slogan "no taxation without representation" was first heard. Australia was also an early adopter of labour reform with the introduction of the eight-hour working day for stonemasons in Melbourne in 1856. This was the first of a series of labour initiatives that paved the way for the country to be hailed in the early twentieth century as possessing the most progressive labour environment in the world. Progressive, that is, if you were a white male.

Despite Australia leading the world in democratic reform, it remained a deeply racist country at the end of the nineteenth century. White Australians had systematically engaged in a program of genocide towards its First Nations Peoples, and its parliaments had introduced the concept of a "White Australia" into official government policy (I still have a wardrobe stamped with the words "Manufactured by European Labour Only").

Australia was also a deeply sexist country, where women were denied fundamental rights and privileges available to men. Despite all this, Dr Moore argues that Australia was universally known "as the social laboratory of the world"[80] – but a male-dominated social laboratory all the same.

# 09

# Bowling Maiden's Over

Women playing cricket in late-nineteenth-century Australia was widely perceived as an incursion into the manly art. When a trickle of brave women did manage to take to the cricket field, they were criticised as participating in an unbecoming, unfeminine sport. Consequently, they were met with derision from the press: "let our women keep their own places in the homes in this day of disregard for the chimeric moral influence". Zedda-Sampson writes that "women's cricketers were accused of being ... unfeminine, or their play was sexualised, their sporting displays likened to burlesque shows".[81] This remained a dominant view in Australia for at least a century.

But then in 1874, twenty-two brave women played the first formal game of women's cricket in Australia. It was a game played for charity and it was a local Bendigo family affair, initiated by the Raes.

The family's patriarch John Rae was the headmaster of a local school and his wife Emily the head teacher. It was John who approached the organisers of the Sandhurst Easter Fair with the idea of staging a women's cricket match as a fundraiser for the Bendigo Hospital and Benevolent Asylum.

Two women's teams, one captained by Emily and the other by her eldest daughter Barbara, took to the field. Barbara's team included her sister Helen, or "Nellie", and both teams were made up of women who had responded to an advertisement in the local press calling on "ladies who are desirous of playing" cricket. There were no shortages of acceptances to the Raes' invitation. Nearly forty eager women applied to play. All clearly needed deliverance from their maternal lamentations stumbling amongst the cracked, quartz-scattered moonscapes of El Dorado.

In the leadup to the game, babies were exchanged for bats and, as sunny autumn days dissolved into the violet light of late afternoon, women as young as fourteen and as old as sixty were coached in the subtle arts of spin bowling and the cover drive by male players from the Bendigo United Cricket Club. The game itself was attended by a large crowd and, as reported in *Bendigo Advertiser* of April 8, the game was "productive of a substantial addition" to the funds of local charities. The *Advertiser* commented on the

> "*very considerable amount of courage on behalf of the ladies to undertake to play a cricket match in public ... The thing was unprecedented as far as Australia was concerned, and such a remarkable event ... Sandhurst has the honour of turning out the first twenty-two lady cricketers, and from the exhibition of their capabilities yesterday in this field of love's labour they added additional charm to the game of cricket, and shown that, as a healthy exercise, it is alike fitted for the gentler as for the sterner sex ... their appearance was very pretty and picturesque and they were loudly applauded by onlookers ...*"[82]

This encouraging – though somewhat patronising – coverage was not to last; the metropolitan press eviscerated the very concept of women's participation as players. Zedda-Sampson writes that one article in the *Melbourne Punch* "ridiculed the cricketers", treating the game as a comical spectacle: "Ms Williams ... was taken by Miss Sharp in slips ... No great catch, you mean thing Miss Sharp, she said, as she returned with her retrousse nose high in the air."⁸³ While the *Melbourne Argus* gave "more prominence to the costumes worn than the cricket played."⁸⁴

Another article, this time from the *Herald*, attacked the game and compared the women to suffragettes: "Let our women keep their own places in our homes in this day of growing disregard for the chimeric 'moral' influence". The *Maryborough and Dunnolly Advertiser* took their lead from the *Herald*, calling the game an "unbecoming spectacle." When John Rae wrote to the paper in defence of the women cricketers, the *Herald* replied with all guns blazing: "such exhibitions under the guise of charity, are indelicate, imprudent and abominable to the well-balanced mind", adding such descriptive adjectives as "vulgar", "unwomanly", "unseemly" and "reprehensible".⁸⁵

Elsewhere, however, the Sandhurst game was well received. Zedda-Sampson writes that the post-match summary that appeared in the *Bendigo Advertiser* was reproduced in both Britain and the Americas, including in the *New Orleans Republican*, the *Public Ledger* in Memphis Tennessee and "many more newspapers published overseas".⁸⁶ No matter the criticism, the Sandhurst match had germinated a sporting seed in other parts of the colony.

The town of Steiglitz near Geelong in Victoria was inspired to stage a second women's cricket match for charity in late May 1874. Zedda-Sampson writes that "some of the community had misgivings but once the match was played, those prejudices dissolved". In fact, one local cricketer, possibly the Victorian male cricket captain Tom Wills, was reported "to be taken aback by the skill displayed by the twenty-two 'Graces'."⁸⁷

Despite the 1874 Sandhurst game's mixed reviews from the Victorian press, the Rae family agreed to organise another charity match at the 1875 Sandhurst Easter Fair. Another advertisement calling for women cricketers appeared in the *Bendigo Advertiser* and again the response was overwhelming.

On April 1 the *Advertiser* reported women playing with "great skill ... indeed the exhibition they made in the field yesterday would go to lead to the belief that the game of cricket is completely compassionate to the female form, and very possibly the female intellect."⁸⁸

But once again the conservative press weighed in with cruel, thunderous outrage. The *Herald* of that same day described the game as resembling a "burlesque ... as performed in Oriental cafés" where women paraded their ankles to the public's gaze: "cricketers are depraving the spectators of the opposite sex. For virtue sake let us hope we have heard the last of the ladies cricket matches ... women should be held to account for the irreverent and rowdy behaviour of the crowd."[89]

The conservative press at this time was clearly engaged in what we would now call a culture war directed at those who would challenge the centrality of maleness in Australia's national sporting mythology. Women were not allowed to challenge the myth of male potency in fear of weakening the veneer of male domination of the country. It's no surprise then that Victoria's women cricketers in the nineteenth century had to battle media censure for daring to publicly "engage in trials of masculine skill," or at best, overcome the perception of women cricketers as colourful, minor additions to an otherwise manly sport.

Consequently, it would take until 1886 before the next women's cricket match was played in Australia, this time in Sydney. It was between Siroccos and Fernlae on Sydney's Association Cricket Ground in front of 1000 mostly male spectators.

The match was sponsored by Sydney cricketing identity Fred Ironside to raise funds for the Bulli Mining Disaster Relief Fund and, as would become a theme throughout the history of women playing cricket in Australia, the game came about because of the determination of an individual woman – or, in this case, the progressive Gregory family.

Ned Gregory, who played in the inaugural Australian men's Test team, was the curator at the Association Ground (or the Sydney Cricket Ground as we know it) and his three daughters Louisa, Alice and Nellie spent their childhoods belting cricket balls around the august oval.

The game featured two teams; the cardinal-and-blue-clad Siroccos, captained by Nellie and featuring her younger sister Alice, while the black-and-gold-uniformed Fernleas were captained by Louisa.[90]

Alice Gregory top-scored for Sirocco in the first innings with a credible 34 out of a total of 83, and in an all-round performance had the bowling figures of 7-14 in Fernlea's first innings. But Sirocco collapsed in their second innings for 53, with Nellie top scoring with 26. The Fernleas took out the game with a 7-94 in their second innings – a score notable for Rosalie Dean's 53-not-out. A further two games were staged at the Association Ground between the same two teams over the coming year.

Full Corset and Stockings 85

*The Siroccos, captained by Nellie Gregory (back row, fourth from left). Source: Clearing the Boundaries: The Rise of Australian Women's Cricket by Fiona Bollen with Matt Bonser. Bradman Museum, 2020.*

The second match, played four weeks after the first, raised funds for the Blue-Ribbon Charitable Institution for Women. It was staged in front of 3500 eager spectators and was notable for the extraordinary all-round performance by Nellie Gregory. She was clearly the player of the match, returning game figures of 14-68 off 25 and scoring 35 and 47-not-out in the winning side.

The third game was played almost a year later and was a truncated affair with the Fernleas easily accounting for Siroccos in an outright performance. Rosalie Deane again top scored in the match with an unbeaten 39. Rosalie would go on to star in a further charity match played between two teams from the newly established Sydney Ladies Cricket Club in 1891. The game was a triumph for Rosalie, scoring 195 in the first innings and 104 in the second, which resulted in her becoming the first woman recorded in *Wisden Cricketer's Almanack*.

Following such a performance, surely the women's game would now hold an established place in the colony's sporting calendar? No, not a bit of it. As Fiona Bollen writes, there were still detractors, men who believed vigorous activity in public – let alone cricket – was not acceptable for women, who must be kept demure and rounded and out of sight! But despite press censure, a few brave, independently minded women pushed on with developing the game. Some drew praise from more progressive quarters for their "keen appreciation for, and a long acquaintance with, the finer points of the game."[91]

In the southern capital, the Australian Ladies Cricket Club was formed in Melbourne in 1891. Soon after, intercolonial matches between New South Wales and Victoria were organised. But they were distracted affairs – the first intercolonial game was shambolic! Victoria could only muster six women players to travel north, while many leading New South Wales players were absent. Consequently, the two teams struggled to field eleven players, much to the amusement and derision of the local press. But Australian women were determined to play the game and one of those women was Emily Whatman – the mother of Donald Bradman.

We all know the story of Bradman hitting a golf ball with a stump against the family water tank in Bowral. But what is *not* widely known is that it was his mother Emily – who represented New South Wales in intercolonial matches at this time – who bowled her left-arm seamers to him every afternoon after school.

Meanwhile, in Southern Tasmania, the Oyster Cove Ladies Cricket Club was formed in 1894 which inspired an interleague competition on the island. In Queensland, the first official women's game was played between Brisbane Girls Grammar and All Hallows Schools in the early 1890s. But it was ultimately Victoria who led the way in the development of women's cricket in the final decade of the nineteenth century.

In Warrnambool, on the state's south-west coast during the screen-door summer of 1897/98, local women were coached by JM Blackburn – then the world's best wicketkeeper. He clearly knew what he was doing! After months of solid training, the call went up to Melbourne from the Warrnambool women's team, dubbed the Forget-Me-Nots, challenging a parliamentary men's team for a game at Allansford just out of Warrnambool. Perhaps they wanted to demonstrate the skill and independence of Victorian women – still denied the right to vote, sue for compensation and hold full property rights.

The women's challenge proved successful: they beat the men, just, largely thanks to Mary Fallahey (the only overarm bowler in the match) and Ethel Dallimore (the game's top scorer with 19 notches).

A notable player on the parliamentary team that day was the future Premier of Victoria, Tommy Bent – that's 'Bent by name and bent by nature'. Bent was a corrupt land-boomer who, while serving as Victoria's Premier Treasurer and Minister for Railways in the early years of the twentieth century, approved the St Kilda to Brighton Beach electric tramway. The new line, opened by him in 1906, just happened to service his substantial property holdings in the area ... no conflict of interest there! Needless to say, the value of his property portfolio and those of his local supporters increased substantially. Given Tommy's rather questionable reputation, it's amazing he didn't bribe the scorer to find a few runs for the parliamentary team at the back of the scorebook just to get them over the line!

Back in Melbourne, on 11 July 1905 at a meeting at St Peter's School in Eastern Hill, the Victorian Ladies Cricket Association (VLCA) was formed. It was Violet Hodson, wife of former Australian Captain Harry Trott, who was the driving force behind the Association's establishment.

Some sixteen ladies cricket clubs were actively engaged in the competition, and membership for all clubs rapidly increased. Teams included Essendon, Maribyrnong, Brighton, Elsternwick, Ascot Vale, Kew, Dunlop Tyres, Tally Ho and some sponsored by various women's organisations such as the Young Women's Christian Association. Players were mainly drawn from middle-class backgrounds; some were teachers, while others were affluent women of independent means. However, women from teams such as Maribyrnong, Dunlop Tyres, Tally Ho and others in all probability included a number of working women members.

But how did they learn to play the game? Perhaps Victoria's 1872 Education Act had something to do with it.

The Education Act was the first of its kind in the Australian colonies, and one of the first regions in the world to offer free, secular and compulsory education for children both boys and girls aged six to fifteen. Although the "purity of male sports" needed to be protected in some schools, girls were no doubt exposed to "boys' sports" such as cricket and Australian Rules Football as well as traditional "girls' sports" such as basketball and "rounders" in the school playground.

If the experience of my mother, Peggy Antonio, Una Paisley, Betty Wilson, Ruth Tucker and many more outstanding cricketers of their age is typical, girls learned the subtle art of the game the hard way by playing their brothers, cousins and local boys in the backyard – or on the killing floor of the suburban street.

My mother described playing cricket with the boys in the playground of her Westgarth Central School in Northcote just twenty years after the formation of the VLCA, then going home to play cricket and football with her brothers and the local boys in the street. Meanwhile, the Victorian Ladies Cricket Association in East Melbourne and its founding president Vida Goldstein were making good progress.

Goldstein, although not a player, was the founding president of the Association in 1905. A left-wing firebrand, she was a force to be reckoned with. The daughter of middle-class Irish immigrant parents, she helped rescue her family from financial ruin following the Depression and subsequent bank crashes of 1892–98 by operating, along with her sister, a successful, preparatory co-educational school in Alma Road, St Kilda. This was just the start of her extraordinary career. Goldstein was a pioneer of the women's suffrage movement. She was political, economically literate and widely read on all matters associated with parliamentary procedure. By 1899, she was the undisputed leader of the radical suffragettes in Victoria. Anti-capitalist and pro-public control of public utilities, Vida was in vehement opposition to Australia's White Australia Policy and campaigned heavily for equal pay for women and a basic wage for all workers.

But that's not all; Goldstein worked tirelessly for women and children's welfare, campaigned for equal property rights for women, and stood several times for both state and federal parliament, being one of only four women to stand for national government in the British Empire. The Victorian Ladies Cricket Association was very fortunate to have Vida's skills as both an administrator and women's advocate. Presiding over the first meeting of delegates at St Peters Hall, she clearly demonstrated her support for women's right to play cricket. Her tireless promotion of the women's game and her social networks drew a number of eminent women to the cause of the women's game. They acted as office bearers, while others became patrons of the sport. Slowly, women's cricket was gaining legitimacy in many influential quarters.

By 1910, an interstate match staged between New South Wales and Victoria held at the Richmond Cricket Ground in Punt Road saw spectators paying 6p entry and a further 6p to enter the grandstand. What the paying customers got for their money was an enjoyable afternoon of sporting entertainment. One press report remarked:

> *"the spirit of the fields-women after the flying leather was good to see. They did not dawdle like some male players but tore after the ball with agility and the grace of antelopes."*[92]

*Group of cricket players sitting and standing in three rows, wickets in centre of front row. c1890–1910. State Library Victoria. Record ID 9917454413607636.*

Shame about the antelope description.

But then Archduke Franz Ferdinand of Austria was assassinated by Bosnian nationalist Gavrilo Princip in June 1914, setting off a chain reaction that led to a war between the British, German and Austrian-Hungarian Empires in early August 1914. The war was fundamentally a land-grab for territory by the opposing imperial forces, principally the control of the oil-rich Middle East. The war had nothing to do with the defence of Australia, but as we have done before and since, we enthusiastically sacrificed our young men and women to the cause of imperialism – in this case, British imperialism.

The result of Australia's imperial sacrifice was - from a population of fewer than 5 million people - 7% of the population served overseas with 60,000 killed and 156,000 gassed, wounded or taken prisoner. If that wasn't bad enough, at war's end, the Spanish Flu pandemic killed a further 15,000.

It's little wonder that the inexorable development of women's cricket in both Victoria and the rest of the country was also killed stone dead by the war. The Victorian Ladies Cricket Association was one of the first casualties. It was a similar story in Britain, although in comparison to the Australian experience, the women's game took longer to recover.

# 10

# Modernism, Flappers and the Depression

During the First World War, millions of British women were recruited to the war effort. They flooded munitions factories, joined the Women's Army Auxiliary and the Women's Land Army – "ruffling" the gender norms of rural Britain. Consequently, many women – especially working-class women – tasted freedom for the very first time. Former domestic servants became gas fitters, while housewives became crane drivers. In many ways, the war was a springboard to liberation. Many newly liberated female workers expressed their freedom by playing competitive sports such as English football and cricket, especially in the manufacturing centres in the north of the country. The wartime authorities were prepared to grudgingly tolerate such an offence against nature, concluding that it was good for morale and sport made women fit enough for work in the factory, the farm or the military hospital.

But once the war ended, the backlash began. As Sheila Rowbotham described:

> "There had been mutterings in letter columns during the war about a decline in sexual morality. Young women were being labelled as 'flaming flappers' well before the 1920s. When the war ended, adventurous (women) found themselves grounded. With no extenuating wartime emergency, admiration and gratitude rapidly melted away. 'Is the Modern Woman a Hussy?' enquired the Illustrated Sunday Herald in 1919. For cultural conservatives, keen to return to a pre-war idyll, this seemed to be an assertion rather than a question."[93]

It's no surprise that, in the immediate post-war period, the tolerance for women playing sport evaporated. Once again, the guardians of respectability reverted to their conservative pre-war default positions, some more than others:

> "Assumptions that cricket playing was an area of male social power and a demonstration of male supremacy. While women's cricket never faced the extreme opposition which women's football had to contend with – the Football Association, angry at the seriousness with which women's factory teams continued to play after the First World War and the massive crowds they were attracting, banned the sport in 1921."[94]

Women's cricket was not banned in the post-war Britain, but it lacked the administrative and financial infrastructural support needed to sustain player involvement and viable competitions. It took until the mid-1920s for any kind of women's cricket organisation to develop - the Women's Cricket Association (WCA) - which was achieved by a collection of middle-class female hockey players in October 1926.[95]

In wartime Australia, things were different for women. At the beginning of the First World War, with their men away at the front, Australian women cricketers left the field to tend to children, take up factory work or work as nurses, or help out on the family farm. In Melbourne, the old Victorian Ladies Cricket Association was abandoned. Could women's cricket in Australia go the way of the German U-Boats and vanish without a trace?

Lilla Brocklebank, a diminutive architectural assistant from East Melbourne, was determined not to let that happen, certainly not in her home city of Melbourne. Pre-war, Brocklebank was instrumental in the foundation of a women's team sponsored by her local St Peter's Anglican Church. She named the team "Coldstream" after the oldest regiment in the British Army – the Coldstream Guards, a regiment that fought in every colonial and international conflict involving the British Army.

Post-war, and despite a blossoming architectural career, Brocklebank – described as a right-hand batter and left-arm slow-bowler – was determined to kick-start the dormant VLCA. In 1919, she took out a series of advertisements in the *Age* newspaper calling for interested women to join a newly revitalised women's competition. The response was underwhelming. It took another couple of years, and repeated recruitment advertisements funded by Brockelbank for two teams – St Peters (East Melbourne) and Preston – to finally put women's cricket back on Melbourne's sporting calendar.

In 1924, St Peter's and Preston took to the field beside the army drill hall in Yarra Park, but it was a shaky beginning to a new era. St Peter's was dismissed for 32, while Preston finished the day's play at 3/81, with 38 of their runs coming from wides. Newspaper reports of the game point to a large crowd of bemused armed forces trainees who paid more attention to the ladies at play than their officers!

But thanks to the persistence of Brocklebank, Victoria was the first state in Australia to form its own women's cricket association following World War I. Within a couple of years, three clubs – St Elmo, Essendon and Semco (an art and needlework firm from Melbourne's southern suburbs) – joined the competition. Women's cricket was alive and well in Melbourne. Perhaps the women's competition was evidence of an emerging confidence in the southern capital. A building boom was well underway and many of its citizens embraced new and exciting technologies – Melbourne was marvellous once again. And so were its women's cricketers.

At war's end, Australians as a whole were keen to move on. They wanted to replace the horror of the trenches, the despair and pain of loss, with all the hope that new beginnings can bring. Those new beginnings took two divergent paths, both driven by innovative new technology.

*Miss Brocklebank 1909. State Library of Victoria.*

*Group portrait of Coldstream Ladies' Cricket Club, including 5 men, a boy and 11 women. Coach, Mr Pat Gooley is at left, 1980. State Library of Victoria.*

In the 1920s, 10% of Australia's population had sought the freedom of the private automobile, with 500,000 registered cars owned by families nationwide by 1928. With the arrival of private transport, together with the spread of electrified tram routes, came the possibility of a new Californian-bungalow home built on a semi-rural gardenesque housing estate far, far away from the disfigurement and grim post-war poverty of the inner city. These new homes housed male-dominated families, excluded liquor, frowned on the modern, and looked to Britain for cultural and political guidance.

On the other hand, in the inner-city of Sydney and Melbourne, the 1920s was defined by the modern Jazz Age, a time when some women emerged from the shadows cast by men. They now had the vote and could work – earning unequal wages to men, it's true, but earning money in their own right nonetheless.

Money meant freedom, and freedom meant that "vulgar", Americanised entertainments were embraced by the new 1920s women and their men in the form of the cinema, the dance hall and commercial music. These new entertainments had arrived on our shores via radio, the gramophone and the movie theatre. Suddenly, inner-city, working-class factory girls jazzed their appearance by bobbing their hair, donning Charleston dresses and art stockings and swinging long strands of beads. These were the flapper girls who, in Melbourne, swung those beads at the Palais in St Kilda, or the Green Mill that stood across the river from the Flinders Street Railway Station. The Green Mill boasted a state-of-the-art rubber sprung floor and modern, atmospheric lighting. In Sydney, the flappers could choose any number of dance halls such the Bondi Casino, the Bondi Pavilion and the Marrickville Town Hall on a Saturday night.

Back in Melbourne, as I wrote in *Roots: How Melbourne Became the Live Music Capital of the World*, flappers even danced to Melbourne's (and possibly Australia's) first all-girl dance band, the Thelma Ready Orchestra. The band had long residencies at the Mayfair Café in St Kilda, the very modern Venetian Room at the Hotel Australia, plus a regular gig at radio station 3DB and two mornings a week at the King's Theatre courtesy of the *Herald* newspaper. Then there was Eve Rees and her Merrymakers, who played every night of the week at Mayoral balls, CWA dances, cafés, lodges, clubs, weddings, funerals, parties ... anything!

Jazz changed Melbourne, but not universally. Anglo-Saxon, suburban, middle-class Melbourne was horrified at the changes. They felt it had infected the city like the Spanish Flu. Opinion leaders said the new Jazz Age was destroying the minds and the morals of the young! If you believed the newspapers, inner Melbourne was awash with jazz, crime and sex.

The *Truth* newspaper was full of articles about sly grog shops sloshing out the back of lolly shops, cafés, hairdressers and dress shops in Fitzroy, Collingwood and Port Melbourne. Fitzroy and St Kilda were wide open to all things American: jazz, flappers, Hollywood movies, cool-cat language and gangsters – like Squizzy Taylor, who emulated his Chicago mobster hero Al Capone by filling the streets of Fitzroy, Collingwood, Carlton and Richmond with bullet-holed bodies, debris and sadness.

Sadness, too, permeated throughout Melbourne and Victoria's Aboriginal people at this time. Many First Nations soldiers fought in the trenches of the Western Front alongside men who came home to openly support a "White Australia" proclaimed at Federation. Despite the brave service of Aboriginal men and women after the First World War, they continued to be marginalised and oppressed by a country dictated by entrenched colonial patterns of racism, notions of superiority and the primacy of "the white race."

My mother was born in 1918 and grew up in the 1920s – meaning her early life straddled two versions of modern Melbourne. On the one hand, she came from a family where her father was one of those who fought in the bloody trenches of Europe and Turkey for King and country. A man's man, who liked a drink with his friends, hunted rabbits on weekends and commanded respect. He dominated his family; a man who was the very definition of a patriarchal, working-class Tory. But he was also a man who was guaranteed – as an essential government worker – employment throughout the Depression, and used that financial stability to encourage his daughter to enter the new post-war age as a modern woman. In this new modern world, some women worked, some played jazz music in orchestras, and others played cricket for Northcote.

Mum embraced her times. By the late 20s she was playing cricket and, as a very young girl, her social life was focused on the cricket club.

> "We practised two nights a week and played on Saturdays. When I was a little older, many of us went to the pictures after the games, or to our homes for cards and supper. Sometimes we went to the Palais, or the dances at the Melbourne Town Hall."

Her life was one of contrast. She lived in an exciting, modern world of change embodied by the opening of the Sydney Harbour Bridge in 1932, air travel, the new information age courtesy of radio, and the freedom and possibilities offered by the motorcar. But at the same time, she lived in a house dominated by her father – a man whose cultural reference was Edwardian England and whose worldview was forged in the trenches of Western France. But this was a familiar story that played out in houses and suburbs all over Australia, and is hardly unique to my mother.

Meanwhile, the VLCA expanded, with factory-sponsored teams, the Pelaco Shirt manufacturer in Richmond and Collingwood's Raymond Shoes joined the competition. Working-class women playing cricket in Melbourne's elite women's cricket competition – now that's what I call modern!


The events of the 30s and the decade that preceded it delineate what we now understand as the modern era – a time scarred by the devastation wrought by war and the Wall Street crash of 1929.

The impact of the 1929 crash was felt immediately in Australia. Almost overnight, the country's commodity exports were left to fester on Australia's wharves and the economy fell over. Hundreds of thousands of workers were thrown onto the employment scrap heap.

Australia was one of the countries in the Western world most impacted by the Depression; unemployment peaked at 32% in 1932. Britain, in contrast had a 22% unemployment rate in the same year. The Australian government had no idea how to respond to the crisis.

Competing ideas on how to best deal with the crisis got in the way of actually dealing with it. Commonwealth Treasurer Red Ted Theodore's proposal, and that of New South Wales Premier Jack Lang, to increase government spending and cancel interest payments on British loans, were rejected by both federal and state governments, sending the Australian economy into free-fall which, in turn, drove whole sections of the population into a state of degradation and poverty. This was the era when conservative Australian politics not only condemned ordinary people to live beyond endurance and even sanity – it was a time when governments manhandled the destitute. My father was one of them.

As the only man of working age in a house of three sisters and his widowed mother, my unemployed father travelled six months of the year in search of work. He picked up a day or two working on farms and towns as he tramped north-west from Melbourne. He lived in homeless camps and survived on 'suso' – pitifully inadequate sustenance payments – all the while incubating a rage against the establishment.

> *"The Communists were the only ones who stepped in to help, they found us places to camp, made sure we had food and often found us jobs like picking fruit or chopping wood for farmers. But it didn't have to be that way. It was when the war came and I joined the Airforce that I finally got my first full-time job in ten years. It was war that made the government invest in jobs, not the poverty of its people."*

As Gandhi pleaded with his British overlords for Indian independence, a battle of "isms" erupted in the 1930s, engulfing much of the planet. Those 'isms' were communism, socialism and fascism, and that war was manifest on the killing fields of Spain in 1936 when a group of disaffected generals – led by Francisco Franco and supported by the growing might of Nazi Germany and Fascist Italy – mounted a coup against the democratically elected Republican Spanish government. The Republicans received only queasy support from Western powers and relied on a ragtag group of modern socialists, writers, communist activists and artists to resist the terrifying, brutal power of Hitler and Mussolini.

Inevitably, the Franco-Hitler-Mussolini army crushed the Republican opposition and Franco, together with his generals, took over Spain. All this, while "Blackshirts marched in the street of London." But the 1930s had another less destructive, more creative side to its personality – modernism.

Modernism – a movement started in the 1920s – was simply modern thinking that rejected traditional and accepted ideas in the arts and in society. Those that embraced modernist thought were, by definition, the rebellious, the progressives, the experimenters; those who were outward looking and saw the 1930s as a time ripe for a new aesthetic. Modernism was Picasso's cubism, Henri Matisse's fluid colour, Duchamp and the jazz age. It was the time when Freud encouraged us all to embrace our uncivilised urges and be free. The time when religion was out, and all things forbidden and lurid were in. When TS Eliot gave birth to the sublime *The Waste Land*, *The Hollow Men*, *Ash Wednesday* and *Four Quartets*.

Modernism was dadaism, futurism, objectivism, Brecht, Faulkner, EE Cummings and Yeats. Modernism was Frank Lloyd Wright, Art Deco and Bauhaus. Modernism was the chaos of Germany's Weimar republic, a time when power went mad, and Einstein danced in the cabaret.

Modernism embraced disintegration and destruction of every conceivable doctrine and notion held sacred by the establishment. And one of those notions was – you guessed it – that women couldn't, and shouldn't, play cricket.

# 11

# 1930s, Modernism and the Golden Era of Women's Cricket

A Pre-History of International Women's Cricket.

As Marion Stell wrote in her book *The Body Line Fix: How women saved cricket*: "In the early 1930s, the streets, alleyways and backyards of Australia were alive with cricket games. Children everywhere tried to emulate the feats they listened to on radio, saw on newsreels, read in newspaper headlines or heard adults discussing at the dinner table. It was a mesmerising, seductive and alluring sport, central to the national psyche."[96]

Those cricket games were mostly played by boys, but all over the country their sisters and cousins joined in, especially in the more economically challenged areas of Australia. That's because during the Great Depression, there were not a lot of recreational alternatives for boys or girls other than street games. But from the 1920s and into the 1930s, those informal games – often played with nothing more than a piece of wood and a tennis ball – became formalised in dedicated competitions. In Australia's southern mainland capital of Melbourne, the girls' competition was known as the Victorian Women's Cricket Association (VWCA).

The VWCA was formed in the mid-1920s with just a half dozen or so clubs, largely sponsored by factories located in the industrial suburbs of inner Melbourne such as Collingwood, Richmond, Footscray, Brunswick, St Kilda and Northcote. Young factory girls slipped out of their drop-waist, knee-length flapper dresses and padded up. These young women ignored the concerns of the medical profession – that playing cricket would negatively impact their sexuality and fertility – and the warnings from many of their fathers that playing cricket was "unladylike".[97] These young cricketers were the very embodiment of the "independent, modern women."

Gideon Haigh wrote of Melbourne's 1930s industrial women cricket movement when profiling arguably the greatest women's cricketer of her age, Peggy Antonio. In profiling Antonio and the competition in which she played, Haigh described not only an outstanding women's cricketer but a unique women's sporting competition that had its own individual identity, separate to that of men's cricket competitions.

The VWCC was a competition where cricket was played competitively, but "played [...] as it should be played"; or, to quote Peggy Antonio's approach to the game: "It was nice winning and all that … but if I made a 50 – fine; if I made a duck – that was bad luck. I never had the killer instinct."[98]

In other words: cricket was played competitively, but it was not win at all costs. Players had fun and enjoyed each other's company; it was a social activity enjoyed independent of men. There was no leg theory practised on Smith's paddock in Westgarth or the reclaimed wetland at Albert Park.

## *Women Cricketers – Taking it to the Streets*

Peggy Antonio was a "child cricket prodigy", affectionately referred to as "the Girl Grimmett",[99] born of Chilean, Spanish, German, French and English heritage. She lived in Port Melbourne, a hard scrabble waterfront community home to wharfies and dockers, and she played and worked making boxes for a women's cricket team sponsored by Nelson Raymond's shoe factory located across town in Easy Street, Collingwood.

*Peggy Antonio, 1936. Kindly donated by the family of Peggy Antonio to the Australian Sports Museum, N2024.8.3.*

Antonio and her Port Melbourne friend and future spin-partner Anne Palmer, had learned their spinning ways playing local boys on the mean streets of Port Melbourne during the Great Depression. In those times, Port Melbourne was a place of dock strikes, mass unemployment, food banks, slum housing and the militant Unemployed Workers Union. As young girls, they must have been tough and bloody good at what they did to hold their own in the treeless streets of the "Burra", as Port Melbourne was known.

They knew those boys could play fast bowling all day, "so they honed their skills devising ways to get the local boys out."¹⁰⁰ "Honing skills," in Antonio's case, meant converting her family's Port Melbourne backyard into a mini-MCG where, as she told Gideon Haigh, she bowled "over upon over of bowling to a single spot on the pitch. No spinning straightaway. Just metronomic pitch and toss until perfect accuracy was achieved."¹⁰¹ But Peggy learned the fundamentals in the local streets playing the boys. She told Stell:

> "I didn't know anything about girls' teams, or anything like that, and my sister happened to meet somebody (who said) how her niece played cricket ... and then my sister said, 'Oh well, 'I've got a sister who likes to play cricket, but she doesn't know anything about it,' so then it was arranged for me to meet up with the girl...'" ¹⁰²

Peggy travelled out to a rough-as-guts oval in Preston to practise and play the game, joining the Collingwood Cricket Club. She met Anne Palmer, who played for local South Melbourne team Clarendon, soon after. The Preston Club struggled to stay afloat – "the sport was expensive," and in the Depression, money was too tight to mention – so the club organised fundraising drives, three-penny raffles and such, to buy equipment so it didn't cost the girls or their families too much to play. ¹⁰³

But play she did: with the help of a local Port Melbourne coach and ex-South Melbourne Premier League cricketer Eddie Conlon, who introduced her to long hours of practise "that ironed out" the kinks in her game. It was Conlon who taught her leg-spin on the turf practice wickets at South Melbourne. Leg-spin, off-spin and a top-spin as well. As the *Herald* newspaper said of her: "A remarkable feature of her bowling is the amount of spin she gets on the ball, considering her small hands and short fingers."[104]

But Peggy could also bat, again thanks to Conlon's coaching. He started with the basics – defence first! By the time he was finished, "she was recognised as Australia's most perfect stroke maker".[105] It seems extraordinary that Peggy was already a state-representative cricketing prodigy at the age of fifteen.

Then, Raymond's Shoes offered her a job making boxes at their factory on the proviso she crossed from Collingwood and played with their cricket team. It was a no brainer: a job and the chance to play cricket in the pit of the Depression? Of course, she accepted Raymond's offer. It was to be the start of a short but staggeringly successful cricketing career for Peggy, a career that would – in a few short years – take her to Britain where she was hailed by august cricket writer and critic Sir Neville Cardus as possibly "the greatest slow left-handed bowler" man or woman, in England – glowing praise, tempered only by the fact that she was a right-hand bowler, not a left.

## *Anne Palmer*

Two other women Test cricketers had very similar stories to Peggy. Her Port Melbourne friend Anne Palmer was born in England, but emigrated with her mother and international-soccer-playing father Billy to Albert Park. Billy saw immediately that Anne had both interest and talent as a cricketer, especially as an off-break bowler and middle-order batter. He encouraged her to practise. Anne, like my mother, admired the work of Bert Ironmonger – who singled out Anne for special tuition – and in a short period of time, she managed to perfect the famous Ironmonger flick.

Like most aspiring women cricketers of her age, she practised both her bowling and batting skills while playing in the street against a couple of local, aspiring male cricketers from her neighbourhood. She bowled to the two boys for hours while they batted, gaining accuracy and control. Reflecting on why this was important, she told Marion Stell:

> *"The idea was to be as skilful as you could to get them out, and you couldn't get them out with a big fast bowl ... so you had to try and trick them by doing something with the ball, and I think I had a natural off-break, anyway."*[106]

But like her friend Peggy, she needed to iron out some kinks in her game – enter, once again, Eddie Conlon. She joined Peggy and Conlon at their Sunday net sessions behind the South Melbourne Technical College in Albert Park: "he would bat and we would bowl to him, or vice versa."[107] Pretty soon, she was starring with the Clarendon Cricket Club as a fourteen-year-old.

She practised two nights weekly with her club, playing all day Saturday and then trying to spin the neighbourhood boys out after school. Anne played a lot, practised a lot and learned a lot.

Palmer was also an athlete, describing herself as fleet of foot. She was a talented basketball player. Even though her Middle Park school didn't offer women's cricket as a sport, they encouraged their girls in sports such as athletics: "each school had a sports day every year where you competed against other schools."[108]

As mentioned, the Victorian state-funded school education system encouraged female physicality. The encouragement of women's sport in Victorian and Australian government-funded schools in the 1930s meant the wider battle for women's agency over their bodies was now further down the path of being won. This was in stark contrast to their British working-class sisters.

Even though some progress was being made in some areas of female leisure activities across all British social classes at this time, progress for working-class women was highly circumscribed against: "a framework of financial, domestic and moral constraints ... prohibiting participation in organised leisure activities."[109] This was not the case, however, for a number of women born into the industrial suburbs of Melbourne or Sydney at this time.

## *Nell McLarty*

Another friend of Peggy and Anne's was the tall and athletic Nell McLarty, who also lived in Albert Park and was destined to play cricket for her country with her two neighbourhood friends Antonio and Palmer. Standing at 180 centimetres tall, she played a variety of sports at her local state-school, but she loved cricket most of all because she loved to bowl fast – very fast!

She learned to bowl with a tennis ball playing with her second cousin in her parents' backyard. She was a natural, and her talent was soon recognised by the local paperman – a man by the name of Leo who recommended her talents to the local Clarendon team in Albert Park. "He said to the captain, this girl can play cricket, how about you give her a game?" [110]

But the skipper wasn't interested: Nell was tall and rangy, and maybe they thought she was uncoordinated. But play she did when one of their bowlers dropped out of the team. "Well, I'd only ever bowled a tennis ball, never used a hardball." But that didn't matter. She picked up a lazy 7 wickets for 2 runs in her first ever game of competitive cricket.[111] From there, it was a short ride to the Victorian state team and then a debut against England a couple of years later in 1934.

## *Amy Hudson*

It was a similar story in Sydney. Amy Hudson grew up in the industrial suburb of Annandale in Western Sydney. Once, it was a suburb of imposing homes and wide streets, but as industry spread west, those large allotments were subdivided and workers' cottages were built to house the incoming industrial workforce, things began to change. Annandale became a tough-as-nails place to live.

But it always had a bit of a rebellious past. It was where Major George Johnston – who sailed in the *Lady Penrhn* with the marine detachment in the First Fleet – led a contingent of colonialists and soldiers in deposing the parsimonious Governor Bligh in the so-called Rum Rebellion of 1808.

Amy Hudson and her mother were also rebels. Amy had two brothers; she was the only girl in her local neighbourhood. But her sex wasn't going to stop her playing sport. Instead, she played with the boys. It was cricket in the street, soccer at Jubilee Park, swimming in Sydney Harbour, you name it. But she was only allowed to swim, play cricket or soccer when accompanied by her two brothers;

a proviso that proved somewhat of a problem if the boys had other plans. By the time she hit fourteen, she'd had enough of the "brother rule": she wanted play in a team, a *women's* team, and her mother was supportive. She had a plan. *Why try to break into an existing club, when we could form a team of our own?* Now that's thinking outside the square! "Her mother went about it in a professional way and placed an advertisement with the Royal Film Theatre in Johnston Street, and within a week she had a team of cricketers" mostly made up of women from Annandale and surrounding suburbs.[112]

The team played on a ground in the Sydney Domain, which involved a bit of travel. The whole team struggled to gain ground, but with the intervention of a kindly male coach, both the team and Amy began to improve – she tempered her aggression and she stopped getting bowled. But the team needed to play closer to home: Amy's mum could see that, and she wasn't interested in "a bottomless well of wishes" – instead, she acted. She successfully lobbied her local council to put in a concrete wicket at a local park. The girls finally had a place to play! Pretty soon, the local blokes started to commandeer the ground for themselves – but those pushy men didn't take into account Amy's indefatigable mother.

> *"It was the Depression time, and my mum had something to do with giving out the coupons and the like, people didn't get money in those days. When the men took our wicket over and came up to get out coupons, she's threatened them – they wouldn't get them unless they got off our cricket wicket, which they did. As soon as the Annandale girls went down there to play, well they got off it ... ALWAYS!"*[113]

In the 1930s all over Australia, working-class women managed to play the sport they loved because a range of state-based cricket competitions had been formed by far-sighted, often progressive middle-class women administrators – or, in Amy Hudson's case, a feisty mother. In New South Wales, it was the Women's Cricket Association formed in 1928, while cricketers in Queensland, South Australia and Western Australia had also formed women's cricket competitions. But some associations were stronger than others, and those strong competitions were gaining the attention of the Australian media and its consumers.

Back in Melbourne, in addition to the Raymond's factory team, the VWCA's A Grade competition included the needlework firm Semco and the shirt-factory Pelaco, plus a smattering of trade union, social and community clubs and teams sponsored by the Young Women's Christian Association. These were the industrial teams that made up Melbourne's A Grade Victorian Women's Cricket Association, and they got the attention of the mainstream press.

As Gideon Haigh observed, the competition was big news in Melbourne with thousands attending local matches every Saturday. In fact, crowds grew to rival most men's first-class Sheffield Shield crowds of the time. As Haigh writes, factories such as Raymond's may have sponsored a women's team because, firstly, it was good for their workers' morale, and secondly it was good publicity for their shoes: "it was reasoned ... that because club matches at the pit of the Depression could draw crowds of four or five thousand people, a works team might in time become a shoe show piece." [114] Plus, the team's best player Peggy Antonio had real star-power. She may not have known it, but she was an unofficial factory sponsor while snagging bags of wickets with her leg-spin deliveries and mountains of runs with her elegant batting.

But I'm getting ahead of myself.

The popularity of women's cricket in Melbourne, and indeed the rest of Australia at this time, was at least partly due to the popularity of men's cricket – especially the Bodyline series of 1932/33. But, as we have seen, women's cricket's popularity also had a lot to do with the deep economic depression – or, to repeat the words of Antonio, "no one could afford to go anywhere so they'd just turn up to the local match".[115]

Such popularity resulted in the mainstream media seizing an opportunity to increase its readership by covering the women's game. This in turn increased the crowds at local women's matches, making stars out of players such as Antonio, Palmer, my mother's Northcote teammate Una Paisley, the soon-to-be-great Betty Wilson ... and yes, even the off-spin bowler with the Bert Ironmonger flick Nesta Williams. And the Melbournians turning up in droves to local suburban grounds such as Smith's Paddock in Northcote and Yarra Bend Park in Collingwood soon came to understand that the women's cricket they'd come to see was the real deal.

# 12

# Women's Cricket and the Media of the 1930s

At first, there was a scattering of reports published in newly emerged Women's Sections of major Melbourne newspapers such as the *Herald* and the *Sun News Pictorial*. But this was only the start. As the years progressed, coverage of women's sport (especially cricket) increased, driven by a new species of journalist that emerged from Australia's primordial metropolitan newspaper swamp at this time – female sports writers. Who knew that the sporting public, both women and men, wanted to read about women's sport? Nick Richardson, writing in the *Conversation* in 2022, described the crucial role female reporters played in the 1930s coverage of women's sport: "there was a readership for women's sport and cricket in particular when it was in the midst of the next phase of its evolution – women's cricket was more organised at a state level – leading to a corresponding growth in interest in the game."[116] As mentioned, this interest was further enhanced by the explosive 1932/33 men's Ashes tour of Australia, forever known as the Bodyline series.

In the third Test in Adelaide, played in front of a crowd of 50,000, Australian captain Bill Woodfood was struck in the heart following a barrage of short-pitched deliveries bowled by Harold Larwood. This was a brutal display of leg theory, where fielders circle the bat behind square leg in the hope of catching out the batsmen trying to defend short-pitched bowling aimed at the body. Larward bowled under strict instructions from his captain, the disdainful Douglas Jardine. Things only got worse later in the day when Australian wicketkeeper Bert Oldfield had his skull fractured by a Larwood bodyline thunderbolt. Needless to say, the crowd erupted!

Fearing a riot, police were rushed to the Adelaide Oval and the English fielding team looked to weapons to defend themselves in case of a pitch invasion. When the English tour manager Sir Pelham Warner entered the Australian dressing room to check on Woodfull and Oldfield's health, Woodfull famously told him, "I don't want to see you Warner ... There are two sides out there. One is trying playing cricket, the other is not."

As Tanya Aldred wrote in the *Guardian*: "Two days later, in an atmosphere verging on hysterical, the Australian Cricket Board sent an accusatory cable charging unsportsmanlike behaviour by the English team through to MCC at Lord's." However, they chose to send their message at the standard rate, which meant that the news hit the London newspapers (whose cables from Australia were marked urgent) before it arrived in MCC hands.

The MCC in high dudgeon fired back:

> "*We deplore your cable ... We deprecate your opinion that there has been unsportsmanlike play. We have the fullest confidence in our captain, team and managers and are sure that they would do nothing to infringe either the laws of cricket or the spirit of the game ... if you consider it desirable to cancel the remainder of the programme, we would consent, but with great reluctance*".[117]

The matter was raised in parliament here in Australia, while the Australian public was incandescent – would the Empire survive?

As Gideon Haigh observed, "the significance is that probably for the first time the relationship between two countries [came] under serious strain ... they were introduced to a species of cricket that for its time was revolutionary, the idea of fast bowlers bowling at very high speed at the line of the body, starving and bombarding the batsmen. And it has gone on echoing down history ever since."[118]

A positive outcome of the series was that interest in cricket, in all of its forms, including the women's game, increased. This contributed to newspapers employing more female journalists to cover female sport and women's cricket in particular.

So – who were the journalists?

Patricia Jarrett: a talented swimmer and junior athletics champion in Victoria, she became the first female sportswriter at Keith Murdoch's *Herald* in 1933, and was the first woman to cover an overseas cricket tour. When she joined the *Herald*, she was one of two female reporters on the editorial staff.

One of her first assignments was to cover the first women's cricket Test series between Australia and England in 1934/35 in Australia, and travelled with the Australian women's cricket squad to England in 1937. Richardson wrote that Jarrett simply asked Murdoch if she could go on the tour, and he readily agreed.

Ruth Preddey was a former cricketer, administrator and national selector who had a weekly column in the newly minted *Women's Weekly* that focused largely on women's cricket but also covered a range of other sporting activities for women.

Kath Cummins, a talented cricketer and tennis player, joined the *Sydney Morning Herald* in 1934 after telling an executive there was a gap in the newspaper coverage she could fill – women's sport. Pat and Carley Hansen, both talented hockey and cricket players, became sports journalists – covering women's sport, especially cricket, in both Brisbane and Sydney. Lois Quarrell established the *Women in Sport* page in the *Adelaide Advertiser* in 1936, while Gwen Varley pioneered the coverage of women's sport, especially sport played at a grassroots level, for ABC radio in Sydney and 3AW in Melbourne.[119]

## *Nesta Williams and Her Memory Box*

I was exposed to the extensive media coverage of 1930s women's cricket when I came across a yellowing pile of newspaper clippings tied with string and buried deep within my mother's memory box in the linen closet of my parents'

Northcote home, that fateful hot summer day in 1960. Those bits of paper contained multitudes.

There was the front page of the *Herald*, October 19 1936, displaying three photos; on the left of the page was a horse, the 1936 Caulfield Cup winner, Northwind, flanked by its trainer, Cecil Goby and his daughter Bunny. On the right, and in keeping with the wind narrative, an upturned railcar, the result of a strong gust that derailed the car on an approach to a "break-wind" (unfortunate name) on an incline into Carterton, New Zealand. Below the photograph of the upturned railway car was an advertisement for a brand-new Hudson and Terraplan coupe on sale for 390 quid at Neal's Motors, 140 Exhibition Street Melbourne.

But there in the centre of the page was my eighteen-year-old mother, full stride wearing her white skirt, supported by a whale-bone corset – or 1930s suspender belt? – and sheer stockings. Her arm is fully extended behind her head: she was about to deliver her Bert Ironmonger-inspired off-break to an unseen batter. The caption read: "Cricket Girl – Miss Nesta Williams swings down a powerful delivery during the Northcote V Clarendon game in Women's 'A' Grade Cricket Competition on Saturday". Under a pile of memorial detritus was that very same photograph, mounted into a soft frame, ready for my discovery – and for adaption into this book's cover, more than sixty years later.

I found more articles: pages and pages of them. The *Star*, Tuesday evening October 8 1935: Dot Debnam reported on the many good performances in the opening round of the VWCA A Grade 1935/36 season. Debnam analysed each match played, including a game between Northcote and Footscray:

> "*Northcote passed Footscray's first innings with 4 wickets in hand. Nesta Williams, for whom last season I prophesised a future as a slow bowler, took 5 Footscray wickets for 6 runs.*"

A match report published in the *Herald*, date unknown, highlighted an outstanding bowling performance: "Northcote's prolific slow off-spinner, Nesta Williams took the bowling honours against Semco on Saturday taking 6 wickets for 35 runs in the first innings and a further 4 wickets in the second." Another article from 1940 had her taking 5 for 25 against Raymond.

On and on they went. An article in the *Herald* in February 1938 reported a hat-trick against Brunswick, describing Mum as "perhaps the best player in A Grade" that day. A story from a December 1941 edition reported her second hat-trick against Collingwood, including the wicket of the soon-to-be-legendary Betty Wilson. A report of Nesta Williams making 108 against Clarendon soon after her Brunswick hat-trick triumph, the article commenting on her "stunning all-round performance". Even the *Brisbane Telegraph* had a significant article dated November 26, 1937:

> "Victoria has bigger plans still for gaining experience for its younger players. They have decided to send a team of eighteen and a manager, such a team to be announced early in December. The five Test players, Nell McLarty, Winnie George, Nancy Clement, Elsie Deane and Peggy Antonio are available for selection, as is the state representative Anne Palmer, and these should form the foundation of a strong team ... Other names who have been listed are Nesta Williams, a medium-slow left-hand bowler who stars in the Northcote club."

More followed: a scorecard from the Raymond V Northcote A Grade final (year unknown) described Mum taking 3 wickets in Raymond's first innings including catching Peggy Antonio for 35. A clutch of paragraph clippings, one of which reported her 3 for 10 against St Kilda. An article reporting on Mum's selection in the Victorian women's squad to play an interstate carnival in Sydney in 1938/39:

> "Northcote's star all-rounder (Nesta Williams) is likely to get her first chance in the interstate tournament. Besides batting and fielding, she is a very promising medium-slow left-hand bowler."

The writer, like the journalist from the *Brisbane Telegraph*, had obviously never seen her bowl: she was a right-hand off-spinner. But she was indeed selected to play for Victoria against Queensland in the Sydney carnival. The *Herald's* Pat Jarrett reported on her performance in the victorious match played at the Sydney Cricket Ground on March 13, 1939 – which happened to coincide with her twenty-first birthday: "Nesta Williams, the only member of the team who had not previously represented Victoria, made a very good impression in the match ... she bowled well and fielded excellently." She also made a quick-fire 10 late in the day in Victoria's first innings.

These articles make it clear that such press coverage of women's cricket had a profound impact on the sport's rising popularity with the public. As Richardson observed, "to appreciate the contribution of these women sportswriters in the 1930s is an understanding of how important they were in supporting women's sport and driving interest, patronage and attendance at games".[120]

Journalists such as Pat Jarrett and the *Women's Weekly's* Ruth Peddey were not only brilliant writers, but they were also sportswomen in their own right and fierce advocates for women's sport and especially women's cricket. Through their brilliant narrative-driven journalism, they helped usher in the 'Golden Era' of the women's game defined by floods of young girls eager to play the game and hordes of curious men and women eager to watch.

What these journalists saw at suburban grounds all over Melbourne were young, independent women demonstrating outstanding athletic ability and remarkable cricketing skill. It was cricket played with good humour: there were no hard feelings at the end of play. No women cricketers threw a bat in anger. Outstanding women cricketers, such as Antonio, Palmer, and more became household names in the 1930s – thanks, at least in part, to the writing of women journalists like these.

At the bottom of my mother's memory box was a letter, written to her family following her maiden first-class game playing for Victoria in the women's cricket carnival in Sydney against Queensland, March 13, 1939 – her twenty-first birthday. She described her first innings playing for her state:

> *"I went in sixth wicket down as the light faded ... I hit 2 fours and a two, then was caught on the midwicket boundary going for a six!... However, Peggy (Antonio, the team captain) played a lovely hand in the first innings, she only hit 2 single runs out of her 38..."*

In Queensland's first innings, Mum reported that:

> *"Peggy never gave me a bowl, but I had one today in their second dig, I got none for 5 off 6 overs, but then Peggy took me off ... I was padded up for half an hour waiting on the steps in the cold, but I never got in ..."*

However, all was forgiven:

> "When we got home, we all had a bath and were told to go to the lounge for a meeting... around 10 o'clock I was told to shut my eyes and when I opened them, Peggy had brought in a cake with twenty-one candles all alight for me ... it was lovely ... all the girls had put in bought me a pretty little gold brooch with three blue stones in it..."

In re-reading her letter to home that March day, I can't help but weep for my beautiful, talented mother standing at the entrance of a life of possibilities. But behind those written words, history conjured a thousand sordid images of insistent, marching feet that were about to trample her every dream.

The 1939 cricket carnival marked the end of an extraordinary era in the evolution of women's cricket in this country. The local game was never more popular thanks to the unprecedented amount of media coverage of women's cricket, championed by the determination and skill of pioneering female journalists such as Pat Jarrett and Ruth Peddey.

The Melbourne- and Australia-wide domestic women cricketers of the 1930s played in an out-of-history moment. The widespread and serious coverage of women cricket during this period challenged the established belief throughout the twentieth century – and before – that cricket was not a feminine-appropriate sport, or to quote English batsman Wally Hammond: "There are some games women can play, in general, actually better than men, but the muscular differences of the sexes prohibits cricket from being one of them."[121]

The 1930s allowed the heady freedom of ordinary suburban women to proclaim potency as sportspeople. And it was the determined and courageous working-class women, living in depressed economic times in the industrial centres of Melbourne and elsewhere, that dared to ditch mealy-mouthed, hegemonic notions of femininity and play cricket as entertainingly and as well as any man.

# 13

# The Dawn of International Women's Cricket

The First Tours: 1934/35, 1937/38

In the 1930s, women's cricket went international. A 3-Test tour of Australia by an English women's team in 1934/35 came soon after the Bodyline tumult, followed by a reciprocal 3-Test series played in England in early 1937. It was a fragile time to mount such a tour, given the ongoing furore caused by Jardine's men just a year before. But, as Marion Stell writes, the tour of the colony by a team of English women cricketers would play its part in reinforcing, restoring and strengthening ties between the two countries. In fact, "retightening the ties of Empire" became a subtext of the whole enterprise. Stell quotes an article written in November 1934 in the *Sydney Morning Herald* reflecting on the first English tour of Australia:

> "In spite of body-line and other occasional impediments, the cricket Tests ... have played a great and enduring part in cementing the Empire tie. And now the women are taking a hand in it ..."[122]

The Australian Women's Cricket Council (AWCC) was established in 1931 as the national governing body for women's cricket in Australia. A key player in establishing the council was Margaret Peden, a twenty-five-year-old Sydney teacher and opening batter for New South Wales. But that description rather underplays both her social background and influence. Margaret and her sister Barbara – who also played for NSW – were the daughters of Sir John Peden, Professor of Law at the University of Sydney and President of the New South Wales Legislative Council. Coming from such a background meant doors opened for the two sisters.

Fundamental to the Council's role was the management and promotion of the game at a national level. Its members were Victoria, New South Wales, and Queensland, with South Australia and Western Australia joining in 1934. The Australian Capital Territory and Tasmania waited until 1977 and 1982, respectively.

It was Margaret Peden who came up with the idea of a tour of Australia by an English women's cricket team. Except there was one big problem – the Council was broke. In 1934, the three-year-old AWCC had only a few shillings to its name, 4s 7p to be exact. But that didn't stop Peden challenging the Council's British rival to send a women's team Down Under.

The Council would cover the tourist's hospitality and billets, but the English players needed to pay for their own passage, an amount pushing £80 or more – the approximate equivalent of £4900 today, or AU$10,000. This appeared to be of little concern to the Brits. Given the cost of travel plus the expense involved in spending four months sailing to and from Australia (plus the time playing tour matches, all without an income), the 1934/35 touring English women cricketers were, by necessity, women born of middle-class if not elite backgrounds.

As Gideon Haigh suggested:

> "That they could find 80 pounds each reflects the differences between the roots of the women's game in each country. The visitors who stepped from the SS Cathay in Freemantle in November 1934 came from a country where the women's game was becoming a sort of polo for the ponyless. The hosts came wholly from working-class suburbs"[123]

*Dean and Archdale (women's cricket team captains, Victoria and England) tossing before the match in Melbourne, 1934. Courtesy National Library of Australia.*

This may be a slight overstatement given Margaret and Barbara Peden's family heritage, but Haigh's description was certainly accurate when applied to the English team. The English captain Betty Archdale was the daughter of a suffragette, and a professional soldier killed in World War I. She was exposed to the game as a boarder at St Leonards School in St Andrews, Scotland, and as she told Marion Stell: "Sport was compulsory and we played whatever we had to play according to the term – lacrosse one term, hockey the next, and cricket the next ... we had a very good cricket coach and I played regularly." After school she lived in Kent where her social connections gave her access to a private cricket and hockey ground: "We played hockey in winter and cricket in summer and of course there was plenty of tennis and golf." [124]

The English tourists were a reflection of the British Women's Cricket establishment, or as Amy Hudson told Marion Snell, "I think you would call them upper class; they were certainly upper-middle class."[125] But it is important to

Betty Archdale, c1934. Courtesy National Library of Australia

acknowledge that these middle-class female cricketers were in their own way denying a broadly held societal expectation about the gendered nature of leisure in modern Britain. Raf Nicholson writes that, at this time, it was expected that women's place was in the home knitting or playing a "feminine" sport such as tennis, while a man's place was outside the home playing manly sports such as cricket and football. [126]

British women cricketers of the 1930s may have been elite, nonconformist sportspeople, but it doesn't mean they had an easy time of it. They were pilloried for playing cricket and not birthing babies. It was a little different for women cricketers 9461 miles (or 15,226 kilometres) away in Australia, largely because they were drawn from more humble backgrounds – the Australian captain Margaret Peden was an exception to this rule.

Given the class divide between the English and Australian teams, how were the tourists received by their opponents and the general public when they finally arrived for that inaugural tour in December 1934? Surely, just over a year after the blood and guts of the men's Bodyline tour, coupled with the Australian disdain of the British class system, the tall poppy syndrome would kick in and be directed at a bunch of privileged ladies from the British establishment. No! Not a bit of it!

Betty Archdale's English team was feted across the country, especially its star batter, the Shanghai-born Molly Hide who was taught her aggressive right-hand opening batting style at the elite girls' school Wycombe Abbey in Buckinghamshire. Curious? Perhaps not – such adulation was not at odds with Australia's national character at that time, given that Australia had long held Britain and the British people in a passionate embrace. For decades, Anglophile Australians born to this country referred to Britain as home. In the 1930s, over 90% of Australians identified as Anglo-Celtic, with any form of Australian nationalism comfortably accommodated within a wider loyalty to the British Empire, as expressed through allegiance to the British monarch.

It's of little surprise that Australia, a place that proudly boasts a mythic, classless egalitarianism, hugged Betty Archdale's English team of largely upper-class women cricketers to its collective bosom. This, from the *Women's Weekly* of December 1934:

> "Seldom in the history of South Australia has a reception to a sports team caused more commotion than that tendered by the Lord Mayor of Adelaide to the English girls. The visiting cricketers had to fight their way through the seething mass of people there."[127]

In Melbourne there was a town hall reception followed by an afternoon tea hosted by the speaker of Victoria's lower house – the Legislative Assembly – which was no small honour considering it was just a year since the first woman, Millie Peacock, had been elected to the Parliament of Victoria. The reception was followed by a luncheon hosted by that bastion of male privilege, the Melbourne Cricket Club.

As Stell observed, the Australians were as star-struck by their opponents as the general public. As mentioned, Sydney-born all-rounder Amy Hudson was in awe: "The majority of them were real class. I don't mean playing cricket, but I mean lifestyle".[128]

## *The Dress Code*

The Australian media were also in awe of the tourist uniform – as they were of the English conservative presentation of femininity in both dress and behaviour of their players. According to Marjorie Pollard, in 1930 it was necessary for women cricketers to play in something that was above criticism – and this meant dresses or divided skirts and the covering of arms and legs.[129] Betty Archdale reported to Stell: "My recollection is people thought our uniform – a divided linen skirt, 'blouse' with sleeves to the elbow and stockings – was pretty hot stuff,"[130] and Australia's national association was clearly eager to conform to the English dress code.

Margaret Peden submitted a new cricketing costume to the association in the style of a divided skirt in linen material to replace the present knee-length

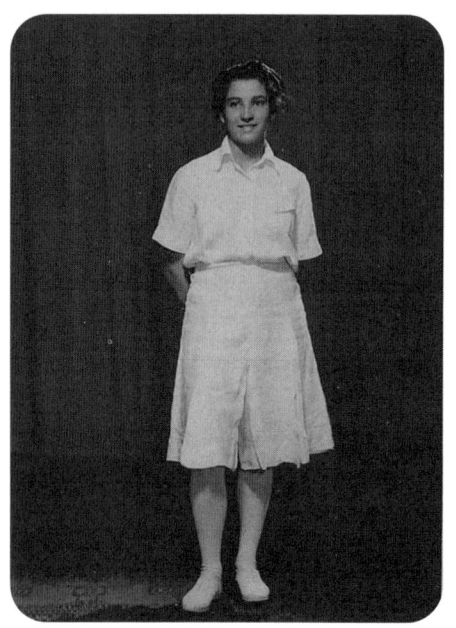

Peggy Antonio. Courtesy Bradman Museum Trust collection.

frock. Why not trousers and long-sleeved shirt or blouse – legs and arms covered, but why a skirt at all?

Ruby Monaghan from Wollongong – who played in the first Test in Brisbane as an opening batter and medium-pace bowler – remembered very sensibly playing in long trousers in her local competition. Why impose a British standard of femininity on Australian women cricketers? A standard that was clearly described in correspondence to the President of England's Women's Cricket Association in 1948: "women should occupy themselves in doing things for which they are fitted and avoid trying to act and dress like a man".[131]

Needless to say, Australian team members were equivocal in their attitudes to the dress code. Nancy Clements "liked the divided skirt ... but the white stockings ... No!" Nell McLarty hated "those terrible stockings ... they were lisle and they were long, and we had to wear a suspender belt to keep them up. Peggy and I couldn't stand them ... we played in tennis socks and had more freedom, oh it was really terrible." Whereas Peggy Antonio was blunt, describing the white stockings as "looking better on a corpse!"[132]

Women cricketers playing in the lower grades of the game were also forced to dress in a way that conformed to the hegemonic notions of English femininity. My mother's uniform at the start of her career in the early 1930s consisted of what she described as a "full harness," or corset and stockings.

> "The corset dug in, and hot! Playing cricket in the heat wearing a full corset and stockings ... it was a wonder I never fainted! It was only when the Association introduced the culotte later in the 30s that I felt comfortable in the field. It was hard to throw yourself about in a skirt and suspenders, but the culotte solved that problem."

The split skirt or culotte was certainly an improvement over the usual one-piece frocks below the knee, but as Betty Archdale told Marion Stell, "I think we were probably, both here and in England, very anxious not to offend anyone, you know, by being too daring."133 Apparently, trousers and a long sleeve shirt to better suit Australian conditions were, indeed, too daring!

Apart from 'the divided skirt,' the Australians admired another thing about the tourists. What was obvious was the professionalism of the team. The Australians were impressed by the English practice methods and their singular approach to playing the game. In the words of Victorian Lorna Kettels, "They were a team and they were sort of together the whole time ... but travel does that to you."134

Victorian Women's Cricket team playing England in 1934. Courtesy Peggy Antonio's family, Port Melbourne Historic Society.

In contrast, the Australians were a factionalised camp on the basis of their state of origin. In the words of Lorna Kettels, the Australians "were sort of segregated ... the Victorians ... stayed with Victorians, the New South Wales with the New South Wales ... that's how it was."135 But when the cricket finally got underway, it was game on – and it was a seventeen-year-old leg-spinner and shoe-box maker from Port Melbourne who stole the headlines.

Victoria played England at the Melbourne Cricket Ground in a warm-up game a couple of days after the MCC luncheon and, all of a sudden, the English players knew they had a fight on their hands. Peggy Antonio returned the match figures of 10 for 48, completely hoodwinking the English batting sensation, the elegant Molly Hide.

"She was a flowing player, graceful casual, four, four, four," Peggy remembered. "But do you know I got her with an ordinary off-break ... I can still remember the look on her face ... she didn't know a thing about it."[136]

Saturation media coverage of the glamorous English tourists, coupled with Peggy Antonio's heroics with the ball, ensured the crowds attending tour matches were very healthy indeed.

## *The Tests*

The first Test was played in Brisbane in front of 3000 spectators, with Australia – captained by the ubiquitous Margaret Peden – bundled out in the first innings for just 47. England then blitzed the home side in their first innings with a score of 154, with Antonio's Port Melbourne spin-twin Anne Palmer returning the extraordinary figures of 7 for 18. Australia would go on to make 138 in their second dig with England, easily achieving the required 34 runs to win the match for a loss of only 1 wicket.

The Sydney Test was another blowout, with England making 5 declared for 301 in its first innings. England's powerful batter Myrtle Maclagan stole the show with the first international women's Test century of 119. Then, in an extraordinary all-round performance, she took 4 for 33 in Australia's first innings of 162. Australia went on to make 148 in its second innings, leaving England to make the required 10 runs for the loss of 2 wickets.

Melbourne was a whole other story. In front of 7000 spectators, England captain Betty Archdale won the toss and batted. The visitors made a credible 162 with Maclagan again starring with 50 – but it was Peggy Antonio who starred on her home turf. Her 6 for 49 was the talk of Melbourne town.

But then Australia almost fell apart in their first innings at 8 for 91, before Anne Palmer (39) and Joyce Brewer (26) got the home side within 12 runs of the English first innings score. England declared their second innings at 7 for 153 and, again, Australia's top six stumbled before the lower order managed to eke out a draw, Joyce Brewer again saving the day with a stoic 31. The home side finished with a score of 8 for 104 when stumps were drawn.

The spin-twins Anne Palmer and Peggy Antonio were the star Australian players of the series; between them, they took 22 of the 35 English wickets to fall in the 3-Test series. Anne Palmer bagged 10 English scalps while eighteen-year-old Antonio's 12-wicket haul included her 6 for 49 in the final game at the MCG where she snared all of England's top order – a tour highlight! According to Haigh: "Peggy Antonio was an adolescent antidote to a grey era."[137] But Anne Palmer was not far behind her childhood friend.

At tour's end, it was clear the Australian Women's Cricket Council's gamble had paid off, both financially and in raising the profile of women's cricket in Australia. There was now undoubtedly an international future for the game.

It's of no surprise that, on the back of the financially successful 1934/5 Test series in Australia, an invitation was extended to the Australian team to tour England in 1937. This, however, would prove to be a difficult prospect for many of Australia's best female cricketers – especially its star spin-twins.

## The 1937 Tour of England

In most parts of Britain, working-class women and girls did not play cricket – but in Australia, struggle-town cricketers were the backbone of the side, with fewer upper-class women making the team. How was the country going to field a competitive side if its best players were stuck at home? Given the cost of funding the passage to England, the months of income-free touring and the cost of living in a foreign country, it was remarkable that Australia could assemble a competitive team at all. Many missed the boat for purely economic reasons. Anne Palmer was one of those women.

Throughout the 1930s, Palmer and Peggy Antonio were undoubtedly the greatest spin bowling partnership in the country, if not the world. But Palmer had one major handicap – she was born into a poor home. Palmer's international career should have been extended to at least the follow-up tour of England in 1937, but the £75 passage (roughly a year's basic wage for a woman at the time), the four months off work and the expense of living away from home meant she never played Test cricket again – although she did continue her first-class career up until the Second World War. After the war however, she chose to move on with her life.

After winning a scholarship to further her education, Palmer joined Victoria Police in 1946 as a uniformed officer. There she stayed for the majority of her working life. Australian women's cricket lost an extraordinary talent, her brief career evaporating into history.

But what of her Port Melbourne spinning partner? Was she resigned to the same fate?

As Peggy Antonio told Gideon Haigh: "I'm not making any bones, my family didn't have a brass razoo. One of my sisters was working and she was married. Going (to England) was just out of the question."[138]

But then Peggy's community pitched in to help the twenty-one-year-old raise the funds. They organised three-penny raffles and a fundraising dinner dance. Even her employer, Raymond's Shoes, contributed a set of travelling cases and a folding Brownie camera for her trip. But all of their combined efforts were still not enough. She was still short of funds.

Then one day, Peggy opened Melbourne's *Herald* newspaper and read an article written by the newspaper's regular women's cricket writer Pat Jarrett: "The Girl Grimmett could go to England after all." She read that a senior executive at McIlwraith McEacharn, James McLeod, had pulled £100 out of his own pocket to pay for Peggy's passage.

Apparently, McLeod had known Peggy's late father on the waterfront and insisted that his financial support came with no ... er ... *expectations*, only the honour of occasionally entertaining her at his palatial Hawthorn apartment. But Antonio told Haigh in 1992: "there was certainly none of that!! He never made any ... how shall I put it? He didn't push himself."[139] We'll have to believe her!

McLeod had not only written a cheque for £100, he also agreed to sponsor her throughout the tour. He would regularly send her letters of credit via the National Bank, alerting her by mail of his latest deposit. He was a gentleman, through and through.

Her benefactor would occasionally send a driver to pick her up at Raymond's factory in his Rolls Royce and bring her to his Hawthorn flat for dinner. A Roller sent to pick up a young, attractive box maker at a factory in Easy Street Collingwood during the height of the 1930s Great Depression? A place once famous for standover rackets, illegal betting shops, sly grog outfits, bullet-holed bodies and debris? A young girl in the back seat of a Roller in Collingwood? That wasn't going to cause a stir now, was it? Well, it certainly did!

Antonio told Haigh that, one day, she was sitting in the back of the car when she happened to pull up beside her Clarendon Cricket Club rival and Victorian teammate, batter Ruth Tucker, on the corner of Smith and Johnston Streets: "I was sitting in the back of the car when it pulled up beside her at the lights ... her eyes nearly popped out of her head!" [140]

Thanks to James McLeod, whatever the arrangement, on April 4, 1937, Peggy Antonio sailed from Perth accompanied by captain Margaret Peden and her teammates to Britain, via a 2-match series in Holland.

The young tourists were certainly kept on a tight leash while on board ship. The rules were strict: no drinking, no smoking or gambling. No husbands, relations or friends. No setting foot on the top deck after dinner. In bed by 10. Then up at 7.15 for physical drills each day except Sunday, and all team members were expected to participate in deck games! Antonio thinks that she especially received special attention by part-chaperone, part-team-manager Olive Peatfield. She told Haigh: "I was the youngest in the team ... a girl from Port Melbourne ... I think she thought ... she'll have to have a brick on her head. But I wasn't the sort, even at that tender age, to put up with that!"[141]

## *Class Barriers Within*

Margaret Peden was one of Australia's great sports administrators and a vocal and highly effective advocate for women's sport – but she was hardly a star Australian opening bat. In the 1934/35 home series she made a total of 32 runs from 6 innings, with a highest score of 11 and an average of around 5. Throughout her entire international career, Peden didn't bowl and in her six Tests she batted in 12 innings, scored a total of 87 runs, with a highest score of 34 and an average of 8.7 per innings.

So why on earth was she captain? It seems her family background, administrative skills and strong personality were the reason she was chosen by selectors to captain the side. Stell quotes a Sydney University friend of Margaret's, journalist Kathleen Commins:

> "She was a very quiet person and never threw her weight around, but she could always get people of all kinds and types moving and doing things ... the name Peden in this state meant a great deal."[142]

Peden's "respectable" heritage meant she was "a safe pair of hands" as Australia's representative – she wouldn't "embarrass the country" while mixing with the lords, ladies, admirals and athletes of the British sporting establishment.

*Joy Partridge signing a bat for Nancy Clements (Victorian women's cricket team), Melbourne, 1934. National Library of Australia.*

Aside from captaining the team, Peden was on another mission: to help ease the tension between England and Australia following the Bodyline furore. I'm sure her diplomatic skills were of equal if not greater importance than her cricketing ability. Her "respectable" background and "good breeding" ensured the "Ties of Empire" would remain securely bound under her stewardship! But her appointment was not without controversy; there were rumblings of discontent within cricketing circles, with whispers of nepotism, especially around the selection of her equally modest-performing architect sister Barbara.

The grumblings began in earnest when England toured Australia in 1934/35, and star Victorian all-rounder Nancy Clements was rushed by selectors from a holiday in rural Daylesford in central Victoria to replace Amy Hudson in the team to play England in the Sydney Test. But when Clements arrived after a mad twenty-four-hour dash from country Victoria, she found her place in the side had been taken by none other than the captain's sister! Nancy sat out the match as the twelfth woman! According to Stell, the controversy featured widely in Victorian newspapers at the time – with the treatment of Clements widely criticised. But more controversy was to follow again involving Barbara Peden's selection in the Australian team.

A decision was made by the Australian selectors to make merit the key prerequisite for players selected for the 1937/38 England touring team. However, after the announcement of the squad, a report appeared in the papers that Barbara Peden, who was working as an architect in England at the time, had been

*The Victoria Women's XI to play England, Melbourne 1934. National Library of Australia.*

added to the touring party. According to Stell, not everyone was happy with her selection: "The feeling may have been that the Peden family seemingly made their own rules ... Victorians Nell McLarty and Peggy Antonio acknowledged it but were tight lipped."[143]

Nepotism may have been the reason the English captain Betty Archdale detected a frisson of resentment towards the Australian captain: "I thought she had a pretty rough time. I may be wrong but I had a feeling that those so and so's down in Victoria, for some reason, thought that somebody else should be captain." [2][144]

Well yes, and maybe they even had misgivings about the standard of performance of both Margaret and her sister at the international level. As Archdale herself told Stell, Margaret Peden "wasn't a good enough player you know ... the captain wants to have something a bit more and I don't think she ever made a score."[145] She didn't, and nor did her sister. In a 4-Test career, Barbara made a total of 94 runs, with a top score of 33, finishing with a Test average of 13.4.

It seems clear that Peden's personality, her experience as both a captain of her state and her acknowledged management skills coupled with her social background and connections out-weighed her cricketing ability. But if merit was the prerequisite for team selection, should she have been chosen as captain for the 1937/38 tour of England? On performance, no. It could be argued there were far more credentialed state captains playing the game at that time. Furthermore, both Margaret and Barbara didn't have the runs on the board to warrant selection in the touring party full stop. But in the minds of selectors, their cricketing ability at the international level was not the point. They were "real class", and class mattered.

*Spear and Partridge fielding (England), Snowball wicket keeping, and Hazel Partridge batting (NSW), Sydney, 1935. National Library of Australia.*

The Australian players who sailed onboard the SS *Jervis* to England that April day in 1937 were women from a range of social backgrounds. Many on board had secured their passage with the help of fundraising matches, local raffles, the odd contribution from relatives and one or two charitable employers. Then there were the Peden sisters, and bowler Pat Holmes.

Holmes came from a relatively middle-class, professional background. She attended Frensham School in Mittagong where she was encouraged in her interest in photography. Following her short international cricketing career, she spent time as a freelance in England and is now recognised as the first woman photojournalist to work on a major newspaper in Australia.

No doubt the Peden sisters and Pat Holmes felt comfortable navigating the behavioural protocols of the welcoming luncheon hosted by Lord Decies at the Savoy London, as well as a similar event hosted by the wife of British Prime Minister Stanley Baldwin, Lucy, at their 10 Downing Street residence. Of equal importance, Lady Baldwin would also easily relate to the Pedens and Holmes – not so much others in the touring party.

At both events, Antonio remained under the eagle eye of Mrs Peatfield who feared the factory girl would do something to disgrace the team: "oh I didn't kick over the traces or make a nuisance of myself," Peggy protested.[146] But Peggy *did* manage to gain an insight into the lives of a whole different social strata when she was billeted with the bursar at Westminster College, a businessman who lived next door to Brookland's racetrack, and the great English batter Molly Hide's parents' five-acre farm at Roundhurst in Surrey. She may have felt a great restfulness, drenched as she was in the tranquillity of the English countryside ... but maybe not. We will never know. There is no record of her "acting-up" throughout the tour. As she said, she "wasn't the type".

When the cricket finally got underway, Peggy was very comfortable out in the middle. She made runs and bagged a significant number of wickets, as she told Haigh in 1992: "the leg-break was unheard of in England at the time ... the leg-break and just the hint of a wrong-un was usually enough."[147]

In the first three-day Test played in front of a large crowd at the County Ground in Northampton, Australia won the toss and decided to bat. The visitors made 300 with Kath Smith top-scoring with 88. England then made 204 in their first innings with Antonio taking Australia's bowling honours with 6 for 51 off 18.1 overs. Australian amassed 102 in their second innings leaving England 198 to make, but they fell 31 runs short. Australian women had beaten England in a Test match for the very first time!

The second Test, played in front of supportive crowds at Stanley Park in Blackpool, was also a tight affair. England made 222 in their first innings with Antonio again taking the bowling honours with 3 for 34 off 9 overs. Australia managed 302 in reply, with Hazel Pritchard starring with 67, though all in all it was an even contribution by all Australian batters.

England in reply made 231 with again, you guessed it, Antonio taking the bowling honours with 5 for 31. Australia, needing 152 for victory in their second innings, could only manage 126, falling just 26 runs short of victory.

Then, in a rain-interrupted decider played at the Oval in London, the game finished in a soggy draw with Australia batting twice with scores of 207 and 224 while England scored 308 in their first innings, then a token 3 for 9 in their second.

In a farewell match at Mitcham Cricket Green against Surrey, a capacity crowd of 10,000 spectators made up of prams, dogs and small children spilled onto the oval to watch the Girl Grimmett's final first-class match played on English soil. Marjorie Pollard, the principal English women's cricket writer, wrote of Antonio: "If I see a cleverer spin bowler than Antonio, I shall not only be surprised but genuinely disbelieving."[148] Pollard covered the women's Test series for BBC radio and persuaded Movietone news to send a crew, so news of Peggy's 19 wickets in 3 Tests at 11 runs per wicket could be spread beyond the boundary. Peggy's "exotic" heritage, combined with her freakish cricketing ability, made her a "poster girl" for the women's game and the star of the English Test series.

"I used to squirm at some of the things they wrote," she said. "I was 'a fluent Spanish speaker', I don't know a word, I was 'a gifted pianist' ... I can just about play a few things by ear."[149]

Antonio came back to Australia to play for Raymond in Melbourne's Women's Premier cricket competition for another season and then captain Victoria in the 1938/39 Women's Interstate carnival held in Sydney. But that proved to be her swansong – and the swansong of Victorian women's cricket for a long while. At the age of twenty-two, she gave the game away. She told Haigh it was because cricket was no longer fun, but maybe there were other reasons. Perhaps she felt she had become a curiosity, an exotic in an increasingly homogeneous game, a game largely played by women with entirely different life stories to her own. There were no hard feelings, and it was time to get on with her life.[150]

## *The End of a Career*

In 1943, Antonio married an English fireman Eddie Howard, who she described as "a sort of undiscovered literary type". They moved to what was, for the time, a bohemian artist colony in the Melbourne semi-rural bushland suburb of Eltham.[151] Back in the 1940s, Eltham hosted an exciting alternate scene of unconventional thinking, a place with a healthy disregard for social norms and traditions. Eltham boasted intellectual freethinkers and early feminists, a place where artistic and literary types – both discovered and undiscovered – thrived. This vibrant scene coalesced around Montsalvat: the provincial medieval, Gothic pastiche village built by Justus Jorgensen from 1938.

It was to this "painterly bohemia" that Eddie and Peggy settled in a mudbrick home built by Eddie to raise daughters – and where Peggy could disappear into the history. Perhaps it was there, amongst the squiggerly gums, in a place where male and female artists came to play with radicals, collectivist Marxists and other assorted ratbags and anti-capitalists, that Peggy finally felt comfortable – no longer a curiosity, but someone who belonged.

Peggy Antonio was and remains a part of my family's mythology. I have a team photo of the 1938/39 Victorian carnival side that she captained; it sits on a bookshelf in my front room. There she is, frozen in her early twenties, raven haired, nearly black eyes smiling at the camera. Surrounding her are her Victorian teammates: Anne Palmer on her left, Ruth Tucker at her back, Betty Wilson at her feet and my mother standing proudly in front of the back row.

These bright-eyed women in the full phosphorescence of their youth were, in their own way, feminists. They were – though some may have queried the label, including my mother – "the new 30s woman" as defined by their embrace, either consciously or unconsciously, of the physical culture movement of the era. By definition, they concurred with the movements first principle that "the actively cultivated body" was fundamental to women's emancipation, along with political emancipation, greater gender equality, and expanding employment opportunities.[152]

It was via the unremarkable act of playing cricket that these young women were remarkable. They challenged a fundamental convention of Australian society at the time – that women were homemakers and servants to men and nothing more. These cricketing pioneers not only stepped outside their traditional societal role they also challenged the idea that playing cricket was the sole preserve of men.

It was the women pioneers of the 1930s who played cricket of a standard that attracted huge crowds and made celebrities of many of the star players. It was these women who organised the women's cricket competitions and the international cricketing tours, and it was women journalists who reported on the women's cricketing heroics in the media. My mother and her contemporaries were exercising a fundamental right to excel in a sport of their choice and did so enthusiastically, not entirely independent of men but largely so. By playing cricket, the women of the 1930s offered an assertive and vigorous statement of modernity. But they weren't alone.

In Melbourne at this time, there was another collection of young, mostly working-class bohemian artists and writers who were also carving out a similarly independent and uniquely Australian artistic vision. Their movement incorporated internationally formed modernist ideas in art and literature and adapted them to form an Australian aesthetic.

The movement centred around two newly married wealthy benefactors living in a farmhouse on the banks of the Yarra River in Heidelberg, just a few stops along the Hurstbridge line from my mother's family home in Northcote. They were attempting to establish a modernist artistic provocation that demanded answers from Australia's conservative establishment. But rather than answers, they were confronted by a vicious backlash unleashed by the usual suspects.

# 14

## The Culture War of the 1950s in Art, Literature, Society and Women's Cricket

The Australia that emerged from the Second World War in 1945 was a different place to the country that entered it. The Soviet Union, a crucial Western ally during hostilities, was now our mortal enemy – along with trade unions, writers, artists, the progressive press, sections of the Australian Labor Party and autonomous, empowered women. The promise of a 30s-style ribald, egalitarian modernist Australia continuing after the war was now perceived as a dangerous sorcery.

In other words, the pre-war larrikin voice as expressed in literature, art and politics, and the idea of an independent woman working or playing sport free of men, were now suspect. Consequently, many pre-war women cricketers retired from the game. In fact, when the annual Australian Women's Cricket

Championship resumed at war's end in the summer of 1946/47, the pool of quality first-class players had reduced dramatically.

Of Victoria's all-conquering 1938/39 championship side only Betty and Gwen Wilson padded up in 1946/47 – although Una Paisley, who had played for Victoria in the 1939/40 championship, was also a Victorian state representative. The tragedy for Australian women's cricket in the post-war era was that many of the country's best pre-war cricketers were now scattered across distant suburbs, ankle deep in new family responsibilities and permanently lost to the game.

*You can further your ambitions nominating as a candidate for Miss Australia 1950. National Library of Australia.*

## Women Cricketers Pull Up Stumps

Once the victory party was over, the serious business of demobilisation and dismantling of the Australian wartime economy began. But it was women who were the first casualties in this post-war economy. While their men served in the Australian armed forces from 1939 to 1945, women had filled vacant essential jobs in the factories and offices of Australian business. Many joined the Australian Women's Land Army and worked as shearers, tractor drivers or dairy farm workers. Then there were the women who served in military auxiliary organisations as delivery drivers, signallers and intelligence officers.

But come the armistice, all women were expected to forget the evidence of their war-time lives with all its camaraderie, worth and meaning and, in deference to a flood of demobbed servicemen, return to their traditional status as what Simone de Beauvoir defined as the "Second Sex". In post-war Australia, it was men who determined what it is to be a woman, and that definition certainly didn't include independent women playing the manly sport of cricket.

The image of woman as homemaker and mother was promoted relentlessly from 1945 – so much so that women's sport (and, by implication, women's cricket) virtually disappeared from the public's imagination. Simultaneously, the crucial role women played in the Australian war effort was devalued, if not entirely forgotten.

Women were defined and valued by post-war convention; not by intelligence, creativity or ability, but in puerile domestic terms: "A woman was either married, or hoping to be married, while girls were in training for their later lives as wives and mothers. Femininity, fashion, grooming and sexual attractiveness dominated women's magazines, along with articles on housekeeping and cooking."[153]

Magazines like the *Australian Women's Weekly* – where former cricketer, administrator and national selector Ruth Preddey's pre-war women's cricket column had helped the magazine grow its readership – was, in the immediate aftermath of the war, replaced with bridal fashion stories, or sewing patterns and grooming advice. Rather than publish profiles of the latest up-and-coming suburban teenage all-rounder, the *Weekly* published recipes suitable for TV dinners and best-selling cookery books. The magazine's features on home design were also very popular.

So, what was the sociology of this new world of suburbs, the wringer and the clothes washer? Did it leave a catalogue of bitterness at the scrubbed front doorsteps of those pioneering women of the 1930s, women such as my newly married mother? Absolutely, it did!

Mum's mother had died during the war, forcing her ex-Air Force maintenance-man husband to live at her family home with her widowed father and three returned servicemen brothers. All five men now worked in jobs with rotating shifts. Mum bitterly described to me some years later how she was expected to provide meals for all five men at all times of the day and night, wash their clothes and their dishes, shop for food and somehow care for her newborn baby along the way. While TS Eliot's *J Alfred Prufrock* measured out his life in coffee spoons, for Mum it was a life determined by an endless production line of chops-and-three-veg, dirty nappies and early morning bacon and eggs.

Of course, my mother was not alone in her post-war domestic drudgery. The experience of many women in this new world was one of being "bombarded with idealised images of family life including advertisements for products from kitchen materials to new appliances presented by perfectly groomed, smiling women, usually with children – all perfectly behaved."[154] This was not the world they knew: the silent husband, his trousers worn at the knee, meat sandwiches, a life of make-do.

How could my mother reconcile with what the propaganda defined as the ideal woman ... married, living in a suburban home with two or three children on her hip with never a day without washing on the line? Mum was living in a crumbling Edwardian home, stuffed with the detritus of war service, disassembled motor-bike engines and ferrets. This was a world where newspaper advertisements for Rinso – brand-new brightness with Rinso's "richer, softer suds" – had replaced images of her full stride, bowling an off-break, or reports of her hat-trick against Collingwood in 1941. My mother shared Betty Wilson and Una Paisley's teasing dreams of a successful sporting career of travel, achievement and independence. But now, living with her husband, son, father and three brothers, she was confronted with a changed narrative. She felt the full blast of what was a conservative backlash not only against women, but modernism in all of its forms.

The late 1940s was a different country to just ten years before. It was the era of the Iron Curtain, a time of espionage and propaganda campaigns, embargoes and the ever-rising threat of nuclear annihilation. It was apparently a world only a man could understand. It was no place for a woman, especially not one who, just a decade previously, defiantly engaged in a cricketing burlesque, a leg show, in a public park. In my mother's mind, she needed to change her story.

To survive this time in history, I believe she needed to conform with the new definition of what it took to be a 1950s woman.

Evidence of her past, independent life was hastily removed from public view and stored away deep inside a cupboard. Hot, sweaty off-break bowling girls who could effortlessly glide a fast in-swinger to the long-leg boundary were, in the world of the 1950s, if not an anachronism, then certainly a bit weird. Mum didn't want to be weird. Consequently, the story of her career remained hidden in her memory box to inexorably crumble and fade.

Her Victorian blazer disappeared; maybe, like Peggy Antonio's, it was turned into a duster. She did manage, however, to keep the pocket. Her hat-trick balls were soon reduced to broken bits of string and leather; my brother and I prised off the shields and belted the covers off them around the backyard.

I used her Bill Woodfull-signed bat for most of my rather unspectacular early cricketing career. I eventually sliced off a huge sliver from the blade when I went for a big drive through cover. I then reattached the splinter with gaffer tape, reinventing the bat for the backyard and the beach. I had, in my own way, exploited my mother's cricketing memorabilia as currency to enter the male canon.

But society's backlash was not restricted to just cricket-playing women, it included anyone who questioned the Persil-white, better-dead-than-red narrative. These included the modernist artists – the poets, painters and writers who challenged the dominant, synchronised artistic and political conservatism of the post-war era. What was done to them was cruel and targeted, and it was done by means of a coordinated hoax executed by two conservative poets, James McAuley and Harrold Stewart, in late 1943.

What does poetry censorship have to do with women's cricket? Well, everything.

## *Backlash: The Menzies Era*

Sir Robert Menzies was voted Australia's post-war Prime Minister in 1949 in the wake of a growing communist panic that manifested around Ben Chifley's promise to nationalise the banks. Menzies was a man who said he would govern for "the forgotten people": "those hard working, great and sober, dynamic middle-class Australians; the salary earners, shopkeepers skilled artisans, professional men and women, the farmers ... those people who placed family, God, hearth and home at the centre of their lives."[155]

The Menzies era ushered in decades of undeniable prosperity, built on towering tariff barriers, mass migration and a dynamic manufacturing industry. But it was also a time when the idea of "an Australian femininity suffered a great leap backwards."

In both the pre-war and war years, hundreds of thousands of women, often for the first time, had felt the freedom to socialise with other women, discuss matters in their life and politics independent of men. But in 1945 and in the years beyond, such female agency provoked a moral panic in the minds of the guardians of respectability. The idea of women cavorting on cricket fields or cycling from home to work an eight-hour day in a factory or office was a distraction from the moral purpose of women's lives – reproducing good British stock and being at the service of their man. The usurping of women's traditional societal role by the idea of a modern, socially engaged and independent woman was confronted by a determined backlash from the patriarchal establishment.

It is hard to conceive just what an incredibly sexist place Australia was in the 1950s. Born of the nation's convict origins, Australia's particular form of sexism has never really gone away. From the latter years of 1940s and early 1950s, women were forbidden to forge a career in the cultural or university sector and married women could not join the public service. Depressingly, Australia refused to ratify the International Labour Organisation's convention on equal pay for women in 1951, condemning a whole generation of women to knowing and relying on the brutal strength of men's arms.

The independent and rowdy pre-war modernism of Australia was now replaced by a conservative quietude, one of nuclear families living in detached bungalows sprouting like mushrooms across the countryside and stuffed with new electrical appliances like radios, televisions and fridges. The "Australian dream" was built on farmland and bush converted by bulldozers and jackhammers into sprawling suburbs filled with young families and migrant workers trudging off to nearby factories, or city offices belching smoke and money into a booming economy.

Female agency, a celebrated quality on the sports field and during the war, now evoked, what the sociologists might described as "a whole repertoire of protests and gender-specific patterns of risk". Social violence is a more succinct way of describing it. Social attitudes in the 1950s placed women, not at the easel, the writing desk, the workplace or the cricket field, but firmly in the home. These women may have watched the *I Love Lucy Show* or *Father Knows Best*. Maybe they flicked through the *Women's Weekly*, read stories promoting the values of domesticated womanhood and consumer culture, never questioning the tailor-made life set down for them, one of "whey-faced anonymity." But on the fringes of Melbourne, a group of bohemian dissenters and rebels with an artistic cause raged against the dying of the light.

## *Heide*

When John and Sunday Reed, a couple born to Australian establishment families – John from Tasmania and Sunday neé Baillieu from Melbourne – acquired an unassuming Victorian farmhouse and a two-and-a half-acre property in Heidelberg for £1000 in the winter of 1934, their plan was to renovate the near-derelict home and fill it with their books, antiques and heirlooms. The area, including the adjacent river valley and sloping, wooded banks, had been used by the Australian Impressionists of the nineteenth century as subjects for their misty, golden gum tree paintings. But there was to be no repeat of the Heidelberg School's Golden Summer at the Reeds' farm.

John and Sunday Reed subsequently acquired a further eleven acres of denuded grazing land from my uncle Alfred Roberts, the husband of my father's sister Jean. In purchasing the land, the Reeds had bought more than an old house and garden; they had acquired a blank canvas on which to create their own verdant Eden, with a walled kitchen garden, a rose walk, laying hens and cattle. It was to be a self-sustaining, garden-to-plate existence.

They named their little farm 'Heide', and soon, their kitchen and dining room were filled with John and Sunday's siblings, landscape gardeners, intellectuals and artists such as Danila Vassilief, Adrian Lawlor, George Bell and Sunday's soon-to-be lover Sidney Nolan. Albert Tucker, Joy Hester, John Perceval, Arthur Boyd and a twenty-two-year-old avant-garde writer and publisher from Adelaide, Max Harris, also gravitated to Sunday's table.[156]

Harris was a swarthy man, a tough little footballer in his day, a rover not easily "bumped off the ball". He was a confident young man who possessed a smooth baritone voice, like Dylan Thomas; Hal Porter described him as "slender and handsome as Flecker's Hassan or a Syrian sweet-meats vendor".[157] Harris was the very image of the avant-garde poet that he was, but destined to be overwhelmed by the raging conservative onslaught to come.

Like the women cricketers of inner-Melbourne, the majority of the Heide artists were self-taught proletarians, children of families ravaged by the depression – Nolan's father was a cable-tram driver, Tucker's father a despondent, downwardly mobile railway worker. Joy Hester, however, came from a bourgeois family of "Spanish saddlers" and schoolteachers. What these artists had in common was a determination for creative freedom and expression.

Under the pear trees of Sunday's garden, or on the boarded veranda of the Reeds' home they plotted to be modern – and modern, at that moment, meant representing the tubercular ravages and Barcoo rot of Depression-era, inner-city Melbourne.

Nolan painted the bathers of St Kilda and later changed the focal point of art by tilting the picture plane so the view of the land became vertical. Albert Tucker haunted the dark streets of the Melbourne blackout and painted the red, smiling mouth of the modern evil he encountered there. While Vassilief revealed the mouldering street life of Fitzroy and Collingwood, filled with bow-legged toddlers, racing tricycle riders, a boy chasing a hoop down a deep lane and Betty Wilson bowling out-swingers to a boy with a bat at a lamppost. Joy Hester painted minimalist, disturbing psychological portraits. Arthur Boyd painted the pain and dislocation of Aboriginal brides. These fresh, spontaneous paintings captured an Australian drama of a largely cheerless time.

Meanwhile John, Max Harris, George Bell and others plotted to form the Contemporary Artist Society (CAS) with the aim of nurturing and promoting modern art in Australia. The Society was a direct response to the then Attorney-General Robert Menzies' plan in 1937 to form an Australian Academy of Art, styled on the English model and "designed to be an arbiter of standards – in particular defending the Australian tradition of landscape painting".[158] The Heide group wanted none of it! It was time to take to the presses.

From the CAS came the publishing firm Reed & Harris, which in turn published the left-wing, modernist publication *Angry Penguins* – a magazine designed to promote the work of the Heide group and publish the work of modernist Australian poets. It was the hope of John Reed and Max Harris that the new publication "might stir the public out of its complacency ... because (Reed) sensed the war seemed to have awoken the latent artistic spirit in Australia and remarkable work was being produced" – though work that went largely unseen and unread.[159] It would be the role of the magazine to bring this work to the public's attention.

But all this modernism set off, to quote Francis Webb, "platitudinous squeaks of the oily-leather bottomed chairs" of the guardians of respectability. It needed to be neutralised or confined, if you will, in full corset and stockings.

But for these "guardians of respectability" to achieve their aims, they needed willing recruits to fight the culture war, foot soldiers who possessed a statue's stare and an assassin's steel. Enter James McAuley and Harold Stewart.

## *The Ern Malley Affair*

As Robert Hughes wrote in the introduction to Michael Heywood's *The Ern Malley Affair*:

> *"It's every editor's dream that one day an authentic genius will drop through his or her letterbox, an unsolicited angel descending in a buff manila chariot."*[160]

Women's cricket had had its genius a decade before in Peggy Antonio, but in 1943 the literary world had theirs when Max Harris opened his morning mail. He discovered a sheaf of poems and a letter from someone named Ethel Malley. It read: "Dear sir, When I was going through my brother's things after his death, I found some poetry he had written. I am no judge of it myself..."

Harris idly flicked through the poems and gasped. He then read them more carefully a second time. Before he had finished that second reading, he knew he had found what he was looking for: a classless genius, what Hughes called the generation's "marvellous boy", "a sort of Rimbaud-cum-Keats ... a dead hero!"

The poet's name was Ernest Lalor Malley, and what poems they were. He wrote of the Spanish war of 1936, when fascist Axis powers overthrew the democratically elected Republican Spanish government. In response to the defeat, Malley wrote:

> *I have heard the shout in the streets*
> *The chiliasms of the Socialist Reich*
> *And the magazines I have read*
> *The Popular Front-to-Back*
> *But where I have lived*
> *Spain weeps in the gutters of Footscray...*

Then Malley delivered the coup-de-gras against those who would weep in Footscray's gutters, with a false quote allegedly from Lenin: "The emotions are not skilled workers." The final line from the poem Dürer: Innsbruck, 1495 – "I am still the black swan of trespass on alien waters" – has haunted Australian arts and artists for 85 years.

Harris was mad for these poems. He devoted a whole section of the autumn edition of *Angry Penguins* to them with a beautiful cover by Sidney Nolan illustrating the Arabian Tree from Malley's *Petit Testament*.

Like Peggy Antonio's British heroics, Malley's poems were an antidote to a grey world. But unlike Antonio's 19 English wickets in 3 Tests for just 11 runs each in 1937, Malley's poems and story were fabrications: a bullshit fairytale supposedly made up in a military army barracks in Melbourne in the course of an afternoon by two young conservative poets, Corporal Harold Stewart and Lieutenant James McAuley. Malley hadn't written them at all – he never existed.

Why did they do it?

To discredit Harris and the Australian literary and artistic modernist movement. They wanted to impose elite British cultural values on those CAS / Reed & Harris modernist larrikins. As Queensland University's Associate Professor Maggie Nolan wrote in the *Conversation* in August 2024:

> "As a nation, Australia was not even fifty years old at the time of the Ern Malley hoax. The hoax arrived at a time of anxiety and deep denial, as settler culture was attempting to build a literary culture that could give expression to an authentic Australian experience under the shadow of Britain's dominance, Australia's convict origins, and the scarcely acknowledged violence of colonial dispossession and assimilation..."

Nolan goes on:

> "In the 1940s, while war raged in Europe and the Pacific, a battle among the intelligentsia was underway in Australia about who had the authority and capacity to construct and define what it meant to be Australian, and how that might be embodied in literary form. Similar debates were taking place elsewhere, but as literary historian Brian Matthews observed in 1988, the 'debate was much more cut-throat, more terminal so to speak, in Australia.'"[161]

A parallel debate raged concerning the appropriateness of women encroaching on the gentlemen's game of cricket. Many men perceived the very idea of female cricket as an assault on traditional values and rejected it as a "feminine-appropriate sport." Remember that local Collingwood Councillor Marshall, who in the 1930s described the act of women playing cricket as a "burlesque and a leg-show?"[162] Such hissing cannon shells of disapproval finally reached their target in the 1940s and 50s and wiped out a whole generation of female sporting talent. When Stewart and McAuley trained their literary guns on the CAS and its *Angry Penguins*, they hoped for the same result – an overthrow of modernism and an enforcement of "traditional aesthetic standards".

In the end, the hoax was an undoubted success. It achieved what it set out to do: it killed off Australia's flirtation with modernism, raised the profile of McAuley, Hope and to a lesser extent Stewart, and ensured the classical English tradition of literature was taught in schools and universities for a generation or more. Consequently, an independent, uniquely modern Australian larrikin voice was silenced by "an imposition of cultural values by those who think they know better." Australian modernists fled in droves: Sydney Nolan sailed for Britain, leaving his iconic twenty-six-painting Ned Kelly series with the Reeds. Albert Tucket travelled to Japan with American writer Harry Roskolenko, leaving his lover Joy Hester and their son Sweeney with John and Sunday. Even the Reeds themselves sailed for Paris in 1948, with Nolan's Kelly series and a young Sweeney in tow. Max Harris stayed to evolve into a well-known poet, critic, publisher and bookseller, but as Maggie Nolan asks, "I wonder, somewhat sadly, if the hoax diminished his boldness and vision."*163* Max Harris may have been diminished by the hoax, but there is no doubt Australia was.

Ironically, as Maggie Nolan observes, the British classists' attempts to impose their cultural hegemony on what was an acceptable Australian literature, at least in the long term, ensured Ern Malley and his poems retained a fascination for his Australian readers for generations to come: "Perhaps he represents, both accurately and fictitiously, a sense of the ambivalent place some of us Australians feel we occupy as culturally constructed subjects on Indigenous Country."[164]

Perhaps the determination of men like Collingwood Councillor Marshall to undermine the legitimacy of women cricketers also had an ironic outcome – it awakened a determination in independent women cricketers such as Betty Wilson, Mollie Dive and Una Paisley, to assert their agency in the coming decades by fighting to play the sport they loved.

But until their arrival, the cricket fields of Australia lay abandoned by the pioneering women cricketers of the 1930s and were instead populated by armies of returned servicemen. My mother was one of those lost cricketers. She had exchanged the cricket bat and the camaraderie of her textile workshop for the woodfired oven, the scrubbing brush and washing mangle. In a short space of time, she soon came to know the stubborn character of money rather than the joy and freedom of the cricket field.

Women cricketers and modernist artists alike had been beaten back by the rising tide of conservatism – but their time would come again.

# 15

# The Cricketing Outliers

## Betty Wilson

Betty Wilson was arguably Australia's greatest all-round Test cricketer, man or woman, to ever play the game. On her debut against New Zealand, she scored 90 and took 4/37 and 6/28. In her second Test, she scored 111 against England, becoming the first Australian woman to score a Test century against the old enemy. If that wasn't enough, she also took 9 wickets in the match.

Then in 1957/58, she produced one of the greatest all-round performances in cricketing history. She became the first cricketer, male or female, to score a 100 and take 10 wickets or more in a Test. On a wet wicket at St Kilda's Junction Oval

*Portrait of Betty Wilson in her cricket blazer, aged 26, 1947. Kindly donated by Betty Wilson to the Melbourne Cricket Club Museum, M16223.54*

in Melbourne, she took 7/7 in England's first innings, including the first ever hat-trick in a women's Test, then 4/9 in their second, setting a Test record of 11/16 in the match that stood until 2004. Wilson top-scored with 12 in Australia's low first innings total and then scored an even 100 in the second. But the St Kilda Test match was also notable for another milestone.

Faith Thomas (neé Coulthard) became the first Aboriginal Australian, male or female, to represent her country in any sport, and the first First Nations Australian to play Test cricket for Australia. It would take until 2019 for Ashleigh Gardner to be the second.

Betty Wilson played only 11 Tests in her career, but made the most of her opportunities, scoring 862 runs at 57.46 and 68 wickets at 11.80. As a batter, this places her ahead of former Australian Captains Ricky Ponting (51.8), Greg Chappell (53.86) and even current player Steve Smith (55.9). Her bowling figures eclipse Australian champion bowler Shane Warne, who finished his storied career with an average of 25.41 (of course, Warne played 145 Test matches, so their scores are difficult to compare).

Born in Abbotsford, Melbourne on November 21, 1921, Wilson was the second child in a family of four children. Abbotsford in those days was a tough place to live; a working-class enclave dominated by the Abbotsford Brewery, or Melbourne Cooperative Brewery as it was then known, before it amalgamated with Carlton and United Brewery later in the decade. Consequently, Abbotsford was home to hundreds of brewery workers.

During the day, they either unloaded trucks of barley and malt, or washed bottles or packed the beer ready for sale. The workers drank on the job; like musicians, free beer was a perk of employment. The workers then took home freebies for a knock-off drink at night. There was no need for the brewery workers to haunt the crumbling Abbotsford backstreets in search of the sly-grog shops operating out of confectioners, cafés, hairdressers and grocery stores. They worked for money, and their beer was free.

However, the brewery employed another class of worker – the skilled coopers and biochemists who lived in the posh, elevated suburb of Clifton Hill just one mile north along Hoddle Street. This was the place where Betty Wilson was destined to live most of her life.

Betty's father was not a brewery worker, he was a skilled boot- and shoe-maker at a local factory in Collingwood. He was paid reasonably well for the times, so Betty's mother was able to stay home and care for her large boisterous family. They even managed to join the brewery coopers and biochemists of Clifton Hill in the early 1930s.

Betty first learned her basic cricketing skills playing with the tough neighbourhood boys in the dusty, empty Abbotsford streets, a lamppost or dented milk-tin doubling as a wicket, a fence post as a bat and whatever as a ball. Betty played all day and into the sun-slanted twilight, only stopping when her mother called her for tea. She was obsessed. It was said that Betty had a good eye, but that's because she practised and practised.

Then one Thursday night a few years later, a ten-year-old Betty happened to be taking a walk with her father down by the Merri Creek in Clifton Hill to watch the Collingwood Ladies' Cricket Club at training. According to the She's Game website:

> "As they walked around the oval, a ball landed at Betty's feet; she returned it from the boundary to the wicketkeeper's gloves. After doing this a couple more times, she was approached by someone from the team and asked if she would like to play a game. Naturally, she said yes – and

*so she was selected in the team to play on Saturday! Between Thursday evening and Saturday morning, a uniform was found for her, courtesy of her new teammates, the Anderson sisters, who shortened one of their own dresses. From there, she never looked back.*"[165]

At the age of thirteen, after three years with Collingwood, she moved to the Clarendon Women's Cricket Club in Middle Park. Maybe that had something to do with her leaving school and enrolling in business college; whatever the reason she was a young woman on fire, a woman untethered by expectations. Upon graduation from college, she fell into a job as an office assistant with a sympathetic employer. He recognised the talent of his recruit and gave her plenty of leave to play cricket. Perhaps, like Peggy Antonio and her Raymond's employer, Betty's boss could see the publicity she was attracting was good for business. Wilson was widely hailed in both the community and the press as a freakishly gifted cricketer possessed of an insatiable hunger for runs, wickets and hard work.

People say you need 10,000 hours of practise to master a skill; Betty Wilson must have committed to three times that number. She practised the things that she couldn't do, the shots she couldn't play or, in her words: "There's no use standing there all day waiting for the ball you want to hit ... There are a lot of other balls that are going to come your way. So, you need to learn how to hit them all ..."[166] And she had a unique method of learning how to do it.

It involved a cricket ball stuffed into one of her mother's stockings and hung on the backyard Hills Hoist clothesline. The ball's jerking convulsions taught her to move and think fast; watch the ball and get her feet in position, and do it until it was a reflex. Practise, practise, practise. She used the clothesline method her entire career. There were no bowling machines in Collingwood in the 1930s – just old stockings stuffed with beaten up balls mixed with a good attitude. Betty never lifted the ball – no sixes, just fours: "you can't get caught if you drive along the ground."[167]

Once batting practice was done, there was no time for idleness. Netflix was ninety years away and social media was an oxymoron waiting for an iPhone. So, what ya gonna do? Bowl! For *hours* in the nets, she bowled at marks on the pitch representing the forward reach of batters of varying heights, and she hit them time and again. After years of practise, Wilson could land the ball on a sixpence, just short of the batter's reach, meaning they over-stretched trying to get to the pitch of the ball. Her accuracy reduced the batter's ability to play shots, and she picked bags of wickets as a result.

At the age of sixteen, she was selected in the state squad. Then in the 1938/39 season, she was again named in the Victorian team as vice-captain, joining the same group of players that included my mother. Betty was cap number 40, while Mum's cap was number 41. Wilson played the interstate carnival in Sydney in a pair of lightweight boots made by her artisan father. She wouldn't risk her footwork being impeded by down-to-earth cricket boots – she was fleet of foot and on her way.

Wilson's talent, dedication and attention to detail meant she rose like a rocket through the ranks, and she loved it: loved the interstate trips, the idle camaraderie of the dressing room. She relished getting out of Collingwood, seeing new horizons, and experiencing new things – like the train trip to Perth across the red and rolling Nullarbor, its wide, flat expanse flooring her. But most of all, she loved plundering bowling attacks. She even managed to keep playing through the grief of war.

In a cut-down version of the Victorian Women's Cricket Association, she topped the batting aggregates three years in a row, 1941/42, 42/43 and 43/44 and the bowling averages in 1943/44 and 44/45.

There were interstate trips after the war: it was safe now, the cannonballs were put away, the war ships were docked and the men came back home. She met one of those, a nice bloke. They courted down by Deep Rock's on the river. He proposed, she accepted. Plans were made.

But then she got selected to tour New Zealand in 1948. Wedding plans were put on hold: "Why would anyone get married in preference to playing cricket for Australia?" she was quoted saying in the *Age* newspaper in 2007. They'd marry after she got home from the New Zealand tour – or that's what she told her fiancé as she packed her whites and her handmade, lightweight boots.

But a blazing 90 in the New Zealand Test – sharing a 100-plus middle-order partnership with Una Paisley, who made a patient 108, the first Australian woman to make a century – coupled with match bowling figures of 10/65, meant Wilson was one of the first Australians chosen to play the touring English team of 1948/49. Wedding plans were cancelled, again.

Her century in Adelaide in the first Test of the series, coupled with her 6/23 in England's first innings and her consistent performances with both bat and ball throughout the three-match series, meant she would sail with the Australian team to England in 1951. Would her fiancé wait a little bit longer to tie the knot? Ah, no.

No hard feelings. Betty chose cricket over marriage: after all, it *was* the 1950s, and if Betty married her man, her cricketing career was over. Birth control was largely made up of hope over science, and in the time of Menzies, marriage and men came first. Betty wasn't prepared to make that sacrifice. She had ambition – she was a woman who wanted to wring every bit of talent she could out of herself, rather than wring sheets through a mangle in a washhouse in Collingwood. She remained single for the rest of her life.

Betty reflected in later years that even if she had stood by her man, rather than leaving him standing at the altar, the marriage would have failed ... and the world would have been robbed of a remarkable sportswoman.

On the 1951 English tour she was a consistent run scorer, her 81 at Scarborough was a classic and she was also a prolific wicket-taker throughout the series. But she saved her best for last. It was the tour of the English women cricketers of Australia in 1958 that Wilson, then aged thirty-seven, finally peaked as a cricketer. Her aforementioned St Kilda heroics and her extraordinary 127 at the Adelaide Oval matched by her 6/71 in England's first dig in the same game have been unmatched in cricketing history, both in the male and female form of the game. Betty's 1958 heroics were to be her last – Betty retired from the game an unmatched champion and like Sid Nolan, Bert Tucker and other modernists from the time, remained in England as a coach and selector. She eventually became England Selector and Chairperson from 1992 to 1996.

Betty Wilson played cricket because she needed to. Without it, she wouldn't have travelled to England to live and work and experience all the international reverence and celebrity her extraordinary career could bring. The little girl from Abbotsford who witnessed the precarity of life, dragging her bat and ball around the dusty streets, got to live an enthralling, independent, though possibly lonely, life – but a life lived according to her own rules and no one else's.

In 1985, Betty Wilson became the first woman cricketer inducted into the Australian Sporting Hall of Fame. In 2015, she was inducted into the ICC Hall of fame and in 2017, she was finally inducted into the Australian Cricket Hall of Fame. Her photo now hangs in the players' viewing room, in the MCG Members' section. She'd like that, I think: she loved the parry and whack of a cricket club room, the player friendships. She loved cricket and she will always be an important part of its history.

## *Una Paisley*

About three kilometres from Betty Wilson's childhood home in Clifton Hill lived my mother's teammate Una Paisley, the "girl mascot" from the Northcote team photograph of season 1933/34.

Like Wilson, she was a woman who resisted the life offered to her by post-war convention. She never married. She unapologetically and determinedly remained her own woman for the entirety of her relatively short time on earth. Not for her, was the clinker brick and terracotta servitude of suburbia – she remained living in her parents' Osborne Street house on the comfortable Sumner estate on the banks of the Merri Creek in Northcote all her life.

*Una Paisley batting. Source unknown.*

Born 18 November 1922, Una Lillian Paisley first came to public prominence in 1935. A newspaper from that time reported that a thirteen-year-old Una Paisley was set to be a champion in women's cricket. Paisley had already played two seasons with Northcote in the Victorian Women's Cricket Association A Grade competition, debuting at just eleven years old. But in those two seasons, she became a prolific runs scorer. My father as her coach always said that she came to the club as an almost-fully formed cricketer. He described a little girl who could play a perfectly executed forward defence and was blessed with an uncanny ability to get into the right position to play a shot.

She had learned the game, like every other young girl at that time, playing with the neighbourhood boys. In her case it was in the local Merri Park, literally at the end of her street. My father's contribution was perhaps to encourage her to use her feet when batting. I remember a conversation we had about Una late in my father's life:

> *"She was very short when she came to Northcote, well under five feet tall. So, to get to the pitch of the ball she needed to use her feet, and she did, she was fearless in moving towards the bowler. And that fearlessness*

*Una Paisley, age 11 centre-front. Behind is Alexander Horne and to her right Nesta Williams. Northcote Women's Cricket Club.*

allowed her to play out of her crease to the faster bowlers, helping her to, not only to get to the pitch of the ball, but to also counter any swing. With her natural defence and uncanny eye, she could easily get out of trouble if she didn't quite get there."

Una's rise through the ranks was fast. At fifteen she played for Victoria, a side she would later captain. Her first game was against South Australia at Unley in 1937/38. Batting at number three, the teenager top-scored with a patient 36, outscoring her more credentialed Victorian Test-star teammates Nell McLarty, Elsie Deane and Peggy Antonio. The Unley game was also Betty Wilson's debut.

It's difficult to understand why she wasn't included in the Victorian team to travel to Sydney in 1938/39 to play the interstate carnival alongside Wilson, Antonio, McLarty, Deane and my mother. Perhaps two players from the Northcote team were simply one too many. But it would be nearly ten years before she played her second first-class match, the war robbing years of her career.

Throughout the war, Una remained focused on her cricket. Like her Clarendon opponent Betty Wilson, Paisley returned to her Northcote club to play in a diminished version of the VWCA competition. There she topped the competition averages in 1941/42 and then in 1944/45, and was the VWCA's top aggregate run scorer with 611 runs at an average of 55.5, just pipped by Betty Wilson's season average of 58.11 per innings. At war's end, even though hostilities ceased in 1945, it took over a year for the national women's cricket competition to get underway.

By then, many women's clubs had disbanded, with almost all of the game's top international players of the 1930s golden era retired. Players such as Anne Palmer, Peggy Antonio, Nell McLarty – women in the prime of their lives – were now lost to the game. Only Amy Hudson and Molly Flaherty emerged from the tangle of armistice streamers to play for Australia against New Zealand in 1947/48. Consequently, international doors opened for the young Northcote-born batter/all-rounder.

It was at the Basin Reserve in Wellington that Paisley made her Test debut. She wasted no time in stamping her authority on the game, not to mention the Australian team. Coming in at first drop, Una patiently accumulated her maiden century by employing her now well-honed technique of using her feet and getting to the pitch of the ball.

Paisley's ability to concentrate, stay at the crease and accumulate runs became a feature of her game. She even managed to score a century entirely in singles. She must have been incredibly frustrating to bowl to! It's difficult to describe her persistence, her dogged determination, her selflessness not to throw her wicket away. She was a fixture at the crease, endlessly turning over the strike to more dynamic batting partners like Wilson. Mountains of runs were added to the Australian scoreboard, game after game, year after year, thanks to her watchful accumulations. Una Paisley was, for over a decade, the constant in a game of variables.

But Paisley was not only one of the country's great batters – she had a great cricketing brain and was a fine partnership-breaking, off-spin bowler. This all no doubt contributed to her promotion to the Australian captaincy in the 1956/57 New Zealand tour of Australia. In the tour's only Test match in Adelaide, Paisley again scored that patient century, helping guide Australia to an innings victory. She went on to captain Australia for a further 3 Tests in the 1957/58 home series against England.

All in all, Una Paisley played in 12 Tests for Australia, batted seventeen times for a total of 471 runs with a high score of 108. She finished with a Test average of 28 and made 2 centuries. She also bowled in 19 innings, sending down 1365 balls conceding 436 runs, taking 19 wickets for an average of 22.9 per wicket. In the 4 Tests she captained, Australia didn't lose a match.

As mentioned, Una played all but one of her Tests alongside the dashing Betty Wilson. They were the perfect duo in the middle order for Australia; one erudite, the other unafraid. Hopefully, the two women remained generous friends after retirement. I know my mother often "bumped into her in the street" as she put it, but I don't remember ever meeting her. I don't think there were regular dinners, no Northcote reunions; perhaps Una evoked a despairing ache of disappointment in my mother that was best unexamined.

Suffering from liver cancer, Una died at the early age of fifty-five in 1977. It's difficult to describe how much Una Paisley mattered, not only as a cricketer but also as a role model for all committed women who struggled to forge an identity in a world dominated by men. I wonder if she mourned those women, who were never able to become the people they could have been. I wonder, too, if in her quiet, solitary moments, she also mourned the life she sacrificed to be the formidable sportswoman she became.

*Photograph of Mollie Dive and Una Parlsey in Australian blazers, walking with a Scottish bagpipe player, 1951. Melbourne Cricket Club Library Collection, 23606.*

## Mary "Mollie" Dive

Further north in New South Wales, the captain of that state's cricket team and soon-to-be-captain of the Australian side, Mollie Dive had also made a name for herself as a powerful batter and occasional leg-spin bowler.

Dive's rapid rise in the cricketing ranks was remarkable; she was an accidental cricketer, first playing the game in her early twenties when called up to fill in for her university side. Unlike Wilson and Paisley, she didn't play cricket as though her life depended on it. It didn't – she had choices. The poverty and decline of the 1930s was not front-and-centre in Mollie's mind.

Born to a comfortable, middle-class family at Five Dock, Sydney in June 1913, Mollie's accountant father was a good cricketer, representing New South Wales as a leg-spinner in 1925/26. The family moved to the prosperous Upper North Shore suburb of Roseville when Mollie was seven. She played hockey, netball and tennis at the exclusive Presbyterian Ladies College (PLC) in Pymble, representing the college in all three disciplines. She lived the life she had been offered; she was unapologetic and determined to excel both on the sporting field and academically.

Possessed of a gregarious drollery, together with her obvious academic and sporting talent, Mollie was popular and able to open many doors. Even at a young age, she was appointed the co-head prefect at her PLC college in 1931. But that was only the start.

She matriculated at the end of 1931 and attended the University of Sydney enrolling in a Bachelor of Science, majoring in botany and mathematics. This in itself was a major achievement – in 1939, a fraction of the Australian population attended a university, just 0.2%, and of those, more than three quarters were men.

For any woman entering a university campus in the 30s, it must have been a sobering experience. Women were discouraged from pursuing courses outside the liberal arts, were denied leadership positions on campus and, when socialising, "both feet were to be kept on the floor at all times" – whatever that means. There were to be no gentlemen callers in ladies' halls of residence, and a strict curfew of 10pm was rigidly enforced. Pregnancy meant instant expulsion!

In pursuing a science degree, Mollie Dive had entered rarefied air. She had joined an exclusive academic club that included pioneering Western Australia botanist Georgina Molloy as well as Edith Dornwell – the first woman to graduate from Adelaide University in physics and physiology in 1885 – and the 2009 Nobel laureate and molecular biologist Elizabeth Blackburn. Dive's academic success was testament to her determination to succeed.

University campuses at that time were very much a man's world. In the perilous mixed spaces on campus, women were prey to misogyny every day. There was always inuendo or the suggestion, from a starved male, of an afternoon on a hillside. Rarely was there the idea of comradeship – there was no chance of being recognised as a fellow student. As many women know, their experience of something exciting – like university – is often spoiled by "the fighting-off of hands". There is the perpetual need to be on-guard, always polite, that careful balancing of tone: friendly but not encouraging. It may have proved all too frustrating for Mollie.

Leaving the mystery dance to others, she sought sanctuary in the university's women's sports clubs, immersing herself in hockey, netball and tennis. It was in those women's-only sporting clubs that she found her comradeship. Then one day in 1932 she was asked to pad up for her university to play her first ever cricket match.

She'd played cricket with her father and brothers in the backyard of the family's Roseville home, but that was the extent of her experience. No matter – she was a natural, scoring a lazy quick-fire 107-not-out in her first competitive innings. The rest is history.

She continued to play cricket and hockey for her university after graduating in botany and mathematics and while working as a technical librarian with Amalgamated Wireless (Australasia) from 1936 to 1941. Putting her science degree to further use, she then worked as a scientific officer for what became the Commonwealth Scientific and Industrial Research Organisation (CSIRO) until she retired in 1973. But ironically, it is her cricketing career that hauls her memory to the surface.

Her rise through the ranks of New South Wales women's cricket was astonishing. It came on the back of her ability to score fast runs for her university, an ability that attracted the attention of the then-New South Wales captain and team selector Margaret Peden. Just one year after playing cricket competitively for the first time, she was opening the batting with Peden for her state.

Following her interstate debut, Mollie was soon heavily involved in the New South Wales Women's Cricket Association – it appears her mentor was grooming her for higher office. That came in 1939, when she was made captain of New South Wales following the retirement of Peden. The rise of Mollie Dive continued at pace.

Dive didn't have the patience of Una Paisley to accumulate runs and build an innings – a right-hand bat, and despite her diminutive build, she was a powerful hitter and liked to score quickly. But it was hit or miss with Mollie – she either went out early or made a few runs. Either way, she made things happen at the crease.

When the war threw an impediment at Dive's cricketing ascension – she was a certain inclusion into the Australian side for the abandoned 1939/40 English tour of Australia that year – she continued to play in the reduced New South Wales domestic competition. It was here that Dive's powerful batting was on full display. Her 184 against Balmain in 1940 was a whirlwind of sixes and fours worthy of a latter-day T20 innings, and her 151 against Ku-ring-gai in 1941 was equally impressive.

During the war, Dive's life was lived according to a rhythm of her scientific work at the CSIRO and sport on weekends. It was club cricket in summer and playing hockey for her Sydney University Graduates Club in winter. She eventually represented her state in hockey at national competitions in 1946 and 1948.

When Australian women's international cricket finally resumed in March 1948, new Australian captain thirty-four-year-old Mollie Dive batted at first drop in New Zealand. She had a good series, making centuries against Auckland and Otago and scored 59 in the one and only Test, leading the team to an innings victory – a victory that went unreported in the Australian media.

By the time England toured Australia in 1948/49, Mollie had dropped herself down the order, making way for Betty Wilson and Una Paisley. It was a tour de force as far as Australia was concerned, resulting in Dive being the first Australian female captain to win an Ashes series.

Mollie went on to lead the Australians on a successful 3-Test defence of the Ashes in England in 1951 where Betty Wilson starred with bat and ball. But the 1951 tour was the swansong for the now thirty-eight-year-old Dive – she retired as skipper having never lost a Test under her captaincy. She finished her 7-Test career having batted 11 times for 111 runs with a highest score of 59 and an average of 16.09. She also bowled 96 balls in 2 innings, conceding a total of 22 runs and taking 1 wicket.

Following her sporting career, Dive spent decades in women's sport administration, both cricket and hockey, and became a state and national women's cricket selector. She was a hockey umpire and managed various New South Wales hockey teams on tours of Canada, California and Fiji.

Inducted into New South Wales' Hall of Champions in 1995 and the Cricket New South Wales Hall of Fame in 2015, she was the first female cricketer to have a stand named after her at a major New South Wales sporting oval – the Mollie Dive stand at North Sydney. She died in Roseville in 1997. Mollie, like Una Paisley and Betty Wilson, never married.

Dive appeared to live externally; her natural habitat was the sporting field and the committee room. Like Paisley and Wilson, she thrived in the light, with the public's eyes upon her.

What defined these three women was their ability to live meaningful lives of determined independence. Betty Wilson emerges as unapologetic and determined, Una Paisley indefatigable and unerring, while Mollie Dive defines intelligence mixed with talent and middle-class confidence. All three women navigated a path through minefields of male expectation and social convention to shape their own destinies.

These were important women whose undervalued contribution, to both cricket and to a form of feminist activism, have been boarded up by the male canon for far too long. By playing cricket at the highest level, they defined a new form of feminist liberation and modernity. Wilson, Paisley, Dive and many other women cricketers from their era were every bit as revolutionary as artists Sidney Nolan, Joy Hester or Sunday Reed. Their determination to play the game they loved and excelled at, to have faith in their ability and the courage to take control of their lives and fulfil their potential – often in the face of external societal censure – was not only heroic, it was tremendously creative, exciting and new.

They had much in common with journalist and writer Martha Gellhorn, the outspoken and uncompromising American war correspondent whose prose during the Spanish Civil War was read by millions. Martha was a seasoned traveller and a recognised writer of talent, but in the masculine arena of war she was described as a "pushing whore," while her fellow war correspondent and lover Ernest Hemmingway dismissed her as a femme fatale. Wilson, Paisley and Dive may have at least partly agreed with Gellhorn, who wrote of men at the end of her life:

> *"I thought men a blight. Men and boys, the lot. They interfered with my liberty of action ... (women) are not free."*[168]

# 16

# The Post-War Era in Britain

While Australians were being ground down under a fresh tidal wave of conservative, British-inspired rhetoric, Britain was, to put it politely, in a bit of a pickle. The war had left Britain threadbare, bombed-out and exhausted. Money was tight, rationing was brutal – it lasted until 1954 – and decent housing was impossible to find. Could Britain ever recover?

They could, in most ways. In just a few short years, in 1957, Prime Minister Harold McMillan told the British people that they "never had it so good". As Dominic Sandbrook has written, by 1957, the nation was basking in the sunshine of the affluent society: wages boomed, towns were reshaped by council housing estates and mega-shopping centres, and British home life was transformed by television, hedonistic consumerism and teenagers. To borrow a phrase from the next decade, the times were a'changing.

From the mid-1950s, Britain was hit by an American wave of rock 'n roll via Elvis, Jerry Lee and Little Richard, who in turn gave birth to British love-children Tommy Steele, Cliff Richard and Lonnie Donegan. Teenagers bought records by the truckload and danced to the music. The 50s was the era of well-educated and assertive young people who marched against the bomb or beat each other up in Teddy Boy-inspired rock 'n roll riots. While millions cheered the coronation of the new glamorous Queen Elizabeth, colony after colony ran for the British Empire's backdoor. Soon after, the Suez Canal fiasco put an end to Britain as a world power.

The face of Britain was changing its hue via mass migration from its escaped colonies, especially the West Indies and India. White Britain didn't like what they saw, and rioted in Notting Hill in 1958. The ugly face of British racism was exposed for the world to see. Despite the distraction of rock 'n roll, the racial riots, and massed protests unleashed by the threat of nuclear war, most Britons in the 1950s spent their leisure time shopping for a new television, or a car, or maybe a sofa.[169]

It's little wonder that, in the immediate post-war period, women's cricket took on the appearance of a village Sunday recreation.

At war's end, the number of women's clubs in England had fallen from 105 pre-war to just eighteen; the number of affiliated colleges and schools had fallen from 103 to just twelve. Thriving pre-war women's cricket competitions that once attracted 3000 cricketers and crowds of 8000 spectators no longer existed.[170] But it wasn't all darkness in the women's game – a small crack of opportunity had opened during the hostilities.

As we've discussed previously, British women generally found the Second World War a very different experience compared to Australian women. In an attempt to make British women ready for work, the British government decided to introduce the wartime female workforce to team sports, to not only "improve the bearing and appearance of female workers" but also, introduce them to "the ways of the organised service".[171]

With 445,000 women serving in the armed services alone, their daily lives involved compulsory physical training and team games, and cricket proved popular with the new recruits. Peggy Scott, a war chronicler, wrote in 1944:

> "A new world of sport has opened out before her, and she finds everyone is anxious for her to find her place ... she plays in a cricket team ... the airmen

*teach the girls cricket, using their left hands as a handicap ... the aim in the unit is not only to do the best for the unit, but spread the ability to play the games to those who have never before had the opportunity.*[172]

Joan Wilkinson was one of those women.

During the 1930s and after leaving school at fourteen, Wilkinson was a weaver in a cotton mill in Lancashire. Like her Australian contemporaries Betty Wilson, Peggy Antonio, Una Paisley and my mother, she had learned the fundamentals of the game playing with boys in the backstreets of her village, Foulridge, before moving on to the Burnley Ladies Cricket Club at seventeen. But the club folded at the outbreak of the war, and in 1941 Wilkinson was conscripted into the newly formed Women's Auxiliary Air Force. This was to prove her lucky break.

In the army, Wilkinson trained and played cricket as part of her everyday duties. She became the captain of an inter-services XI and continued her career in the Air Force at war's end, catching the eye of the English selectors and touring Australia in 1948/49. Wilkinson was an exception on that tour and the subsequent tour in 1957/58, requiring outside financial help (like many of her Australian counterparts and unlike many of her English contemporaries). Her WRAF colleagues raised the £275 for the boat trip plus the £100 to buy her cricketing kit, and the WRAF authorities granted her leave to play.

Wilkinson was described as an entertaining batter who liked to cut and hook and was also a useful off-spin bowler. She went on to play 13 Test matches for England during the 1950s with modest success. From 24 innings she scored 436 runs at an average of 19.81, but as an English working-class Test cricketer, having a career at all was a triumph!

As a single woman, Joan lived with her sister until she died in 2002 at 110 years of age. As with many successful sportswomen of the 1950s, she rarely talked about her cricketing success. This is a familiar story to me – as was the case with my mother, her disappearance from the public imagination meant people were either uninterested, disbelieving or (at worst) disapproving of women participating in male sports.

In an ironic twist, the war had allowed Wilkinson and thousands of other servicewomen the opportunity and means to play cricket and, in Wilkinson's case, the means of upward social mobility into a permanent job with the RAF and then to a professional career in the 1960s. This was slowly becoming a familiar story in Britain.

As the British economy began to recover at the end of the 40s and early 50s, and as unemployment virtually disappeared, life became more comfortable for families. As a consequence, the minds of thousands of wartime cricket-playing women turned their attention to those happy times.

By the early 1950s, active women's cricket clubs began to resemble pre-war affiliation figures. England's captain Molly Hide wrote that "the number of women and girls wishing to learn and play cricket has increased enormously, and there has been a great demand for coaches." There can be little doubt that this sudden burst of interest in the game in the early 1950s was the result of women being exposed to cricket for the first time during the war years.[173]

But was the relative democratisation of the women's game during the war carried over into the post-war years? Ah, no!

At the grassroots level, most affiliated clubs tended to be based in more affluent areas of Britain or had support from unusual sources. Nicholson gives as example Dukesmead in Chiswick, London, with its strong links to the civil service. The club thrived in the post-war era due to financial support it received from the Civil Service Sports Council and the "very favourable conditions of both leave and pay" granted to its members who were selected to tour Australasia in 1957/58. "Overall, only twenty-eight women's cricket clubs managed to survive continuously, twenty-one from 1950 until 1970; six of these were training colleges, and thirteen others were based in the Home Counties." "Surrey for example boasted eight women's cricket clubs while Middlesex supported six.[174]

The reasons for this are familiar. The costs associated with playing the game – clothing, equipment, transport to and from games, plus the cost of affiliation – were often prohibitive for working-class women, who needed financial support from governing bodies or from benevolent employers. The lack of it was terminal. Britain was transforming in many ways, but onerous expectations were still being placed on working-class women living in impecunious, patriarchal families:

> "The gendered expectations about teenage girls' use of their free time precluded cricket as an activity for some ... housework and other 'pressing family needs', as well as opposition from parents towards girls'

*involvement, [were] two factors preventing working-class girls from participating in sports like football and cricket.*"[175]

No doubt many a potential international women's cricketer saw her talents wither as a consequence.

In post-war Britain, women's cricket was once again dominated by middle-class, white women. The English touring party to South Africa in 1960/61 was a typical example of cricket's monoculture. Nicholson writes that the English team did not include several players who would have qualified on merit but were unable to travel due to their inability to raise the funds. Nicholson concludes that English women's cricketers in the ten years following the conclusion of World War II were, "generally, from comfortably middle-class families, enjoyed the opportunity for a grammar or private school education, often attended training college or university, and themselves settled in middle-class professions."[176] She writes:

> "The twenty-six women who represented England between 1945 and 1955 form a manageable data sample, with information available on the backgrounds of twenty-two of them; this data is suggestive. Only one attended a council-run elementary school. Seven attended grant-aided secondary grammar schools; two attended private Catholic schools; one attended a voluntary-aided Methodist school; and six attended independent day or boarding schools, with five of these falling into the category of large, elite 'public' girls' schools."[177]

Elite women's cricket of 1950s Britain continued the hegemony of class power that had been so evident in the 1930s. Even more remarkably, the English women's cricket team embodied pre-war British notions of privilege and subordination. Specifically, many of its members maintained a belief in the superiority of white Britain over the "coloured" peoples of their Empire.

The popular culture of imperialism after 1945 continued to impart "a general belief in the superiority of whites over coloured [sic] people" into the minds of the British people. Certainly Netta Rheinberg (English team manager for the 1957/58 tour of Australia and New Zealand) was fully at ease with the white privilege still apparent across the Empire. The team's British host in Colombo, where they disembarked for a practice match en-route to Australia, owned a large bungalow, which Rheinberg described as "beautifully and luxuriantly furnished ... black

Cingalese [sic] servants everywhere. One claps one's hands and there they are". Additionally, on their tour of Panama City en route to New Zealand in 1957, she wrote: "Ended up at the Panama Hotel – glory me – what a place. £5 a day for a room in season excluding meals is the cheapest. Maids and servants are ten a penny and get paid about $10-20 a month."[178]

English women's cricket emerged from the war with its middle-class foundations fully intact.

The British team's class exclusivity remained despite attempts by authorities to democratise both sport and access to women's sporting activities through legislation. A key element of the 1944 Education Act, which legislated free secondary school to all British children, was an attempt to address the physical health of working-class children, both boys and girls, through physical activity:

> *"It shall be the duty of every local education authority to secure that there are adequate facilities for recreation and social and physical training, and for that purpose a local education authority may establish, maintain and manage camps, holiday classes, playing fields, play centres, playgrounds, gymnasiums, and swimming baths (s.53)."*[179]

The reality was quite different. According to Nicholson, the war had done little to alter the segregation of British society by social class. This was a factor deliberately built into the legislation, which continued the divide in the education system along both class and gender lines. Most state-funded modern secondary schools were single sex, with only a smattering of co-educational schools.

The class divide was particularly evident in the range of sporting facilities available for girls at what we in Australia understand to be government schools. Nicholson quotes a report touching on the problem:

> *"Many of these [secondary modern] schools have no playing space other than the tarmac of the playground, the girls never handle a tennis racquet or a hockey stick [... they spend] hour in the playground practising netball, under difficulties since some 200 other girls are milling around in various forms of unorganized play and a good deal of shouting and laughter."*[180]

Under these conditions, girls (and boys for that matter) playing any form of cricket was almost impossible. Compounding the whole situation for working-class, would-be cricketers was a paucity of physical education or cricket-coaching staff employed in the state-funded school system, a problem recognised in the 1949 state school sporting syllabus. It advised that cricket should not be attempted unless the services of a "first-class coach" were available.

As the 1950s progressed, the situation in "modern" state-funded secondary schools did change, especially for boys, courtesy of an initiative of the Marylebone Cricket Club. Following the humiliating 4-0 defeat of the English men's team by the Australian "Invincibles" in 1948, the MCC called an inquiry into the state of English cricket. The inquiry recommended that cricket authorities look beyond their traditional, elite, fee-paying public-school nurseries to improve the standard of their English Test players. In other words, develop the game in the untapped industrial areas of the country. But how?

The MCC formed a partnership with local education authorities to run coaching clinics and to subsidise cricket material and facilities in government schools, especially co-educational schools. The approach proved a limited success. A trickle of talented working-class cricketers did eventually appear in first-class men's cricket teams – they were, of course, team professionals and, as such, due deference still needed to be shown to their "gentlemen" amateur teammates. Up until 1962, even British scoreboards noted the distinction between amateur players and professionals, with amateur initials preceding their surnames, whereas with professionals, their initials always followed their surname.

But the women's game remained a solidly middle-class sport; gender bias at government schools proved to be too much of an obstacle to overcome. It's no surprise that at the majority of single-sex, government-funded secondary schools, boys-only schools enjoyed a monopoly over available cricket resources and programs, leaving girls' schools bereft. Similar gendered attitudes also prevailed at co-educational state schools, where boys were encouraged to play the masculine game while girls were cautioned to keep to their knitting. Nicholson quotes the headmaster of Holland Park School, a government-funded non-selective comprehensive school in West London. He was responding to a query about girls not playing cricket at his school:

*"Tradition decrees that almost as soon as they can walk boys start playing cricket ... For girls there is no such compulsion ... They play in smaller groups than do boys and it is seldom that they are found playing team games ... When they take part in organised games at school the boys readily and naturally take to organised cricket ... For girls ...organised games is often an introduction to team-playing ... A few of them may take to cricket ... but they will be a small minority, a minority which will dwindle when faced with the hazards of the hard ball – and it is no good appealing to a girl's manliness if she declines to accept a chance of catching a full-blooded drive. Girls will not enjoy a game in which they have neither aptitude nor interest."*[181]

# 17

# The 1960s and 1970s
## An Unflagging Dance of Nerves

*"O to be in the news again – now that fashion runs everything"*
– Robert Adamson

In the 1960s and 1970s, the emergence of the Women's Liberation Movement and Second Wave Feminism in both Australia and England made the personal political. Women won the right to vote decades before, but they still did not have the right to control their bodies. Nor did they have agency over their lives – defined as they were by marriage and motherhood. But then in the 1960s, and especially the 1970s, traditional gender roles were challenged: calls for abortion rights, a focus on the issue of domestic violence, workplace equality and an end to discrimination based on sex, were all part of a period of feminist consciousness. However, the political and economic struggles of women were always the main focus of second-wave feminists – sport did not figure in any of their campaigns.

Raf Nicholson believes there are spurious ideological reasons behind this:

> "For many feminists, sport has ... been identified as a supremely male activity and therefore eschewed, both in practice and as a topic of interest. This suggests that ... women's increased involvement in sport is in fact anti-feminist."[182]

Nicholson points out that if ...

> "'the personal is political', it is surely the case that participating in an everyday male-dominated activity like sport becomes highly politicised. For those women who participated in sports like cricket, the lack of autonomy which they faced in their leisure lives could be an everyday issue; by rejecting sport as a masculine institution, feminists overlook a key struggle faced by women, that of access to spaces of leisure. Indeed ... women's cricket can and should be viewed as a 'feminist' activity."[183]

But women's cricket wasn't viewed that way, and the reality was, as a game, it was again in rapid retreat in the 1960s. In England for example, by 1980 there were only fifty-five clubs affiliated to the Women's Cricket Association, down from what had already been considered a low point of sixty-eight in 1970.[184]

A similar story was being told in Australia. During the 1960s and 70s, the sport was virtually invisible. By and large, the papers didn't report it, and radio and television were silent. But this was also true of the more traditional women's sports such as netball. Could it be that women's sport at this time was simply "uncool" – experiencing, as it did, a dramatic fall in interest and participation during those decades.[185]

With the introduction of the contraceptive pill in 1961, many women gained freedom across two key areas targeted by second-wave feminists, sexuality and life outside what Germaine Greer would later describe in *The Female Eunuch* as the prison of the consumerist suburban home. The pill proved to be a catalyst for radical change in many women's lives.

In addition, the 1960s and 70s were decades of protest. Hundreds of thousands of men and women marched on the streets of Britain and Australia demanding the banning of the bomb. In Australia, young and old raged against Australia's involvement in the Vietnam War and the government's policy to conscript twenty-year-old men into the army to fight it. These were the decades of liberation: from parents, and from 50s conservatism, consumerism and convention. Many women also released the straps of social convention and rejected men, capitalism and sexual hang-ups. Young women and their male allies marched for women's rights and gay rights; they marched against uranium and for the environment. It was the time both in Australia and Britain when women demanded access to a workplace free of discrimination.

In contrast, in the 1960s and 70s, the idea of women playing cricket was not an act of modern liberation, rather it seemed to be from another time, a time before the Beatles came to Australia and lay waste, in a flash of a rifle's eye, the black and white humdrum decade of the 1950s.

This was an era when skirts were shortened, dope was smoked, and boys' hair grew longer. It was a time when the music of the Beatles, Bob Dylan, the Rolling Stones, Cream, Hendrix, Muddy Waters, Howlin' Wolf and more inspired a whole generation to tune in and drop out.

At this time, most young girls wanted to be where the boys were – in the dark, loud, sweaty, smoke-filled inner-city clubs like the Marque in London, the Surf Riders in Sydney and Melbourne's TF Much Ballroom; places alive with electric sounds, groovy lighting, long-haired boys and the promise of the mystery dance. Girls no longer practised their footwork belting a cricket ball in a stocking from a Hill's Hoist for hours; they had other things on their mind like jumping headfirst into the zeitgeist of the time. Shame the zeitgeist was lost on women's cricketing authorities.

While Germaine Greer argued in *The Female Eunuch* that the idea of women's femininity was a tool of social control that led to a loss of sexual agency, women's cricketing authorities at this time clearly missed the memo. As Nicholson points out, the authorities were continuously exhorting players to always engage in ladylike behaviour! The strict uniform codes forbidding club players "turning up to practice and matches in the briefest of flimsy tennis shorts ... however slim, young and beautiful she may be," seemed to be from another age.[186]

But that's not to say women's cricket didn't survive – it existed on the fringes of Australia's consciousness, like an antiquated underground movement, a bit like Morris dancing.

Many cricketers resisted these "femininity edicts": the English players that toured Australia and New Zealand in 1968/69 deliberately shortened their skirts to be more in line with the fashions of the time. But change was incremental in the world of women's cricket. Perhaps most women who played in this era avoided popular magazines, Germaine Greer, rock 'n roll and the Moratorium to concentrate on what they wanted to do – play cricket.

With the exit of 50s star-power, the Australian team of the 1960s was now largely made up of inexperienced, unknown players. They were like traffic lights – neither here, nor there. Luckily, there emerged from the red glow of cricketing indifference a couple of green-eyed stars that would sustain the game in Australia for the next two decades; all-rounder Miriam Knee was one of them.

## *Miriam Knee*

Born in 1938, Knee grew up in the then-rural hamlet of Wonga Park, 30 kilometres northeast of Melbourne. As it had been for most women cricketers for decades before, she learned the fundamentals of the game playing with her brothers – not in humble inner-city backstreets, but on the family's orchard.

As a teenager, she joined the Mitcham Women's Cricket Club, making her debut for Victoria in 1958 as an all-rounder after catching the eye of Test player-turned-coach Nell McLarty. She did well at the interstate level; her bowling in particular landed her in the Australian team to play a one-off Test against New Zealand in 1961. In many ways, the Dunedin Test was a pivotal moment in the evolution of Australian women's cricket.

The Test was the last for Knee's Victorian and Australian captain Una Paisley. Although the corsets and stocking were long gone, there remained a thrumming conservatism swirling about women's cricket. For generations, women cricketers had fought for recognition as legitimate, independent sportspeople in their own right. But the fight was always informed by male-constructed stereotypes of acceptable female behaviour and presentation; specifically, the dress and behavioural code of the time that stipulated that player dress must be modest and their behaviour "feminine, polite, accommodating and nurturing at all times". It was a classic case of stay under the radar, don't draw attention to yourself and don't make the pissed old duffers sitting in the MCG's Members' Pavillion vibrate with outrage!

Knee reported the words of Paisley to her Victorian teammates before play at an interstate game. Paisley was nearing the end of her career but, as Knee recalled, she was a stickler for protocol – clearly Una had misread the memo from the zeitgeist: "I can remember Una Paisley saying to us when we went out, 'girls, make sure your socks are correct. You must not touch them when you are on the ground'."[187]

With a concerted program of fundraising by her brother's Wonga Park Cricket Club, Knee was able to join the reigning Ashes Australians on a 3-Test tour of England in 1963. Unfortunately, Australia lost the Ashes series, finishing 1-0 down with 2 matches drawn. Knee, however, was the series-leading wicket-taker with 16 scalps.

Over the next five years, Knee continued to play for her home club of Mitcham and dominate the domestic first-class competition while playing for the all-conquering Victorian women's team. But it would take until the 1968/69 tour of Australia by England before she got to play again at the international level.

Once again, the tenor of the times was the saboteur of the Australian team – women were simply not playing the game in sufficient numbers to field an evenly strong Australian team. At the local level numbers were down, and at the first-class level, talented players were leaving in droves in their mid-twenties. Clearly, too many women cricketers were distracted by 1960s distractions. It's amazing, given the circumstances of the times, that the 1968/69 series finished in a nil-all draw.

Knee, however was a constant; a veteran of 4 previous Tests with an impressive record with 20 international wickets, at 15.45 apiece and a highest Test score of 82 at Scarborough, from her 4 Tests. But the new-look Test squad did include a smokey[188] in the form of Anne Gordon.

## *Anne Gordon and the 1968/67 Test Series*

Born Christmas Eve 1941 in Moe in Victoria's Latrobe Valley (a place the Victorian Premier at the time Henry Bolte described as Victoria's Ruhr Valley, referring to Germany's coal and industrial heartland), Gordon was a very fast bowler who could move the ball off the seam. She was also an elegant batter who made an impact in the middle order. Gordon grew up playing vigaro at school but wanted

*Photograph of the 1976 Australian women's cricket team walking out onto the field at Lords, England. Melbourne Cricket Club Library Collection, 23608.*

to play cricket. Her grandparents had a plan: have her travel the 137 kilometres to Melbourne to stay with them in the southern suburb of Cheltenham on the weekend and play for South Hawthorn in Melbourne's domestic competition on Saturdays. But that took a lot of effort. It meant criss-crossing Melbourne on buses, trains and buses again, all the while dressed in her whites and carrying her gear. But she persisted. She was good at what she did and wanted to keep doing it; and, like Knee, her family was supportive.

When Gordon was selected to play for Victoria against Western Australia in Perth, she managed to scratch up the money to buy her uniform and the second-class fare from Melbourne to Perth:

> "[It] meant sitting up all night in the train from Melbourne to Adelaide, changing trains from Adelaide to catch the Express across the Nullabor and we had to then spend two days traveling across the Nullabor, stop at Kalgoorlie, change trains and then back on to Perth. So, it was quite a long trek there and back. And then to have to play cricket. It was quite an experience."[189]

But it was an experience that didn't interrupt her ascension to an international career. In 1968, she was picked to open the bowling against England in the first Test in Adelaide. The Test match was played at the modest Thebarton Oval in

West Torrens. A scattering of spectators sat amongst wattles, *corymbia ficifolia* trees and jacarandas and watched Anne make an impressive debut for her country. She scored a solid 26 in Australia's only innings and took 2/35 in England's second. But it was Miriam Knee who was the outstanding bowler in the drawn match, returning figures of 8/68, bowling a mixture of medium pace and off-spin. Knee also scored an impressive 55 in Australia's only innings.

The team then travelled by train to Melbourne to play the second Test at the Junction Oval in St Kilda where both Gordon and Knee starred. Twenty-eight-year-old Gordon opened the bowling, and in just her second Test sent down 28 overs in each of England's 2 innings, finishing with the remarkable match figures of 10/18 (or 5/61) and 5/57 in each of the 2 English innings. Gordon joined Betty Wilson as the only other Australian bowler to claim 10 wickets in a Test match.

Knee, for her part, rescued the team from certain defeat with a gutsy 96 in Australia's first innings of 215. With wickets tumbling around her she holed out at deep mid-off going for a six: "I did fall for the full toss, I tried to hit it over the fielder's head but was caught at deep mid-off. I didn't feel anything at all. I was fighting for the team. I was so thrilled to fight for the team."[190]

Despite the heroics from the two Victorians, the match ended in a tame draw.

The Sydney Test was a bit of a non-event, with England putting up the shutters to play out time. It was a disappointing end to an Ashes series where the Australian no-name team had shown real spirit and fight. But the real positive that came out of the series was the emergence of two future captains of Australia. Miriam Knee became Australia's sixth captain when she led the side in a one-off Test against New Zealand in Melbourne in 1971/72 and then, in 1973, became the first captain (man or woman) to lead an Australian team in the ODI World Cup.

Following Knee's retirement soon after the World Cup, Anne Gordon took over as Australia's seventh women's Test captain; but little did she know that in a few short years she would play a major, defining role in the history of women's cricket.

## *Transitional 1970s*

Anne Gordon became captain of the Australian women's Test team in 1975, the year when Australia's Prime Minister Gough Whitlam's government was sacked by the Queen's representative John Kerr, ending what was the greatest reforming government the country had ever seen – and it was women who were amongst its chief beneficiaries. In the four years of Whitlam's Labor Government, he introduced no-fault divorce, funded specialist women's health care, the single mothers' benefit, removed restrictions on oral contraceptives, appointed a women's advisor to the Prime Minister and reopened the 1969 Equal Pay Case leading to both a pay increase of 30% for women and the adult minimum wage being extended to women for the first time. The Whitlam Government's reforms changed the lives of many Australian women for the better – but the lot of women cricketers? Not so much.

Women's participation in cricket was still in the gutter. Some of the problem lay in the amateur status of the sport, especially in England. In fact the governing body, the Women's Cricket Council, stipulated it be the case, meaning the game remained a middle-class recreation played largely by women of means.

In Australia the situation was not much different. As Anne Gordon recalled: "The only thing I received from the Victorian association was the big wide V that went onto the pocket of the blazer." She was still paying for her cricket gear and travel costs well into the 1970s. Playing cricket for working-class women in the 1970s and early 80s was a luxury, especially when wider economic opportunities were opening up to them.

The female workforce participation rate for twenty-five-year-old Australian women was at an all-time high. It stood at around 50% of the total workforce compared to less than 30% for the previous generations. The opportunity for economic independence for women in the new age of liberation no doubt trumped the financial and social sacrifices demanded by cricket's amateur status.[191] Patsy Payne, a pioneering ODI international cricketer in the late 1960s and 70s, played for Australia in the 1976 Lord's One Day International, returning figures of 2/8. An article published by *Cricketing Australia* highlighted just what sacrifices she made to become an international cricketing star:

> *"Payne was twenty-eight when she took stock of her reality and didn't particularly like what she saw. Playing international cricket at the time was, in many ways – notably financially – a liability as opposed to an asset. That fact was rammed home to her at a ten-year high school reunion. Payne said: 'All my classmates were married, had houses and mortgages, children, and I had nothing, she says. "I thought to myself: Why have I got nothing? It was because I'd been playing cricket. I'd been going interstate, I'd gone to England twice, and I was broke. I thought: This is ridiculous. It was far too early to give up. But I did."*[192]

Of course, there was also the lingering objection to women playing the manly sport of cricket in both Australia and England. Nicholson cites the example of 1970s English school girls approaching male Physical Education teachers with the request to play cricket and being refused on the grounds that it was a man's game. She goes on to quote an article from the *Evening Standard* from 1973 that described the English players as having "that weathered, muscly-thighed [sic], broad-beamed, wind-blown look of gym mistresses – as indeed most of them are or have been. Only three of the sixteen in the team are married."

There was clearly still some currency in the view that sport had the capacity to "masculinise" its female participants.[193] Again quoting Patsy Fayne:

> *"In New South Wales back in the 60s and 70s, you didn't mention you were a cricketer ... (People would say) 'are you a boy or something? Do you stand up to go to the toilet, do you?' Just really nasty comments, so you didn't tell anyone. You just did it. I remember, years later, my sister actually said to me, 'I didn't know you played for Australia'. It just wasn't something you talked about."*[194]

## *Women Storm the Male Bastion*

When Anne Gordon led the Australians on the 1976 tour of England, women were riding the crest of second-wave feminism, demanding equality in all areas of life, politics, work and family. Equality for women's cricket seemed to come when Gordon led Australia against England in the first ever women's fixture played at the previously male-only bastion of privilege – the Lord's Cricket Ground.

Until Gordon and the England captain Rachael Heyhoe-Flint walked through the fabled Long Room en-route to tossing the coin before the historic ODI on August 4, 1976, the only woman to have previously graced the Lord's pavilion was Her Majesty Queen Elizabeth II. Gordon said of the game:

> *"It was an honour for us to be playing. You know, I can't get over that fact, the first women to play at Lord's. The MCC had given us the match because Middlesex, their team that usually plays there, had not made the semi-finals, first time for ages. And of course, these fixtures are not built*

*in that year, they're made two years before ... That's when it was decided that Australia would play England there in that one-day match. And it was a huge honour."*[195]

This was an out-of-history moment for women's cricket. But the triumph of the occasion was inevitably imperilled by the sneer of reductive sexism. Anne Gordon again:

*"Prior to the match [at Lord's] we had a very nasty experience where a photographer (Hilaria McCarthy of the Daily Express) managed to smuggle herself into the rooms (before a practice session). And we're all in a state of undress where she takes this photo, huge big photo that goes out worldwide. I couldn't believe it."*[196]

Under the headline "CAUGHT BEHIND: Ladies Your Slips are Showing", the English tabloid reported the preparations for the game.

Back in Australia, things were not much better. The revealing dressing room photograph was reproduced by the salacious *Australian Post* with the headline "Our Cricket Girls Caught in Slips" and reported: "male domination has quietly surrendered to the sex war. It has slowly vanished under the weight of ladies' underwear". Whereas the Murdoch *Sun* in England wrote:

*"Television sport suffers a takeover today by the women. And I refuse to call them ladies. Particularly those who pranced around Lord's this week showing their knickers and screeching like Apaches on the warpath. I don't think I have ever seen a more undignified sight than women trying to play cricket."*[197]

The more things change, the more they stay the same.

Despite the sexism and misogyny, was the Lord's ODI a turning point for women's cricket? After all, the game was televised and hundreds of thousands of British viewers tuned in. Anne Gordon, for one, initially thought so:

*"Well, in 1976, after the Lord's match, we thought, right, women's cricket is now on the (map). And we were quite happy that at last women's cricket*

*had got some recognition. And now, everything should open. [We] came back to Australia and I couldn't believe nothing was happening. Nothing, we couldn't get sponsorship for anything. I shouldn't say we couldn't get it. But it was hard to get sponsorship because we weren't known. And they want to be known. They'll go for a known product and we weren't a known product as far as they were concerned."*[198]

Anne retired from cricket after the 1976 English tour and became a respected selector and administrator of the game both in England and Australia. She finished her 9-Test career having taken 22 wickets at 23.09 and a batting average of 19.50, scoring 195 runs from 11 innings with a highest total of 38-not-out.

Given the widespread public indifference to the women's game and its consequential poverty of funding, the future of women's cricket was bleak. Over the next decade, international women's cricket resembled not so much a triumphant march as an unflagging dance of nerves.

# 18

# Women's International Cricket in the 1980s
Same Old, Same Old

The 1978 ODI World Cup played in India looked a bit like the US Baseball World Series – only four teams competed: Australia, England, India and New Zealand. Other cricketing nations couldn't raise the funds to field a team.

Despite the limited competition, it was a tight series. Australia only got over England in the final match played at Hyderabad to take home the cup, largely thanks to Sharon Tredrea's 4/25 and a solid innings of 57 from captain Marg Jennings.

But public indifference and a poverty of funds meant the future of women's international cricket was on life support. The game couldn't attract publicity, sponsorship or crowds – and when the press did report a game, the same old sexualised (and racist) tropes were trotted out. The *Guardian's* chief sportswriter Frank Keating's article, published on the eve of the 1978 Women's World Cup in India, carried a distinctly erotic and racist undertone:

> "Whatever will [India] make of three lots of sixteen short-skirted peaches and cream sports girls? Certainly on my one experience of touring India ... it became for all the obvious reasons, a recurring dream that you might play next day against three squads of sixteen short-skirted peaches-and-cream sports girls, and later that evening get a decent whisky. And if that's chauvinist piggery, I'm sticking to it because dreams don't count!"[199]

Meanwhile, the Australian women's team with Sharon Tredrea as its tenth captain managed to notch back-to-back ODI World Cups by winning the 1980 tournament held in New Zealand. Then it was back to India in 1983/84 to play an inaugural 4-Test series against the host nation. The three-day Tests meant the possibility of a result in any of the four games were negligible and so it proved to be. Australia did however achieve a clean sweep of the four ODI games played during the series.

The Indian tour was tough, but it did throw up some outstanding individual performances by the Australians. All-rounder Karen Price's 10-wicket haul in the second Test at Lucknow (6/72 off 34 overs in the first innings and 4/35 off 17 overs in the second) was outstanding, as was her 104-not-out in the follow-up Test at Ahmedabad.[200]

Price became only the second Australian woman to achieve the 10-wicket/century double after Betty Wilson. However, the stark photograph of Price walking unbeaten towards the dressing rooms against a backdrop of a near empty stadium is a reminder of the near invisibility of women's cricket at the time.

Back in Australia, Price's heroics escaped the attention of the Australian press. Instead, many stands of glorious Mountain Ash were felled, pulped and converted to newsprint, where reportage of Australia's victory in the 1983 America's Cup – the first time an American yacht had been beaten in the event in 132 years – was printed and made available to the Australian public. Prime Minister Bob Hawke certainly wasn't referring to Australia's Indian ODI clean-sweep or to Karen Price's stunning all-round Indian performance when he famously told the Australian public that "any boss who sacks anyone today for not turning up is a bum."

But soon after the Australians returned from India – to paraphrase Leonard Cohen – a crack opened in the gloomy silence around the women's game.

When England arrived in Australia in December 1984 to play a 5-Test Ashes series celebrating the Golden Jubilee of Test Cricket, they did so as the reigning holders of the trophy. In fact, they had held it since 1963 and, worse still, Australia had not won a Test against England since 1951. But that was all about to change.

The aforementioned Hawke Labor Government was voted to power in March 1983, and Australia's twenty-third Prime Minister was sport mad. Hawke particularly loved his cricket. Could this be the reason his government contributed $25,000 towards the costs of the English tour? Who knows, but it wasn't enough to cover the costs of the Australian players' uniforms – they paid $200 each for the honour of wearing them!

The opening Test was played at the WACA in Perth and finished in a draw, despite the heroics of Australia's Jill Kennare who scored a century in the second innings. The Perth opener also marked the final Test for Australia's great captain and possibly the world's fastest woman bowler of all time, Sharon Tredrea. She snapped her Achilles tendon early in the game:

> "The disappointment when it 'gave way' during the game is indescribable. Had dreamt of playing a full Test series against England in Australia – then puff, gone."[201]

England went on to win the second Test – a see-sawing affair at the Adelaide Oval that was notable for Australian opener Denise Emerson's century in Australia's first innings. The third Test at Brisbane's Gabba again finished in a draw, leaving Australia needing to win the next 2 Test matches to regain the Ashes.

At Gosford in New South Wales, Australia declared overnight at 8/232, with Emerson again top-scoring with a patient 58. Then, left-arm seamer Denise Martin's 4/24 and left-arm orthodox spinner Lyn Fullston's 4/53 demolished the English batting, handing Australia a 117-0-run victory in the Test; the first against England in 34 years.

It all came down to the fifth Test, played at the birthplace of Australia's women's cricket – Bendigo. In front of the biggest home crowd at a women's cricket match since the 1950s, England won the toss and decided to bat. Australia's stand-in captain and opening bowler Raelee Thompson ripped through the English top order, finishing with 5/33, restricting England to a modest first innings score of

196. Then Australia took a 100-run lead in their first innings. England's second innings didn't fare much better than their first, and was 5/140 at stumps on the penultimate day.

Even a bout of team gastro didn't stop Australia's winning momentum! Needing just 116 to win the Test on the last day, they achieved it with 7 wickets to spare. Australia had wrestled the Ashes from English hands for the first time in over a generation!

The all-conquering women's team then deconstructed England in the three-match ODI series in a clean sweep, a victory notable for the Australian Broadcasting Commission's decision to televise the first match of the series to a decent, nation-wide audience. Change would surely come ... well, maybe not. The women's Ashes triumph was drowned out by the gush of money pouring into the Australian economy, thanks to Australian Treasurer Paul Keating.

The 1980s was a transformative time in Australian history. The Hawke Government's decision to deregulate the financial system, slash tariffs and open the economy to overseas competition meant invisible barriers had been crossed. By embracing a very Australian style of neoliberal economic reform, the nation's hopes now rested with white-shoe-wearing entrepreneurs and those great aviators of civilizations – bankers. What could possibly go wrong?

The decision fuelled a take-over splurge that in turn led to a number of high-profile business busts. *Bang!* went Alan Bond's Bond Corporation, *Boom!* went Christopher Skase's Qintex Group, and *Phhhht!*... went the State Bank of Victoria, thanks to cowboy lending by its venture-capital arm *Tricontinental*.

However, business busts and the emergence of world-leading corporations didn't solely define the Australia of the 1980s; we had other, more creative works to offer the world – and the world couldn't get enough!

The movie *Mad Max* was a hit right across the planet, as were the bands AC/DC, Men at Work, Midnight Oil, Crowded House and Michael Hutchens' INXS, while Kylie Minogue spun around to great effect and Olivia Newton-John got *Physical*. Let's not forget Paul Hogan, Dame Edna Everage, Nicole Kidman and more – all household names both in Australia and overseas.

Through it all, Australia did become a more outward-looking nation at this time, accelerating its engagement with Asia and especially with China. The 1980s saw the emergence of companies such as Macquarie Bank, the world-leading cochlear implant company Nucleus, and the software innovator Computer Power. As a result of the 80s reforms, Australia would go on to enjoy over three decades of economic prosperity.

Australia's economic realignment wasn't restricted to business: a confident nation also challenged the world via its sporting teams. International cricket, for example, had been redefined and modernised by Kerry Packer's World Series Cricket in the late 1970s, and come the 1980s cricket was more commercial and professional. Packer introduced night cricket, coloured clothing and one-day internationals. By focusing on slick television coverage, Packer's cricketers became celebrities and the cricket they played bold, combative and widely popular. "Come on, Aussie, come on! Come on!" was heard ... ad-nauseam.

Given all that, the obvious question is this: was anyone paying attention to women's cricket? The answer is, not really.

## *All is Change and only Change is Changeless*

By 1987, a whole new batch of Australian female cricketers travelled to England to play a three-game ODI series and defend the Ashes over 2 Tests. There were six debutants on that tour.

Why? You could guess.

Despite all the money pouring into the men's game, women's cricket was treated as the poor cousin; it remained an amateur sport where players paid to play. It meandered around sporting neighbourhoods, hoping someone would buy it a drink. But no one ever did, and so players dropped out of touring sides, their bank accounts threadbare, because they couldn't access childcare, or because their partners got shitty – once again, their wives were off playing cricket while they were left holding the baby.

It's of little surprise that droves of 80s women cricketers emulated Patsy Fayne and quit the sport when they hit their mid-to-late twenties, because the cost of playing the game was simply too great. Having said all that, the team that travelled to England in 1987 proved themselves to be pretty damned good. It was notable for the emergence of twenty-four-year-old Belinda Haggett, a hard-hitting batter who scored a match-winning Test century on debut at Worcester. Then, in the second Test at Collingham, opener Lindsay Reeler held Australia's first innings batting together, scoring an unbeaten 110, alongside Denise Annetts who scored a brilliant 193. The match ended in a draw, but it was enough for Australia to retain the Ashes with a 1-0 series win.

Another notable performance by the Australians during the two-month tour was their first ODI victory at Lord's. Not that you'd notice of course – there was still bugger-all media coverage of anything to do with women's cricket, both in Australian and England. Raf Nicholson describes the state of women's cricket of both nations at this time as "limping along."

In Britain, it was the era of the "Iron Lady" Margaret Thatcher and her neoliberal, slash-and-burn economic policies. Thatcherism meant everything that wasn't nailed down was privatised, throwing millions out of work and into poverty, while others did very well out of it all.

A whole new English species emerged at this time – the female Sloane Ranger – young, upper-middle-class women, often working in banking. They emulated the doe-eyed, pleated skirt, Gucci loafer-look of Princess Diana while their equally entitled men wrapped themselves in Hermes scarves, drove Renaud 5s and made a motser working as traders on the now-booming stock exchange. They all congregated near the Mayfair Hotel and were, for five minutes, the darlings of Britain's voyeuristic media. Once again, British female cricketers struggled for airtime in this heady atmosphere of money and *Downton Abbey*-like privilege.

Thatcherism entrenched commercial values into British sport – which was all very well if one could attract sponsorship (the Benson and Hedges Cup anyone?). But of course, as Nicholson points out, "amateur sports like women's cricket faced a struggle to adjust to this new environment." It was Catch 22: how does women's cricket attract sponsors if it doesn't attract media attention? Thatcher's cuts to local-government funding impacted grants to local amateur sports organisations, including women's cricket. Reduced funding equalled reduced participation in the sport. Women's cricket seemed to be in a death spiral with community-level clubs now on life support. Compounding the whole situation, reduced funding to the government-backed Sports Council prevented the Council adequately tackling the underlying class inequalities in sports participation – a particular problem (as we have seen) for the women's game.

To make matters worse, those women's cricket clubs that managed to survive often played on local, government-funded school grounds that were sold off via Thatcher's privatisation program. It's no surprise that in the face of

Thatcher's scorched-earth economic program, many local women's cricket clubs simply disappeared, never to be seen again. Consequently, throughout the 1980s, women's cricket hobbled along as a fringe, white, middle-class pastime in Britain despite a massive influx of cricket-mad migrants from Southern Asia. In contrast, in Australia, a sense of restlessness could be detected within the women's game – was something significant about to happen?

1988 marked 200 years since the First Fleet, made up of nine transport vessels and a couple of war ships, sailed into Botany Bay with 850 convicts accompanied by their Marine guards. The whole scruffy venture was under the command of Governor Arthur Phillip – and its celebrations 200 years later seemed equally shabby.

The Bicentennial was celebrated with a First-Fleet re-enactment voyage into Sydney Harbor, a World Expo in Brisbane, a camel race from Uluru to Brisbane, sporting events, Bicentennial number plates, tea towels and a Bicentennial one-off Australia vs England men's Test match played in Perth – but not the land rights and treaties promised to First Nations groups, thanks to vigorous lobbying from the mining sector.

Australia and England competed against New Zealand, Ireland and the Netherlands in the Women's Cricket World Cup. India didn't compete in the tournament due to lack of money – the same went for the West Indies, South Africa and Pakistan. This was the first time that the Women's World Cup (and the Australian women cricketers specifically) were sponsored by the government – but only via crumbs fallen from the Bicentennial table and the Shell Corporation.

Unsurprisingly, against this backdrop, Australia easily accounted for England in the final played on December 18, 1988, at a largely empty MCG in Melbourne – just 3000 spectators bothered to turn up to watch the win. The victory was in no small way thanks to two outstanding players; the batting of Lindsay Reeler, who scored a total of 448 runs in 8 innings during the tournament at an astonishing average of 149.4, and the performance of left-arm orthodox spinner Lyn Fullston who, in her last international series, took 16 wickets at an average of 11.9. Fullston left the sport at age thirty-two, the world record holder of most wickets – 39 – taken in World Cup matches by an individual female cricketer. Tragically she died at just fifty-two in her hometown of Adelaide in 2008 after a long illness. Her death received little or no attention in the South Australian or Australian media, prompting sports psychologist Jenny Williams to form the *South Australian Women's Sport Network* in an attempt to promote South Australian women's sport.

In many ways, the 1988 Women's World Cup was a turning point for the women's game, especially in Australia. Firstly, the Australian Broadcasting Corporation's decision to televise the final live to Australian audiences gave the sporting public a chance to witness the skill and elegance of the women's game from the comfort of their own homes. But of equal (if not greater) importance, the money men recognised that the game was worth sponsoring – in a limited way, of course.

# 19

## The 1990s
### A Game Changer

At the start of the decade, sponsorship money began to slowly trickle into the women's game, courtesy of the Commonwealth Bank. A shrapnel of corporate dollars meant training facilities marginally improved and elite pathway programs were enhanced. The best that can be said of the sponsors' support was that elite women's cricketers were no longer eating from tins. Meanwhile, a splutter of funding was made available to local women's cricket clubs, associations and schools. Baby steps.

The 1990s had opened with a bang – or, rather, a bust. The Japanese economic boom of the 1980s burst, making the record prices they paid for Australia's mineral resources unsustainable. Australia – the mineral resource supplier to the world – was in big economic trouble. Inflation took off and interest rates hit 17%. Many highly geared celebrity entrepreneurs of the 80s were reduced to penury while others, like Alan Bond, were exposed as frauds and sent to jail. Something had to give – and it did, in the form of a recession.

It was, as Treasurer Paul Keating said in 1991, "the recession we had to have". It was a tough time, especially for those thrown out of work. But Australia's reformed economy – specifically the floating of the dollar and its internationalisation – proved resilient and the country soon recovered. Australia emerged from the recession largely intact, so much so that in the coming years, per capita national income increased by two-thirds.[202]

For a time, Australia became a more confident, engaged and outward-looking nation. Even the country's First Nations peoples had cause to hope. In 1990, a national consultative representative body, the Aboriginal and Torres Strait Islander Commission (ATSIC) was established to advise on programs specifically affecting Aboriginal Australians. Then in 1992, the High Court recognised the Meriam people of Mer (Murray Island, in Torres Strait) as the traditional owners of their Country. The case was brought by Eddie Mabo and others against the state of Queensland, and was the first in Australia to recognise pre-colonial land interests of Indigenous Australians.[203]

The 1990s were a wild ride in Australia, but against that backdrop, our women cricketers were quietly going about their business. The national team ushered in the decade with a series win in New Zealand, thanks to a mesmerising spell of aggressive fast bowling by recalled speedster Debbie Wilson. In the third Test held in Christchurch in January 1990, she finished with match-winning figures of 9/92 and a series average of 13.7.

The first 2 of the 3-Test series had been marred by rain and finished in draws, but not before Wilson again nabbed 4 wickets in New Zealand's only innings of the first Test in Auckland, then followed this up with a 91-not-out batting at 9 in Australia's only dig – a record for a women's Test score in that position or lower that still stands today.

In 1990/91, India mounted a 3-Test tour of Australia, playing the first match at Sydney's North-Sydney Oval, a match remembered not so much for the result – it ended in a draw – but for the debut of one of the greatest female cricketers to ever play the game: Belinda Clark. Clark made a hard-hitting 104 in Australia's first innings, sharing a 178-opening stand with Belinda Haggett.[204]

## *Belinda Clark*

Newcastle-born Clark was a prolific right-handed opening batter who started life dreaming of winning Wimbledon. When that looked to be impossible, she turned her attention to cricket. Like a latter-day Don Bradman, she honed her hand-eye and footwork skills hitting not a golf ball on a water tank, but a tennis ball against her family's garage door. The neighbours must have been happy! She played her first game of cricket at school, aged thirteen. She was a natural, a run-scoring machine – she played her first international as a twenty-one-year-old and, as mentioned, scored a century on debut against India.

Clark was then made Australian captain following a team overhaul, and the rest is history. The team blossomed under her leadership with ODI victories over Pakistan – inspired by Clark's 97-ball 131 – and a drubbing of New Zealand where Clark smashed a 142 against the hosts. Australia's 1997 World Cup victory came on the back of a series of Clark's unmatched batting performances. In a lead up game to the final, she was the first cricketer – man or woman – to score a double century at 229-not-out. And, in the final against New Zealand, Clark's top score of 52 guided Australia to victory.

A century in the third Test against England in 1998 was her second, and a hint of what was to come. She then led the Australian team to seventeen consecutive ODI victories between 1998 and 2000. After a brief stumble in form, more Women's World Cup victories followed, including the 2002/03 final against New Zealand, where she scored a match-winning 89 before leading the team to a 98-run World Cup victory over India in 2005.

In retirement, Clark continues to promote the women's game. She held down a number of managerial roles, serving as a member of the ICC Women's Committee for a number of years before being appointed as the Director ICC T20 World Cup 2020 Organising Committee. It's of little surprise that, today, Australia's best women's player of the year is awarded the Belinda Clark Medal.

But all of that was to come. Meanwhile, back in 1991/92, Australia still had a Test series against India to win – and that they did.[205] Australia went on to win the series 2-0, beating India by 10 wickets in Adelaide and 9 wickets in Melbourne thanks to a blistering spell of fast bowling by Debbie Wilson in India's first innings. She returned figures of 5/27 off 21 overs.

*Batter Belinda Clark watches her shot. Won last Test to defeat India 2-nil. Bradman Museum Trust collection.*

But the 1990/91 Test series was the last played by Australia's women for eight years. International women's cricket reverted to the One Day International format for most of the decade, in a desperate attempt to raise the profile of the game. While the successes of the Australian men's cricket team made front-page news for the entirety of the decade, the heroics of Australia's women cricketers went largely unreported. It seemed Australia's insatiable appetite to bask in the glory of its male sporting teams' successes evaporated when forced to acknowledge the achievements of its women. Consequently, Australian women's cricket continued to struggle financially. Fiona Bollen described just what 'the struggle' looked like for one Australian women's cricketer:

> "*Cathryn Fitzpatrick was recognised as the world's fastest bowler in women's cricket but supplemented her stellar career with jobs as a garbage collector and postal deliverer. The reality for women was that representing your country came at a real cost, with players continuing to raise funds or pay their own way for the honour.*"[206]

I wonder if Shane Warne or Glenn McGrath needed to work a milk run when playing for their country? What to do? Women's cricket and its cricketers tried everything to raise the game's profile, like playing in a 50-over exhibition game against hero male cricketers from the past and present.

Western Australian all-rounder Zoe Goss was the only woman invited to play in a novelty televised match featuring a combined "Bradman XI" – which included Goss playing alongside past Australian players such as Denis Lillee, Bob Simpson, Greg Chappell, Doug Walters, David Hookes and Jeff Thompson. The Bradman team faced a World XI that featured Brian Lara, David Gower, Sunny Gavaskar and Graeme Pollock.

The stands were filled with over 17,000 people: Australians love acknowledging past male sporting heroes. But it was Goss who "won over the crowd." In the Bradman team's 50 overs, she made a hard-hitting 29, stumped by Jeff Dujon from a Brian Lara tweak. But she got her revenge when it was the World XI's turn to bat. Bollen described what happened:

> "Goss angled two into Lara's pads ... then moved the luminous orange ball away on the third. Lara – probably the world's greatest batsman at the time – edged the delivery and was caught behind by Steve Rixon ... for 23. Goss then completed her revengeful spell having Dujon caught by Lillee in covers for 8".[207]

The crowd went nuts! And something went *Click*! in the minds of hundreds of thousands of young women watching the game on television. According to Bolton, this televised novelty match had the effect – for the first time in living memory, at least – of "making people sit up and take notice ... it put female cricket on the agenda, creating an injection of interest and respect [for] the women's game".[208]

From the mid-1990s, women's cricket took on a whole new professional look. In 1996, the sixty-year-old annual domestic interstate carnival was restructured as a 50-over domestic competition – the Women's National Cricket League (WNCL) – replete with snazzy, coloured uniforms for players and catchy names for teams such as the NSW Blues, Queensland Fire, Western Fury, South Australian Scorpions and the Victorian Spirit. It was an attempt to make women's cricket more sellable to the public, and it proved to be a winning formula; the public lapped it up like peaches and cream. Meanwhile, members of the Australian women's team drained their bank accounts to fund their appearance at the 1997 Indian World Cup.

Early in the tournament, Belinda Clark made aforementioned history with 229-not-out. Australia had failed to make the 1993 50-overs final, so it was clear they had a bit to prove in India in 1997. They crisscrossed the country on buses and trains, playing matches at colourful venues such as army barrack parade grounds. But they ground out wins wherever they went, making the final against New Zealand in front of a world-record crowd for a women's sporting event at Eden Gardens in Calcutta (Kolkata). Women had been bussed in from all over the city courtesy of the Indian Sports and Transport Minister to watch the final.

Australia prevailed with 2-and-a-bit overs to spare on the back of Belinda Clark's innings-high 52. It was Australia's fourth World Cup victory; an extraordinary achievement considering the team operated on the smell of an oily rag in the way of sponsorship, media coverage or acknowledgement by the Australian public. But all that was about to change – and just in time to usher in the new millennium.

## *British Women's Cricket in the 90s*

The 1993 Women's 50-over World Cup almost didn't happen. England was host, but they didn't have enough money to cover costs – in fact, the tournament was within days of being cancelled. It was only the last-minute intervention of a charity – the Foundation for Sport and the Arts, contributing over £90,000 to the running of the event – plus some desperate local fundraising that got the whole tournament over the line. Lucky it did – the final result led to a minor revolution in the public's perception and support of English women's cricket.

In the lead-up to the final, Australia had missed the cut and so England played New Zealand at Lord's in front of a healthy crowd of 4500 spectators, including the British Prime Minister John Major. In a first, the final was televised live by the BBC and attracted over 2.5 million viewers. In what proved to be a decisive result, England defied the odds and got up to win against their more-favoured opponent. According to Raf Nicholson, the following day, women's cricket dominated the front and back pages of all the national newspapers for the first time in the sport's long history.

The win clearly changed a lot of minds both in terms of the quality of the women's game in Britain and its popularity with the public. Even a couple of stuffed shirts from the MCC and the media came over to the cause – the then-president of the club Dennis Silk effusively wrote to the Women's Cricket Association Chair: "It was the best day's cricket at Lord's this year and between you all, you created a magical atmosphere. You have done the whole of English cricket a great service."[209] While the previously sexist and patronising *Guardian* reported witnessing:

> "High quality skills with the bat, old-fashioned virtue with the ball, superb fielding ... and not a single no-ball to blight the memory. Make no mistake, these are terrific cricketers."[210]

When the triumphant World Cup English women's team failed to win the BBC Award for Team of the Year, all hell broke loose. The *Daily Mail* wrote:

> "This space is not exactly renowned for its fiery pro-feminist sentiments but I felt like marching with Germaine Greer and the rest of them when England's women's cricket team were left standing there like spare nuns at a wedding. Too well-brought-up to express their feelings in public, they have left it to me to do it for them: 'What the hell do we have to do next to win a little public recognition?'"[211]

The response to the World Cup win from young English female cricketers, however, was nothing short of overwhelming. WCA figures showed a surge in schools playing women's cricket competitively. There were fifty schools affiliated with the Women's Cricket Council in 1993, but after England's World Cup win those affiliations had jumped to 114 by 1998, while school participation by schoolgirls had increased 42% in five years.

In addition, a new high-speed form of the game – Kwik Cricket (or Kanga Cricket in Australia) – was aimed at getting school-age children interested in the sport. It was an attempt to recruit more children from less-exultant family backgrounds into the game – and it was successful.

Nicholson points to future England captain Charlotte Edwards, discovered by a scout for Huntingdonshire Boys when playing in her regional Kwik Cricket final. In fact, during most of the 1990s, many of the best female cricketers in the country – Clare Connor, for example, who captained England between 2000 and 2005 – emerged from a background of playing junior cricket with boys at a local community men's club. Of the fourteen players who participated in the 1997 World Cup in India, seven had come through boys' clubs or school cricket. Was this the moment when women's cricket in Britain became democratised?

Young female cricketers competing with boys at the community level may have had the added societal advantage of boys being aware of the skill and ability of their teammates; girls playing cricket was seen by these boys as normal. Nicholson points to Charlotte Edwards, who captained Huntingdonshire Boys from age twelve:

> "The boys were fine. The boys had grown up with me playing cricket, so for the boys I played with it was 'Charlotte, she plays cricket', boy or girl, they didn't care." [212]

With more mixed club cricket being played at the local level, girls were empowered – for many, it was a life changing experience. Nicholson quotes future international Beth Morgan, who first played club cricket aged thirteen:

> "I was a very shy kid ... I was very socially awkward and struggled with any social situation really ... But [cricket] completely gave me confidence and friends, a social network, and a confidence in myself ... it changed me in a massive, massive way." [213]

Barbara Daniels, who represented England between 1993 and 2000, reported a similar experience:

> "I found sport, for me, was absolutely a liberating thing ... I knew I was good at it I suppose, because I could play with the boys, not just my brothers but their friends and stuff. Not just I was good, but I loved it ... I was a very shy child, and sport became a vehicle for me to be confident really." [214]

A more inclusive women's cricket environment in Britain in the 90s may have contributed to broadening the social profile at the elite level of the game. But as we shall see, all female players were not universally welcomed to play in mixed-gender teams – and then there was the little matter of money, and the expense involved in playing the game.

Elite players still contributed over £1600 a year to cover travel, accommodation and training costs, and were expected to prioritise cricket over career, killing any chance of most cricketers who lacked a source of independent income. Despite this,

Nicholson writes that the fourteen players selected for the 1997 World Cup in India included a van driver and a service station attendant:

> "England captain Karen Smithies had in fact attended her local state school; her father was a designer at an electrical machine firm, her mother worked in a factory, and she herself left school with 6 O levels and 1 A level, married a welder, and became a manager at a local bookmaker." [215]

Despite the successes of the English women's cricket team during 1990s, the women's game still lacked a major sponsor while government support was minimal. Added to this, the game was mired in female tropes, with media coverage focused on "the feminine nature" of women's cricket, with divided skirts still universally the cricketing uniform over "masculine" trousers.

Of course, the media strategy adopted by the sport's British administrators didn't help. They continued to offer the more attractive Anglo-Saxon representatives of their international players to the media for stories and profiles that reinforced a perception in the public's mind that women's cricket was a sport played by middle-class, "white young things". This from a speech by British Prime Minister John Major in 1992:

> "Fifty years on from now, Britain will still be the country of long shadows on county [cricket] grounds, warm beer, invincible green suburbs, dog lovers, and – as George Orwell said – old maids bicycling to Holy Communion through the morning mist."

As Raf Nicholson commented:

> "Not only did this vision of Britain explicitly exclude non-whites, who were generally located in urban areas, it also harked back to past days of greatness, and was an attempt to promote an image of an imperial past where Britain was the dominant force in cricket, a past which had existed prior to the arrival of non-white immigrants. It was the promotion of the myth of the 'whiteness' of cricket which led to the publication of articles in the cricket media during the 1990s questioning the 'loyalty' of non-white England cricketers, even those

*who had been born in the UK. The long association of cricket with British imperialism had left its mark."* [216]

Back in Australia in 1998, the women's game received a major shot in the arm via a well-established source. Following Australia's Indian World Cup triumph, the Commonwealth Bank decided to significantly increase their investment in the women's game. Suddenly, a whining shrapnel of money turned into a bombardment of cash. But the battle for parity with the men's game still needed to be won. Sure, the bank's sponsorship meant Belinda Clark and her teammates no longer needed to drain their bank accounts to pay for playing kit and travel costs. But they were still paid a relative pittance to play for their country.

So where did all that sponsorship money come from?

At the end of the 1990s, Australian entered a new era politically with the election of the Liberal Howard Government. Howard's timing in coming to government was impeccable; the economic good times had arrived via hundreds of billions of mining dollars pouring into Australia's Treasury coffers. All that mining money came courtesy of a massive increase in demand for Australia's iron ore and coal from China, and the Prime Minister graciously shared Australia's good fortune with his middle-class supporters. He showered them with middle-class welfare via superannuation and family tax benefits. He super-sized negative gearing and capital gains tax discounts on their investment properties. He raised their personal income tax-free threshold and reduced their top marginal tax rate. He massively increased funding to their children's private schools that, indirectly, improved their child's sporting programs. In just a few years, Howard cemented into the Australian middle-class psyche what political commentator Laura Tingle describes as a "culture of entitlement". Alternatively, Howard used the language of fiscal restraint to slash funding to programs that benefitted those who didn't vote for him: migrants, refugees, people who lived in public housing or relied on public health or women's services, trade unionists, Indigenous Australians and the families of public-school students.

Of course, Howard was most generous to his biggest supporters, Corporate Australia. Sections of the media, mining industry and the finance sector especially were rewarded with unprecedented tax holidays, incentive payments, direct government assistance and a watering down of an already-pale system of environmental and corporate governance. They couldn't believe their luck! But such government sponsored corporate rapacity came with a degree of risk. It could generate wide-spread revolt by Australia's plundered population. Companies saw the need to engage in a program of brand management to maintain their social license to continue normal operations. Why not sponsor arts programs, cultural institutions and (yes) sporting teams to show just what responsible and generous corporate citizens they were? It helped that such sponsorship deals were tax deductable. They were regarded as "advertising" and, as such, a legitimate business expense. Win-win!

Australian women's cricket shared in the corporate largesse. At the end of the 90s, a relative truckload of money via media deals and corporate sponsorships was backed into the game's front door – recognition (finally, and admittedly from a strange place) of the surge in interest in the phenomenal story of Australian women's cricket.

Consequently, as women's cricket entered the new millennium, its players were exposed to a wider audience. Thus, player payments increased, coaching and player facilities improved, and the overall financial health of women's cricket was ensured. But was something lost in all of this? Has the game become more commercialised? Has it lost some of its unique identity and cultural significance? I'll let you be the judge.

# 20

# The Australian Women's Cricket Team
## A Sporting Behemoth

The new millennium started, not with a bang but a whimper – a Y2K whimper to be precise. For the whole of 1999, portents of havoc predicted death-by-coding-malfunction. There was constant talk of computerised systems not recognising the numbers 00 and shutting down, thus ending life as we knew it. No, I don't understand it either – but at the time, it gripped collective consciousness.

As the clock struck 12 midnight on January 1, it was feared banks would be non-operational, utilities across the world would grind to a halt, air conditioning, lifts and medical equipment would switch off and – most alarmingly of all – passenger jets would fall from the sky. In a frenzy of global alarm, hundreds of billions of dollars were spent upgrading computers while people threw themselves into preparations for Y2K parties, rationalising that it was better to die dancing than be obliterated by a computer error. Then at midnight, nothing happened ... other than a giant, global hangover the next morning.

Disaster averted, Sydney was now free to host the 2000 Olympics, while Prime Minister John Howard was able to do what he promised he never would – introduce a GST – and South Australian scientists cloned the first sheep in Australia, Matilda. Life went on. But the new century started badly for the Australian women cricketers, who lost the 2000 World Cup final to New Zealand by 4 runs in the fiftieth over.

Not to worry. In 2001, Australia easily accounted for host nation England in a clean sweep of the Ashes. Australia's first Test victory, played at the quaint, suburban and sparsely attended Denis Compton oval at Shenley, was thanks largely to a Michelle Goszko double century on debut.

Australia's women then trounced England in the second and final Test at Headingly, with highlights including Cathryn Fitzpatrick's match-winning figures of 9/112 and Karen Rolton's record-breaking innings of 209-not-out.

Nothing succeeds like success. Women's cricket was now recognised as the real deal, and the game's administration recognised the need to improve its overall governance. And so, in 2003, the crucial decision was made to integrate Women's Cricket Australia with the Australia Cricket Board (ACB). This was another key turning point in the game. Women's cricket could now access a professional, streamlined back office, better training facilities and enhanced elite pathway programs. But most important of all, games were now played at first-class venues: meaning better wickets, faster outfields and more entertaining matches.[217]

The Australian initiative was replicated internationally in 2005 with the merging of the International Women's Cricket Council with the International Cricket Council – "a move that greatly impacted on funding, marketing and broadcasting of world events" such as the Women's World Cup.[218] Women's cricket was indeed entering the game's mainstream, especially in Australia.

The Australian women won the 2005 World Cup staged in South Africa, blitzing India in the final led by a brilliant century by Karen Rolton. They then followed up with a five-game ODI series tour of England a few months later, winning the series narrowly by 4 runs in the final match. Lisa Keightley and Kate Blackwell were the outstanding batters for the series, but it was the left–arm orthodox spin of Shelley Nitschke that stole the show in the second of the 50-over matches, finishing with 7 for 24 off 7.4 overs.

## *The GOATS – Australian Women's Team and Players*

In Australia, the 2010s was a decade characterised by the climate culture wars – encapsulated by an ideological, head-shaking refusal by some, a science-driven acceptance by others, and calls to do something about it by many. That "something" included five prime ministers in ten years being axed by their own parties for daring to utter the words "carbon tax" (and, alternatively, "repeal the carbon tax"). Meanwhile, as coal and gas exports boomed along with the profits of mainly multinational exporters, the planet cooked and the Australian public received next to nothing in tax revenue from the exploiters of the nation's resources – especially its gas reserves.

In stark contrast, things were pretty stable in the world of Australian women's cricket. In 2010, Australia played New Zealand in the second ICC Women's World T20 final in Barbados in the West Indies – the first, played in Britain the year before, was won by the hosts, also over New Zealand.

The 2010 final was a tight affair, with Australia struggling to a modest total of 8/106 after its allotted 20 overs. However, when nineteen-year-old Ellyse Perry picked up 3 early wickets, the skies began to darken for the White Ferns. Then a hard-hitting innings of 38 by Sophie Devine put New Zealand back in the hunt. It all came down to the final over. Needing 14 off the final Perry over and then a six off the final ball to win – or a four to force a super over – Australian spectators couldn't look. Perry ran in and bowled a ball full of length – Devine belted it straight back at the young rising star.

If Argentina scored the winning 1986 World Cup quarter finals match against England with Diego Maradona's "Hand of God" goal, then Australia won the 2010 final with Ellyse Perry's golden right foot. Perry – who represented Australia in soccer at sixteen years of age, subsequently appearing eighteen times for her country and scoring 3 goals – instinctively put out her right foot and deflected the ball for a single. Australia won the Cup by 3 runs!

There's no doubt that Ellyse Perry would go on to fulfil her potential as a generational cricketer. She was a driven and extraordinarily talented all-round sportsperson. Perry became a three-time Belinda Clark Award winner and ICC Cricketer of the Decade. She is, if not *the* greatest, then indeed *one of* the greatest players of her generation. Her masterful 213-not-out in the 2017/18 Ashes series at

North Sydney Oval, then the highest score by an Australian woman in Tests, only cemented her reputation as a formidable force in the game. But Ellyse was just one of a clutch of extraordinary Australian women cricketers playing for Australia at that time.

Meg Lanning as an eighteen-year-old displayed her talent when she made a hard-hitting 104-not-out in only her second international match, a T20 against the old rival England in Perth in 2010/11. Then, a year later in the third match of the 2012/13 Rose Bowl series against New Zealand in Sydney, she demolished the New Zealand attack with a startling 103 in just 50 balls. This was just a foretaste of things to come.

Captain of the Australian team in 2014 at just twenty-one years of age – the youngest ever Australian skipper, male or female – Lanning presided over arguably the greatest Australian sporting team of all time. She led the nation to a record five T20 World Cup crowns (played in two others), and was the winner of the ICC ODI Cricketer of the year and the Wisden Leading Woman Cricketer in the World titles. She also won three Belinda Clark Awards, made the most ODI hundreds of all time, and was the youngest Australian – male or female – to score an international ODI ton.

She led Australia to victory in 3 Ashes series: 2015, 2019 and 2021/22. Australia lost the 2013/14 series when Lanning stood in as captain replacing the injured Jodie Fields mid-way through the series and did not play in the 2017 event due to injury. Lanning retired from international cricket at the end of 2023, scoring 8352 runs from her 241 international appearances to play in the domestic Women's Big Bash League, the 50-over National Cricket League and the lucrative Women's Premier League in India.

But wait, there's more!

When Alyssa Healy first played for her country in a T20 against New Zealand in 2010, she was a bit of a slogger and an accidental wicketkeeper – she only became the wicketkeeper for New South Wales when its established stumps person Leonie Coleman retired in 2009.

She eventually replaced Australian wicketkeeper and captain Jodie Fields in 2014 when Fields was seriously injured mid-way through the 2014 Ashes series.

Full Corset and Stockings 199

'The three amigos' Alyssa Healy, Meg Lanning and Ellyse Perry. Courtesy The Age (Nine Publishing).

Healy always had talent both as a batter and wicketkeeper but was a little impatient. But with hard work and excellent coaching, she developed into a punishing opening batter and brilliant wicketkeeper, especially to spin.

Named Australian women's captain in 2013 following the retirement of Meg Lanning from the Australia team, Healy has been integral to Australia's astonishing success for over a decade. She has played in six T20 Women's World Cup finals, two Women's ODI World Cup wins and three Women's Ashes victories including the clean sweep in 2025. She's a big-game player: at the 2018 T20 World Cup held in the West Indies, Healy capped off an Australian victory by winning Player of the Series as the tournament's leading run scorer with 225. Then later in the same year, the ICC named her the T20 Player of the Year. If that wasn't enough, in 2019 she made the highest individual score of 148-not-out in a women's T20 match while playing for Australia at the North Sydney Oval against Sri Lanka. But the best was yet to come.

Leading Australia at the 2020 ICC Women's T20 World Cup, played in front of the biggest ever crowd for a women's cricket match in history at Melbourne's MCG, Healy (as mentioned) made a rapid-fire, player-of-the-match innings of 75 off 39 balls, all but securing the trophy for Australia – its fifth. Just to add to her outstanding record in the short version of the game, Healy holds the record for the most dismissals as a wicketkeeper – male or female – in T20 internationals.

In 2025, Healy topped off a magnificent career by overcoming the disappointment of a semi-final exit to South Africa in the Twenty20 World Cup played in the United Arab Emirates in October 2024, to lead the side in a historic clean sweep of the 2024/25 Ashes series.

Healy, a fierce advocate for women's cricket and women's sport in general, has captained one of the most successful Australian sporting teams and played through an era of extraordinary growth for the women's game. She has seen women's cricket evolve from a semi-professional game to a fully professional sport. In 2009, her first international contract was worth $5000, but oh, how things have changed for both Healy and her sport since those times.

The three amigos of Australian women's cricket – Perry, Lanning and Healy – have also had some pretty handy sidekicks during their time in the game – like the prodigiously talented Beth Mooney. The top-order, left-hand batter and backup Australian wicketkeeper became the first Australian female to score a century in all three formats of the game when she made a century at the MCG during the triumphant 2024/25 Ashes series. Her innings of 106 was only eclipsed by the rising star of Annabel Sutherland's 163. But these are only some of the women who have contributed to Australia's world dominance in the 2000s.

We can't ignore the talent of the former Australian captain and star all-rounder Lisa Sthalekar, Jodie Fields, Alex Blackwell, Nicole Bolton and Rachael Hayes – and who could forget Sarah Elliot's hat-trick at the Bankstown Oval to seal the 2010/11 Ashes series? Ashleigh Gardner has also been a team constant – a proud Muruwari woman and only the second First Nations women's cricketer to play for her country. She is a prolific all-rounder who can bamboozle her opposition with her flighted off-breaks then come in to bat in Australia's middle order and turn things around if they get shaky. Then there's the quick Megan Schutt, who moves it off the seam and gets early wickets and happens to be one of the best fast bowlers the game has seen.

Australia's star power seems endless – but why all of a sudden, over the last twenty years or so? What's the secret? The formation of the brand-based T20 Women's Big Bash League (WBBL) in 2015/16 has had a lot to do with it.

## The WBBL

The WBBL, from the outset, attracted the best female cricketers from all over the world to come to Australia and play in the city-based team competition – and money has a lot to do with it. As Andrew Wu wrote in the *Age* March 8, 2025:

> *"The top Australian contract holder with a WBBL (Women's Big Bash League) deal can earn $800,000 and more than $1 million by playing in the Women's Premier League (India) and the Hundred (England).*[219]

By playing the best cricketers in the world, Australia's women are able to test themselves on an almost weekly basis, allowing them to work on deficiencies and improve. But there's more.

WBBL has been a runaway success; broadcast live on television, it achieved immediate six-figure ratings. Channels then moved games to prime-time television which improved audiences even more. More eyeballs on screens attract eager sponsors wanting to be associated with the game. Not only that, but higher ratings also led to a bidding war between television stations scrambling for the rights to broadcast the game. Ka-ching!

Money, money, money – not only makes the world go around, but it also leads to even better training facilities and attracts the very best in professional coaching. Best of all, it acts as a bargaining chip for players when negotiating for a better pay deal, which is exactly what happened in 2017.

After months of often bitter bargaining – with threats by women cricketers to black-ban the up-and-coming Ashes series – Cricket Australia finally agreed to a revenue-sharing deal over a five-year period. The deal meant women's cricketers for the first time would share in the substantial television broadcast rights paid to Cricket Australia. The deal resulted in a 100% increase in international cricketer payments.

Suddenly, elite women cricketers were being paid $179,000 per annum, plus a minimum retainer for those cricketers granted an Australian contract of $87,609 – an increase of 119% from $40,000. State cricketers, too, enjoyed a big pay boost of 148% from $11,000 per year to $27,287 as a result of the deal, while Women's Big Bash League players saw a 65.5% increase in their pay packets in the final year of the new Memorandum of Understanding to $11,584 per annum (from the previous $7000).

CA chief executive James Sutherland was quoted at the time saying that neither side has got everything they wanted out of the negotiations, but "enduring outcomes depend on the needs of both parties being recognised ... and in that spirit I think we have reached a good compromise ... one that will be good for the game and good for Australian cricketers."[220]

As a result of the deal, Australia's international women cricketers no longer needed to pay to play or work outside of the game. With serious money now entering the sport, elite women's cricket is now fully professional and, crucially, it is now able to attract and keep Australia's best female athletes playing the sport.

As mentioned, Ellyse Perry was a gifted international soccer player as a teenager, while Alyssa Healy was initially attracted to hockey as a sport, Australia's current opening bowler Darcie Brown was a South Australian Schools representative in netball, and opener Phoebe Litchfield played hockey for the Australian Under-16 team. Super-star leg spinner Alana King's first love as a young teenager was tennis ... you get the picture. Most of the Australian women's Test squad have multiple sporting talents, but the lure of a professionally administered, lucrative cricket alternative proved irresistible.

Such athletic excellence has another spin-off – elite athletes *understand* excellence. To achieve it, they know they must possess a relentless commitment to everything they do in terms of focused practice and physical preparation. Both of these elements have defined the Australian women's cricket team for over two decades.

Ellyse Perry is typical of Australian player preparations. On a typical training day, Perry packs in three or four high-impact sessions, usually made up of a skills workout, training in the gym, running and recovery. She told online blog *Balance the Grind*:

> *"My week looks different depending on our schedule, but I train most days. I never really count the hours, but it's similar to a full-time job," she says. "Our [national team] training consists of three components: skill work – so batting, bowling and fielding; the physical stuff, like weights and running; and then all the tactical preparation, which is looking at footage and discussing in groups how we want to play a game."*[221]

But then, Perry often goes that little bit further. She once revealed she can perform twenty-seven burpees in a minute, while her workouts focus on core strength, explosive leg power and shoulder stability – all essential elements for one of the greatest all-rounders the women's game has seen. One England commentator reported surprise when, during the 2024 T20 World Cup held in Dubai, he observed Perry wheeling her racing bike into her hotel lift with an attachment to allow her to statically train in her room. The same commentator also expressed astonishment when he observed Phoebe Litchfield fresh off the plane, preparing to open the Australian batting in a 2025 Ashes ODI played in Hobart by sprinting solo around the city's waterfront. As the commentator wrote, "training day or not, (Australian) players take responsibility to be machine-like athletes."[222]

Success, of course, breeds success. As a result, things have only got better for Australian women cricketers, especially in 2024. That's when a deal was again struck to increase the pay packets of domestic cricketers holding either a state or WBBL contract by 66% across the board, with an average income now of $151,000 per player and most earning over $100,000 per year. Cricket Australia also increased the women's national contract list from fifteen to eighteen, and gave them a 25% pay increase. This means the game's highest earners now pocket close to a million dollars per year across all contracts. The weighty pay packets are the result of the success of the Australian team and recognition that the team's success has generated enormous revenue for the sport.

Australia is currently ranked by the International Cricket Council as the top women's team in global rankings, having won more World Cups than all other nations combined (1978, 1982, 1997, 2005, 2013 and 2022). It had similar dominance in the Twenty20 competition, winning the T20 World Cup in 2010, 2012, 2014, 2018, 2020 and 2023. Then at the Commonwealth Games held in Birmingham in 2022, the team won gold by defeating India in the final.

The Australian women have won 12 Test series since 2000, including wins against India in 2004/05, South Africa in 2022/23 and multiple Ashes series including 2001, 2005, 2015, 2017/18, 2019, 2021/22, 2023 and a first-time series clean sweep in 2024/25.

But what of Australia's main sporting rival?

England has clearly not performed to anywhere near the same level as Australia, despite emulating Australia's administrative arrangements and player payment contracts. What makes the difference?

English cricket reporter Henry Moeran writing in *BBC Sports* in January 2025 pointed out that England's last Women's Ashes success came eleven years previously, and the last time they beat Australia in an ICC knockout match was in 2009. As Moeran observed:

> "Eleven tournaments have passed since then, with England's solitary success ... in 2017. Australia, meanwhile, has amassed eight World Cups (T20 and ODI), (plus) a run of Ashes triumphs."[223]

Moeran points to Australia's ability to attract the nation's top female athletes to the sport. In contrast, England's top female sportspeople are more likely to play more lucrative sports such as football (or soccer), therefore limiting the talent pool. While England *has* increased the salaries of its top female cricketers, Moeran contrasts England's chaotic domestic cricketing nursery with Australia's well-resourced and well-established domestic league structure. Up until 2019, England supported a thirty-five-team county competition of varying standard. This was replaced in 2020 with an eight-team regional competition that has since been disbanded to be replaced by ... something. Not sure what, though – or when.

Despite all the chaos, England still manages to produce world-class players: Sophie Ecclestone, Heather Knight and Nat Sciver-Brunt to name three. But still, they fall short in the big matches. Moeran believes that's to do with the Australians' ruthless focus on physical fitness which leads to high performance on the field. He quotes Australia's current Under-19s coach Kristen Beams: "There's always another edge or another way we want to go about it, whether that's athleticism, or the way that they're working on [their] strength."

Moeran concludes that, over the last decade, England was not remotely as dominating as Australia physically. Australia's physicality means they save dozens of runs in the field and take the catches that need to be taken. Even the England coach Jon Lewis admitted: "I would say yeah they are, they're a much more athletic team than us, they're more agile, they look faster, at times they look more powerful." They also "consistently show game intelligence, that seems to be ingrained as cricketers from an early age, and [that's] something sorely missing from England."[224]

An inability to attract top female sporting talent to the women's game, a lack of physicality and poor game intelligence may explain, in part, Australia's domination over England in recent times. But perhaps there is also something more profound at play here. Perhaps the unique and historic interplay between race and class in Britain has restricted the talent pool from which England's elite female cricketers are selected.[225]

# 21

# 2024/25, An Ashes Clean Sweep
'Why is England so Shit?'

February 1, 2025. Australia completed a historic Ashes whitewash when they beat England in a day-night Test at the Melbourne Cricket Ground – the first women's Test played at the 'G since 1948/49 – and they did it inside three days.

A record women's Test crowd of 35,365 across three days was entertained with a record-breaking 163 by Annabel Sutherland in Australia's first innings – her third in Tests – and Beth Mooney's maiden Test century of 106 in the same innings. As great as these two performances were – the two batters are the first women to score a century on the famous ground – their heroics were eclipsed by a couple of Australian spin bowlers late on the third day.

First, there was the masterly display of leg-spin bowling by Alana King who finished with 5/53 in England's second innings, giving her match figures of 9/99 off 46.4 overs. Her Test-winning performance meant she was the second woman to have her name etched into the MCG Honour Board for achieving a 5-wicket haul in an innings. The first was that leg-spinning wizard Peggy Antonio who snared a 6/69 against England in the third Test of a three-game series back in 1935.

As with Antonio, King put on a clinic on the last day of the Melbourne Test. Bowling from the Shane Warne-end throughout, she regularly fizzed balls past the edge of the English women's bats and beat them with wrong-uns and flight. Defending and hoping for a loose ball was useless. King was on the money from the start, runs were scarce, plays and misses the norm. But it was the ball that bowled England's Sophia Dunkley in England's second innings that got the whole world talking.

King pitched the ball well outside leg-stump; Dunkley lunged forward trying to play down the line. But the super-revving ball landed, spun prodigiously and clipped Dunkley's off stump. Unplayable! Sitting in the stands watching King weave her magic was thrilling. I saw Shane Warne's hat-trick against England at the same ground in 1994, but Alana King's performance was equally as spectacular.

But it takes two to tango. Enter Ashleigh Gardner.

The Australian quicks had not particularly troubled the English top order in the first session of play on day three, but it was after the break – with England at 2/100 – when the real damage was done. Gardner was the first of the spinners into the attack, closely followed by King. I would argue the next two hours of play produced possibly the greatest display of partnership spin bowling ever seen at the MCG.

Gardner provided the pressure while King produced the pyrotechnics. They both got wickets – *lots* of wickets. In two hours of spellbinding spin-bowling, Gardner and King broke the back and spirit of the English batters. In just 60 balls, England lost 5/18, with Gardner finishing with the astonishing figures of 25 overs, 11 maidens and 4 wickets for 39. The Ashes clean sweep was now assured.

Gardner's Melbourne bowling performance was, in a way, the cherry on top of an Ashes series that saw her rescue Australia from a possible ODI defeat in the third of the 50-overs series played in Hobart. Coming in on a slow pitch with Australia teetering at 4/59, the all-rounder proceeded to demolish a dangerous English attack with a powerful and flawless run-a-ball 102.

With able support from a Beth Mooney half century and a couple of hard-hitting cameos from Tahlia McGrath and Georgia Wareham, Australia was able to post a formidable total of 8/308, setting up a thumping 86-run win over the old rival.

Oh, and Ashleigh Gardner also happened to take the catch of the series in the same Hobart match: fielding on the boundary, she launched herself at a Sophie Ecclestone hoick off Alana King and caught the ball with one hand just inside the rope. Fearing she would stumble over the boundary and, with one motion, she threw the ball forward and re-caught it just before it hit the ground. Extraordinary! King's 5/62 for the match was also amazing. Although Alana King was rightly named the player of the Ashes series, Ash Gardner provided the platform from which King could perform her heroics throughout.

I witnessed first hand the spin-twins' genius a little earlier in the series. On a glorious Melbourne January summer's day, I saw just how important the King/Gardner combination is to Australia's current domination of women's international cricket.

In the second ODI of the Ashes series, played at Melbourne's Junction Oval, Australia had posted a modest total – all out for 180 off 44.3 overs, thanks largely to a sound Ellyse Perry innings of 60 off 74 balls and a couple of cameos by Alyssa Healy and Phoebe Litchfield, both smashing 29 apiece. But once it was Australia's turn to field, the result was never in doubt. Kim Garth did the early damage with a fiery 3/37 off her 10 overs. But then the King and Gardner show took to the stage. Bowling in tandem, Ash Gardner tied up an end (her figures of 1/23 off 10 overs are self-explanatory), while King, in a player-of-the-match performance, picked up 4/25 off her allotted overs – England all out for 159 off 48.1. Amazing stuff.

Alana King, Ashleigh Gardner, Annabel Sutherland, Beth Mooney, Alyssa Healy, Ellyse Perry and more. The greatest Australian women's sporting team of all time, perhaps Australia's greatest sporting team *period*. Compared to England, the Australian team is in another league – not only due to our own amazing players, but also England's deplorable performance in the field. On the Friday of the Test, England dropped 10 catches and gave twenty-three-year-old Annabel Sutherland three lives, including a regulation catch in the gully off the dangerous Sophie Ecclestone. By stumps, she was 135-not-out and the damage was done.

Beth Mooney, the series-leading run scorer, also benefited from England's fielding largesse when she was dropped three times in her first twenty-five deliveries. The English team's ground fielding was almost as deplorable, with balls travelling through and under legs to the boundary, poor throwing and a lack of urgency between overs.

As Andrew Wu writing in the *Age* rightly pointed out, the decision to send the youngest member of the team, twenty-year-old Ryana MacDonald-Gay, to explain the side's worst day of the tour to the press was, well, not thought through. Where was the captain or the coach? It wasn't MacDonald-Gay's responsibility to explain why England had performed so dismally – she was playing in just her first game of the tour. Talk about a lamb to the slaughter! MacDonald-Gay was out of her depth after a game where England was out of their league. Maybe this incident pointed to deeper problems within English women's cricket and cricket in Britain in general.

## *Racism, Sexism and Elitism Define English Cricket*

Exiting the MCG that February evening in 2025, the most common question I heard being asked was, "Why is England so shit?" With a history of English and Australian cricket now under our belts, we have some answers to that question – including England's inability to attract the country's best female athletes, the lack of commitment to a vigorous physical training regime by its players, and poor "game intelligence". But a more fundamental answer to the question asked by Melbourne spectators may have been provided eighteen months earlier in June 2023, when a long-awaited report examining the state of the English game was released.

The Independent Commission for Equity in Cricket (ICEC) compiled the report,[226] and what they found was not pretty. It's headline findings? English cricket was infected by institutional racism, sexism and class-based discrimination. It seemed like nothing much had substantially changed in British cricket for over a century or more. The ICEC was particularly critical of the state of the women's game.

At all levels of women's cricket, players were routinely treated as subordinate to men, meaning women had little or no power, voice or influence within cricket's decision-making structures. As a result, women were often demeaned, stereotyped and treated as second-class citizens.

At the grassroots level, women's subordination played out in many disturbing ways, starting with inequities in accessing playing equipment, grounds to play on and women-friendly facilities. But worse was to come: women cricketers playing at mixed local clubs were often seen as easy prey by their male colleagues. Many were subjected to gross, "laddish", predatory behaviour. At the elite level, the marginalisation of the women's game manifested itself economically. At the time of the report, English women's average salaries were 20.6% of English male players, and funding of the sport grossly favoured the men's game – for every £5 spent on men's cricket, just £1 was allocated to the women's game.

It's no surprise the ICEC also found both men and women's first-class English cricket remained elitist and exclusionary, favouring private school networks within cricket's talent pathways. Look no further for evidence than at the women's Test team in 2025. Four of the eleven players (or approximately 36%) who took to the field in the 2025 Test match attended an elite private school, while two others were educated at select-entry elite grammar schools – a clear over-representation of private school alumnae, given only 7% of the general population is privately educated. Why? A simple matter of class blindness and inequity.

The report discusses

> "the scarce provision of cricket in state schools, the widespread links between cricket and private schools, the cost and time associated with playing youth cricket, the lack of a systematic, contextual process for talent identification, and the relative absence of diversity amongst coaches on the talent pathway: these are all important factors which present significant barriers to an equitable system."

The ICEC found such factors combine to ensure British cricket remains dominated by "private school and old-boy (and girl) networks and cliques that permeate throughout the game to the exclusion of many. The report cites stories of children from state schools who enter cricket pathway programs being called peasants or having their working-class accents mimicked.[227]

It goes without saying that a sport displaying such misogynist and elitist discrimination will have a fundamental problem attracting and retaining players of talent. Why, for example, would a woman tolerate a drunken, slobbering yob feeling her up at the end of day's cricket?

The report was particularly scathing when it touched on cricket's entrenched racism. It highlighted the experience of former Yorkshire player Azeem Rafiq who reported to a Commission hearing that he was a victim of racial harassment and bullying throughout his ten-year tenure at the club.

"Do you believe you lost your career to racism?" asked the ICEC.

"Yes," he said, "I do".[228] Rafiq finished his testimony by telling the hearing that, as a result of his experience at Yorkshire, he would not want his children anywhere near the English game.

There have certainly been some attempts, through programs such as Kwik Cricket, to democratise English cricket – but with limited success, evidently. Even the Marylebone Cricket Club – described by a former celebrity president of the club, Stephen Fry, as a place that "stinks of privilege" – has made programmatic gestures towards those social classes underrepresented in the English game. But are such attempts a form of box ticking?

## *Marylebone Cricket Club and Alsama*

David Talalla is a force of nature. Born in Malaysia but raised in Australia, Talalla was captain and subsequently vice-captain of the Malaysian cricket team debuting in the 1994 ICC trophy in Nairobi. It was there he scored the team's only century for the tournament, 112-not-out against Gibraltar. Talalla played over 100 ODIs for Malaysia, including tours of Africa and Asia, as well as the 1998 Commonwealth Games held in Kuala Lumpur.

A lawyer, Talalla studied and worked in England before landing permanently back in Australia to become what can only be described as a one-man cricket behemoth: a coach, elite level Cricket Australia match referee, umpire, mentor, cricket tour organiser, talent spotter and Marylebone Cricket Club member.

David is also a man with extensive experience and specific expertise in the inclusion and diversity space. I was able to observe first hand in my local community these traits in his capacity as head coach of the female-administered women's team of the community-based Northcote United Cricket Club in inner Melbourne. David is a hands-on coach. Women with limited experience of the game are taught its finer points, such as running between wickets, the high art of the cover drive and square cut. Encouraging and inclusive, David is the antithesis of the elitist, male authority figures described in the ICEC report. So, as man of obvious inclusive principles and also as a member of the MCC, I was interested in his opinion of the ICEC's findings. He pointed me towards a partnership the MCC had with the Alsana Project, a refugee education program that targets displaced school-aged children living in Beirut, Lebanon. This is what I discovered.

The program uses sport, and in some cases cricket, as a platform for learning and the development of leadership skills in children suffering trauma and dislocation stemming from their refugee status. The MCC, through its charitable arm, funds a number of cricketing hubs focused on supporting Syrian refugee boys and girls in Lebanon.

In September 2024, the UN Refugee Agency (UNHCR) officially registered 770,000 refugees from Syria staying in Lebanon. About 60% of Syrian refugee children of school age (approximately 470,000) do not attend school. Whereas the Asana Project is admirable in its aims (which are understandably modest in scope), it can only address the needs of a very limited number of girls and boys.[229] The same is the case when looking at similar MCC Foundation-funded programs based in Britain.

As it did in the immediate post-war period in Britain, the MCC Foundation has reached out to children from the government-funded education system by funding a network of hubs across the UK proving free coaching, match play and support to more than 3000 state-school-educated boys and girls. The MCC's aim is to encourage more children from working-class backgrounds to play the game. Children that demonstrate aptitude for cricket are then encouraged to join local community clubs where, in turn, the most talented are channelled into elite pathway programs. Of course, government-school boy and girl cricketers who manage to find their way into the pathway or development stream may then encounter many of the game's systemic misogynist and elitist issues highlighted by the ICEC report.

There are 9.1 million children attending state-funded schools in Britain as of 2023/24 as compared to approximately 557,000 private school students, but as the findings of the ICEC report illustrate, cricket at all levels of the game (but especially at the first-class, contracted and international spheres, both men's and women's cricket) is over-represented by players from middle-class, white, privately educated backgrounds.[230]

A recent study by Tom Brown of Birmingham City University found that of the specialist male batters that debuted for England since 2011, 95% have been white, while 77% of them have come from private schools. The research further found that of the full cohort of English professional cricketers, those who were white and from a private school background were thirteen times more likely to be granted a county-level cricket contract, despite the fact that only 7% of the school-age population attended an independent fee-paying school. In fact, Brown's report highlights that the English team's batting top order is a more elitist cohort than the House of Lords![231] It may be the case that a similar class bias exists in the English women's Test team.

The MCC has, for over 250 years, been the custodian of a game that has maintained and promoted ideas of white privilege and hegemonic English "values" to the peoples of Britain's Empire. Through the custodianship of the game, the MCC has, to quote Dr Thomas Fletcher from Leeds University, used cricket as:

> "the symbol par excellence of imperial solidarity and superiority epitomising a set of consolidatory moral imperatives that both exemplified and explained imperial ambition and achievement"

Within a majority of British colonies' cricket elites, they quite consciously sought to maintain and promote a specific moral code which revolved around white hegemonic masculinity.[232] The ICEC report highlights the MCC's reliance on its 250-year history as evidence that, as an institution, it is reluctant to change, especially around issues of class and class consciousness.

The report gives as example the traditional annual fixtures of Eton vs Harrow and Oxford vs Cambridge held at "the Home of Cricket" Lord's. It comments:

> "Those who argue for the continuation of the historic fixtures do not seem to understand the damage they are doing to the reputation of the MCC and Lord's in the public's imagination – compounding a view, whether fair or not, that the MCC members are out of touch, elitist and unrepresentative of the wider population and those who play cricket."[233]

There is clearly still a lot of work to do in English cricket before it can say it is truly a representative, inclusive sport welcoming players from all racial backgrounds, social classes and genders. When women's cricket in particular takes itself seriously as a professional sport that incorporates talent over social connection, then maybe it'll stop "being so shit" and challenge Australia as the world's dominant cricketing nation.

But what of Australian women's cricket? Does the women's game face similar challenges as their British rivals?

## *Class-Based Discrimination and Elitism*

Australian women's cricket is not immune to elitism, the scourge of sexism or racial discrimination – perhaps not at the same levels as highlighted in the British ICEC report, but there are issues within the code nonetheless.

Similar enquiries into the state of the women's game in Australia have, for example, pointed to the sociology of class as a barrier to universal access and participation. The Inquiry into Women and Girls in Sport and Active Participation, commissioned by the Victorian State Government in 2015, made the generalised point that "participation rates are lower for women experiencing social and economic challenges regardless of the cause (for example those from culturally and linguistically diverse backgrounds, those with a disability and those from low socio-economic families)."[234]

As discussed earlier, cricket is a relatively expensive sport to play; bats, pads and gloves are all costly. Annual club fees, a weekly match payment and travel costs all create barriers for low-income women and girls' participation. In addition, low-income families have choices to make about their children's sporting activities, and male participation opportunities are often prioritised.[235]

Social class is a key determinate affecting participation in the game by both boys and girls. As social commentator Frank Bongiorno recently observed, Australia may have avoided the worst aspects of British class-snobbery, but it never quite abandoned its taste for hierarchy and class difference. We've just been reluctant to talk about it. Class is present in the women's game in Australia, especially at the elite level. I think our taste for hierarchy and class difference in our education system may go some way to explain it.

Australia likes to think of itself as egalitarian, a place where "Jack is as good as his master" and for some of its history there was arguably some truth to it. Following World War I and through to the 1970s, Australia was one of the most egalitarian countries on the planet. Historian Donald Horne (no, there's no relation), wrote in the 1960s that Australia was a place where there was no possibility of determining status by accent, topics of conversation, clothes or manners. However, over time, and for reasons already canvassed, Australia's egalitarianism has been slowly eroded. Nowhere is this erosion felt more than in Australia's education system.[236]

With the passage of Victoria's Education Act of 1872, Victoria was the first Australian colony and one of the first regions globally to offer free, secular and compulsory education to children – and for a century or more the vast majority of Australia's school-aged children attended their local neighbourhood school. Of course, a minority attended a community-based Catholic School, and an even smaller number of children attended a fee-paying independent college or grammar.

But all of that has changed over the last twenty years or so. The reason for the change is money; fee-paying, independent and religious schools have been funded by state and federal governments between twice and five times the rate of traditional community-based state schools.[237] In the space of just over two decades, Australia's secondary education system now holds the mantel as one of the most segregated in the world.

As in Britain, women cricket players attending well-funded private schools gain an advantage in sport, in particular due to access of better facilities such as well-equipped gyms, superior training facilities including turf wickets and specialised equipment like bowling machines, video cameras and more. Many private schools also provide specialist high-level coaching and intensive match play.

Affluent families are also generally able to grant their child the time, resources and support allowing them to follow their all-consuming passion for the game – such as being part of overseas cricketing tours.

It was David Talalla's Team Sports Travel Company that Melbourne private schools (such as Melbourne's Ivanhoe Grammar, Marcellin College, Caulfield Grammar and Wesley College) engaged to arrange overseas cricketing tours – to Singapore, in the case of Wesley; the UK and Singapore, Ivanhoe; Marcellin travelled to the UK; and a senior team of boy and girl cricketers from Caulfield Grammar travelled to Sri Lanka. Students' families paid several thousands of dollars for the privilege of playing on the first-class grounds of host nations, and experienced specialised coaching held at international-level training facilities. In addition, the tours offered student cricketers leadership and development programs as well as local cultural experiences. Such unique experiences can be life changing for an aspiring cricketer; they help grow their knowledge of the game, develop vital cricketing skills and improve game-day performance. With improved performance comes the possibility of selection into elite cricket pathway programs. It's no surprise that the tours were, as one parent commented, the experience of a lifetime. It's a whole different story in the state-funded school system.

Australian government schools do not universally offer students a cricket program. However, in states such as Victoria, an introductory cricket program is offered in association with School Sport Victoria and Cricket Victoria. Enthusiastic teachers or community volunteers provide coaching, often on community ovals where interschool matches are played. Children who show interest and aptitude are then encouraged to join local, community-based cricket clubs and play regularly on the weekends.

For those government school students who demonstrate particular cricketing ability, they have the option of applying to enrol at one of two low-fee, select-entry, specialist government-funded sports schools: either the Maribyrnong Sports Academy or Rowville Secondary College. At these specialist sports colleges, students study a comprehensive secondary educational curriculum while accessing a full cricket-skills development program overseen by elite coaching staff. Coaching and practice sessions are generally held at local community sports facilities. Student cricketers then play tournaments organised by School Sport Victoria as well as friendly matches against a range of private schools on the manicured cricket ovals of their private school opponents.

While the government schools cricket programs are a huge improvement on eras past, when gifted cricketers such as Betty Wilson learned the basics of the game playing the boys in the street of her neighbourhood community, they can't compare to those offered by the private school system, given the quantum of taxpayer resources that have poured into the sector over the past two decades or more. It goes without saying that such an inequitable school funding system produces differentiated results that favour private schools, especially in the area of sports.[238]

Looking at the Australian women's contracted player list for 2024/25, of the eighteen players where information about school background was available, six attended an elite private school, a further six attended a lower-fee-paying Catholic College, with the balance educated at either a select-entry government-funded sports secondary college or a "normal" government school.[239]

Cricketers from my mother's era would shake their heads in disbelief at the resources and the opportunities now available for women cricketers of talent and motivation. My mother and teammates would, however, certainly recognise the misogyny that is still embedded at all levels of the game. It's a case, once again, of the more things change, the more they stay the same.[240]

A recent study by Melbourne's Deakin University described how young male cricketers often behaved like "emotional Brownshirts" (my words) towards young women cricketers: the report highlights the relentless levels of sexual harassment, misogyny and actual threats of sexual violence experienced by some female cricketers participating in elite pathway programs via mixed teams in country regions.

Up until relatively recently, it was suggested that the best way talented female cricketers could build resilience to the harsh realities of the elite level game was to play in men's community teams. That's often when the trouble started. The Deakin report highlighted just what that trouble looked like:

*"Boys as you know are quite different to girls. I've had some – we had a super talented girl that plays who had an incident where she played senior men's cricket and she got a bloke out. He came off the ground and the boys [jib] him because he went out by the girl and his response is, 'That's alright I'll fuck her up the bum later on'. So that sort of environment. It's a stupid comment by a bloke, but they all laugh and think it's funny." (Coaching staff member).*[241]

In another incident a coach of a country mixed cricket team reported:

*"One of the girls in country Victoria was on a boys' team and was getting bullied by the boys, even to the extent where they were all calling her a lesbian because she played cricket. But then one of the boys sent her a text message and said, 'If you send me nude photos, I'll tell everyone you're not a lesbian'. Now that's horrendous."*[242]

It's of little surprise that the attrition rate of girls was alarming when they reached the end of their junior pathway programs. Something had to be done and the answer was simple: remove the misogynists.

In states such as Victoria, the governing body – in this case, Cricket Victoria – made significant changes to underage player pathway programs in 2023. One of the key changes was to offer female-only elite pathway options to shield girls and young women from the abhorrent sexism of the bright young (and not so young) men of local community clubs.

In Melbourne and in regional areas, elite cricket coaching academies were established specifically for Under-15 girls progressing through their formative year.

These talented players then played female-only representative competitions such as the Country Cup and Marg Jennings Cup. From there, the most talented are selected to play in a Premier Under-18 competition.

The very best Under-18 players then follow the gilded pathway into the state's highest level of club competition, where elite women cricketers are ushered into professional level state representation. From there, it's the Women's Big Bash League and finally a Cricket Australia contract.

The pathway system has been revolutionary, as it takes into account the embedded misogyny in both Australian society and, by definition, the sport of cricket. Apart from perhaps a few coaches and mentors, talented female cricketers need never confront the male sense of entitlement. No longer will they lay awake in the dark and worry about what ugly male sting awaits them the next day on a green and rolling cricket field. Perhaps now women cricketers can be seen as talented sportspeople and not objects for male derision or objectification.

Cricket Victoria's reimagined pathway programs are clearly working: in 2023, Cricket Australia reported an increase of 26%, or 50,377, in the 2022/23 season of women and girls registering to play in local cricket clubs. Clearly the success of the Australian women's team has something to do with the surge. There is also an understanding that the massive increase in women's incomes for those playing in the WBBL competition and for Cricket Australia, courtesy of the new Cricket Australia contracts, means women's cricket is now a viable career option for players of talent.

However, there is one glaring problem that still exists in the women's game: the national team is very white. Alana King and Lisa Sthalekar are possibly the only women of Indian origin to play for Australia, despite the Indian diaspora numbering over one million people in this country. As King told SBS television in Australia recently, while growing up she didn't see a lot of girls like her playing cricket, but now she hoped her example will encourage more women and girls from the South Asian region to follow her lead and play the game.[243]

But it's not just the South Asian diaspora that is under-represented in the game. Australia is one of the most multicultural nations on earth. Australians identify with over 300 different ancestries, with 29% of its population born overseas and 48% with one parent born overseas.[244] There are well over 1.5 million ethnic Chinese Australians resident in Australia, or 3.5% of the total population – in addition, there are around 150,000 Vietnamese and 120,000 people of Philipino origin. But still Alana King is, at the time of writing, the only woman of colour to hold a Cricket Australia contract.

Putting aside our multicultural community, representatives of the oldest living culture in the world, our First Nations peoples, have seen just two women's representatives at the highest level. Clearly more work is to be done by Australian women's cricket to make it an ethnically diverse game that better reflects the broader population.

It's clear we've come a long way in making women's cricket a fully inclusive sport in Australia. It's equally clear that there's still a long way to go. But cricket authorities are working on it, especially at the grassroots level.

# Conclusion

# A Return to the Village

Women's cricket in Australia and England is typified by periods of rapid growth and high visibility, followed by rapid declines in both participation and public interest. It's been boom and bust for over a century and a half.

We have discussed the role of the Rae family in Bendigo, or Sandhurst as it was then known, in initiating and organising the first official women's cricket match on Australian soil. It was an initiative that came with a tsunami of censor and derision from the Australian press. It was then twelve years before the next official women's game was played, this time in Sydney courtesy of a male ally and coach of women's cricket, FJ Ironside and the Gregory sisters, Nellie and Rosalie. The usual patronising rancour blossomed like blue-green algae. But, slowly, times changed.

In Melbourne, women such as Violet Trott and Agnes McDonnell championed the establishment of the Victorian Ladies Cricket Association in 1905.

Vida Goldstein was not only a leader of the suffrage movement in Australia and international activist for women's rights, but also the Association's first president and vital to the Association's success. By the end of 1905, twenty-one women's cricket clubs had joined the Ladies Cricket League, and their membership boomed. But then all that momentum came to a shuddering halt with the outbreak of war in 1914. Boom and bust.

Between the World Wars, it was women like the well-connected Australian women's cricket captain and administer Margaret Peden and others who got women's cricket re-established in the public eye. Peggy Antonio captured the public's imagination with her beguiling leg-spin – because female journalists like Pat Jarrett at the *Melbourne Herald* fought to tell Peggy's story. Post World War II, it was the heroics of the great Betty Wilson and Una Paisley who once again kick-started interest in women's game. What goes down must come up.

The revitalisation of women's cricket over the years has been driven by extraordinary women in both administrative and player roles. It has taken an enormously sustained effort over almost 150 years for women's cricket in Australia to reach a level of professionalism on a par with the men's game – and it will take a similarly sustained effort to keep it there. Addressing the disparities of class and ethnic representation and ensuring equal access to gender-appropriate facilities and grounds will be crucial for the continued growth and development of the game.

## *Liddy Clark and the village game*

Australian women's cricket has undergone a boom at the grassroots level in recent years. Of course, the success of the national team has a lot to do with it – young girls and women all over the country savour the histrionics of the WBBL competition and are inspired by the astonishing talent of Ellyse Perry, Meg Lanning, Alyssa Healy, Beth Mooney, Ashleigh Gardner, Tahlia McGrath, Alana King and more. Dedicated women and their male allies all over the country are working hard to accommodate this surge in demand from young and not so young women in playing the game. One woman working hard to accommodate this interest is Liddy Clark. Her aim is to return cricket to the women of the village.

Born in Adelaide at the end of 1953, Liddy soon moved with her family to Melbourne, growing up in the city's leafy south-eastern suburbs, finishing school in 1971. This was when Labor's Gough Whitlam was setting about redefining how we thought about Australia and being Australian. We have discussed his women's reformist agenda, but Whitlam's plan was also aimed at ensuring all Australians had access to art, culture, sport and entertainment, especially Australian-made entertainment. This was a time that clearly shaped the person Liddy Clark became.

After school, Liddy plunged headlong into a performing career, joining the Melbourne Theatre Company as a repertory actor soon after leaving school. This led to a significant career in television drama and film that then morphed into a role with the Entertainment Arts Alliance as an Industrial Officer. From there, she made the huge leap into state politics as an Australian Labor Party candidate.

In 2001, she won the previously safe Queensland Liberal seat of Clayfield for the Party under the Premiership of Peter Beattie. She was re-elected in 2004 and briefly served as the Minister for Indigenous Affairs in the third Beattie government, but lost her seat, standing as she was in the most marginal electorate in the state in 2006.

Clark moved back to Melbourne and settled in the northern inner-city suburb of Clifton Hill. She now lives just a few hundred yards from where Betty Wilson practised her cover-drives under a streetlamp, and a kilometre away from where Peggy Antonio made shoeboxes.

Like most of Melbourne's inner-city, Clifton Hill has gentrified. The old factories and warehouses are now transformed into "desirable studio living" apartments and the once-empty, dusty Collingwood streets are now filled with Teslas and Range Rovers. Clifton Hill's Victorian and Edwardian-era workingmen and women's terraced cottages, once considered slum housing, are now worth millions.

But Clifton Hill remains a secluded piece of Melbourne history that is at once divided by the Hoddle-Punt corridor, the city's only north-south arterial route, a railway line, the Merri Creek and the Yarra River to the south and Queens Parade to the north. Melbournians don't go there; in fact, most of the city's population doesn't know Clifton Hill exists.

But they should. The factories, tanneries and refineries have long gone, its quarry-turned-tip is now verdant, rolling parklands and the Merri Creek and Yarra River, once polluted drains, are now free-flowing waterways bordered by revegetated bushland alive with careering, colourful birdlife.

It was in the rolling parklands of Clifton Hill that Liddy Clark happened to be walking one Sunday afternoon when she noticed a group of women playing cricket.

Curious, she asked a local what was going on. It turns out the men's Clifton Hill Cricket Club was hosting a four-week cricket training program for interested women cricketers. Liddy was interested. Even though she had never played the game, except for the occasional hit in the backyard at Christmas, she thought she'd give it a go. She enjoyed the experience so much she wanted to unravel the game's ontology, but she could only do that if there was an actual women's team she could join. So, in 2010, she fronted the blokes at the Clifton Hill Cricket Club with the idea of extending the four-week training program into an ongoing Clifton Hill women's team.

The club agreed. Calls went out for interested players and the response was overwhelming: mothers came with their daughters, aunts with their nieces, and over time a team came together. Libby was made the inaugural captain.

> *"I didn't have a clue what I was doing. In one of our first games, I noticed before play that the opposition captain called her team into a huddle, so I did the same ... bring it in, bring it in! With the team surrounding me I said ... I've got no idea what to tell you but that's what the other team is doing so I guess my message to you is ... let's – I dunno – win! Yay!"*

And the Clifton Hill women did win, often. Over the next few years, they took home multiple premierships. They did it with talent nurtured by one or two male coaching allies and by forming a tight community of women amongst what was an established men's club. Liddy writes:

> *"I tried hard to fit into the club's expectations. I emulated the men's team by giving each player a nickname and tried to get as many of our players to hang around the clubrooms after the game and have a drink ... But some of the women had kids and needed to get home as quickly as possible, especially after spending a long afternoon on the cricket field. We had players that were still at school, while others felt uncomfortable drinking with the blokes, speaking publicly and generally conforming to the dominant male club culture. Over time I could see there were a few problems ... so I stopped trying so hard. I realised it was difficult for women to integrate comfortably into what was previously an all-male sporting club."*

It all came to a head when some of the veteran players couldn't understand why the women's team had priority over the use of the club's home ground on Sundays – Sunday being game day for women's cricket – rather than the men.

> "It became obvious that while many of the members of the Clifton Hill women's team could meet the blokes on their own terms, others struggled. As much as I appreciated Clifton Hill giving our women's team the opportunity to play the game, I decided that it was best for all concerned if I moved on."

But Liddy was not done with the game:

> "I heard good things about the Northcote United Cricket Club,[245] so I contacted them about forming a women's team. They were keen. Almost from the start I felt welcomed and supported. They 'got' what I was on about. We wanted to join a club that was inclusive, where players new to the game would not face judgement but rather were encouraged to improve ... where all players, young and older, were able to play cricket in an environment where they could feel comfortable and supported. I knew my time was up as a player, so I took on the team manager role. But I needed some help."

Liddy recruited the help of the ubiquitous David Talalla. She saw David's role as head coach, where he would not only teach players crucial cricketing skills but also offer game-day technical and tactical advice as well as mentoring women into coaching and leadership roles. It was a role he was happy to take on. Liddy explained:

> "We play in Melbourne's Eastern Women's and Girl's Cricket Association, where one of our opponents is awkwardly Clifton Hill! Our home ground is Alphington Park a superb oval on the banks of the Yarra River ... It's a place that was once home to the Wurundjeri-Willum people of the Woiwurrung language group, the traditional custodians of Naarm (or Melbourne) for over 65,000 years."[246]

*Northcote women post match at Albert Park.*

I visited Alphington Park to watch the Northcote women play a couple of games throughout the year. Each time I parked my car at the far end, behind the changerooms and near the community barbeques where local men sipped beers and women balanced a chardonnay and discussed house prices and superannuation. The only thing missing was a bookie taking bets. But I came for the cricket, not lunch or idle talk.

Northcote was playing Clifton Hill, the same team many of the Northcote women had played for the previous season; a cause for friction perhaps between the two teams? I saw no hostility; I saw the batting team sprawled like picnickers on the lawns in front of the players pavilion and Liddy encouraging her niece who happened to play for Clifton Hill. There was competition, but there was calm and friendship, a lot of smiling and good cricket set against a painterly, community setting.

It was a scene that reminded me of the stories my mother told of her playing days; the rivalry with Collingwood, Clarendon and Raymond. She played to win and played well, but not at all costs. After the game, rivals talked, friendships were earmarked and worked out over time. Invitations were made and accepted to play picnic games on straw-coloured cricket grounds on the banks of the Yarra in Eltham. Between innings, the billy was boiled and the sausages cooked while hands trailed in

*Alexander and Nesta Horne. Summertime in Eltham.*

the river and all thoughts of work and economic struggle disappeared into the blue, green canopy of red gums waving in the warm, summer breeze.

The season went well for Northcote United. They won 7 out of 12 matches in their inaugural season, finishing the year in second place on the ladder. By any count the team – consisting variously of a paediatric surgeon, a head of paediatrics at a major Melbourne hospital, a teacher and teacher's aide, a political advisor to a Federal parliamentarian, a PhD candidate, a social worker, a teacher, a housing loans broker, a business analyst, a student and a full-time mother – had progressed well by year's end. By round eight, Northcote held an even four win/loss ratio, but then won the next three games on the trot, before being knocked out in the first week of the finals.

Women's cricket has surely returned to the village where it all started 300 years before. But today, with more investment in women's cricket, coupled with broad societal change, the cricket played looks and feels very different from when Betty Wilson, Peggy Antonio and my mother were making their way in the game. Today, cricket is a more inclusive and welcoming sport for women and in the post #MeToo era, many more women have agency and independence to play the game they love. It's important, therefore, that the sport makes the new wave of women entering the game feel safe and supported. Reflecting on the Australian experience, cricket's governing authorities have introduced a range of protocols and policies that deliver greater safeguards for female cricketers, including gender diversity directives, flexible uniform standards and codes of conduct that stipulate zero tolerance of sexual harassment within grassroots clubs. In addition, there are now greater opportunities for players to develop both their cricketing and life skills through coaching and leadership roles within clubs. In some cases, private travel companies offer well-resourced grassroots players unique cricketing and personal growth experiences overseas.

My mother, living with her father, three brothers, husband and young son, would look at the opportunities available to some young women cricketers of today in wonder, while brushing away cobwebs and waiting for the washing copper to boil. The village game has certainly travelled a long way from Smith's Paddock in Northcote or the Yarra Bend Parklands of Collingwood. What are the challenges that lay ahead for the women's game, especially in Australia?

As Frank Bongiorno said, we in Australia may have avoided the worst aspects of British classism and snobbery, but we have never quite abandoned our taste for elitism and class hierarchy; women's cricket at the elite level remains largely a mono-cultural sport, played by women of relative privilege. Having said that, things are changing for the better, and that change is being driven upwards from the grassroots.

Cricket Australia reports that in just one year (2022–23), there was a 26% increase to 50,377 in registered participation by women and girls in cricket programs. Even more pleasing, Cricket Australia reports a 60% increase in five-to-twelve-year-old girls registering for club or Big Blast cricket programs from South-Asian backgrounds.[247] In addition, in many Australian areas such as Melbourne's less affluent outer-northern and western suburbs, there are a number of thriving women's cricket clubs offering Master Blaster programs and team-based competition to sub-teenage girls right through to U-16. From there, girls transfer into the senior female ranks of the sport. Surely, with more girls and women from both multicultural and less affluent backgrounds playing cricket at the grassroots level, such diversity will eventually be reflected in national and international player profiles – let's hope so. But for that to happen, there still remains a lot of important work to do.[248]

Australian women's cricket has seen many transformative moments in recent years: the 86,174 fans packing the MCG for the T20 World cup final and the 2024/25 Ashes clean sweep over England, which both demonstrated (once again) why Australia's women's team is simply the best in the world. But to maintain Australia's pre-eminence in the women's game, it is vital the sport continues to strive to be fully inclusive – to be a game that empowers impassioned, cricket-loving women and girls to reach their full potential, no matter their family origin, what school they went to, or in what postcode they live.

# *Acknowledgements*

The idea of this book came when I was walking along the banks of Birrarung Marr in Fairfield, Naarm, with Hilary McPhee. I was describing how my sixteen-year-old mother swam and easily won a mixed-sexes, open-age mile challenge back in the 1930s when the river was known as the Yarra. The race started and finished at Deep Rocks swimming hole, the place where Hilary and I sat watching the brown water boil and slide towards Dights Falls just around the bend – the very same place where Mum's ashes are now sprinkled. As the sun warmed our backs, I told Hilary about my mother's remarkable sporting career as a cricketer, baseball pitcher, street footballer, you name it. But my mother had the misfortune to live as Richard Flanagan said of his mother; 'at a time that wouldn't allow her to be who she really was'. Hilary encouraged me to write about her, to tell the world just who Nesta Williams was, and for that I thank her.

I also thank David Tenenbaum of Melbourne Books for once again taking a punt on my idea. I thank my editor, Georgia Cooper; her advice, patience and good judgement made this a much better book than it otherwise may have been. Holly Lambert has designed an engaging and highly readable book, so thank you, Holly. Thank you also to Belinda Clark for her extraordinarily supportive foreword, along with David Talalla, whose support, encouragement, advice and comment is also much appreciated.

Thanks also to Liddy Clark, who introduced me to the new world of community women's cricket. Liddy has been nothing but supportive and encouraging, and her advice has been invaluable. Thank you to Margret RoadKnight, who read an early draft of the manuscript, corrected spelling and grammar, and said of the book: 'it could be a winner'. Thank you to the *Age* newspaper, the Bradman Museum, the Australian Sports Museum, the Melbourne

Cricket Club Library, the National Library, the State Library of Victoria, as well as the Port Melbourne Historic Society for their enormous support with photos and historic documents. Thanks also to Hamish Jones at Cricket Victoria.

A special thanks and appreciation to my sister-in-law, Jen Doherty, and her eagle eyes; my wife Karen, for her support throughout; and our children, Alex and Dylan. Finally, to my brother Peter, who filled in a lot of gaps, corrected errors of fact, and was able to share with me warm memories of our mother's unconditional love.

# *Endnotes*

1. Andrew Lemon, The Northcote Side of the River, 1983, p213
2. Light, Robert: http//www.cambridge .org/core. University of Warwick
3. Light, R: op. cit.
4. Duncan, Isabella: Striking the Boundary. Source: Isabelle Duncan, Skiting the Boundary, The Robson Press, May 1, 2013
5. Heyhoe Flint, Rachael, Rheinberg, Netta Fair Play, the story of women's cricket, Angus and Robertson, London ,1976,  p14
6. Duncan, Isabella: op. cit.
7. Heyhoe Flint, Rachael, Rheinberg, Netta, op. cit. P15
8. ibid p.16
9. Light, Robert, op. cit.
10. Light, Robert, op. cit.
11. Boyce, James Imperial Mud, The fight for the Fens, Icon Books, London, 2020, p, 18
12. Land Management Magazine, A Short History of Enclosure https://www.thelandmagazine.org.uk/articles/short-history-enclosure-britain
13. England's forests: A brief history of trees, The Guardian July 27, 2013
14. Howitt, Mary and autobiography online resource https://archive.org/details/maryhowittautobi00howi/page/n21/mode/2up?view=theater
15. Land Management Magazine, op. cit.
16. Piketty, Thomas, Capital, Harvard University Press, 2014 (http://piketty.pse.ens.fr/files/Lindert86.pdf) p, 1140
17. Dr Thomas Fletcher The making of English cricket cultures: Empire, globalisation and (post) colonialism Paper accepted by Sport in Society, Leeds University. Of course, notions of fair play and sportsmanship were a remarkable case of early British gaslighting especially when viewed from the prism of Britain's record as rulers of their Empire.  In India British rule is seen as an exercise in opportunism, violence and shameless, heroic greed. British administrations blew Indian rebels from canons, massacred unarmed protesters and forced farmers to grow cash crops like cotton and opium rather than food while millions died of starvation. On the Australian frontier tens of thousands of Australian First Nations peoples were murdered, dispossessed and marginalised while in Kenya, Mau Mau rebels were massacred at will. Meanwhile in every corner of the British Empire the 'imperial gift' of institutional racism became entrenched in their societies.
18. Light, Rob, op.cit.
19. https://www.worldhistory.org/Storming_of_the_Bastille/
20. https://amp.theguardian.com/news/2017/sep/07/how-the-aristocracy-preserved-their-power
21. Bradley James Dr., Cricket, Class and Colonialism, PHD thesis awarded by University of Edinburgh, 1991, p 65)
22. Bakkapatnam, Raghu: https://www.theroar.com.au/2017/10/23/when-england-played-as-amateurs-and-professionals/
23. For further discussion of Srdjan Vucetic's argument see his paper published in  National Identity and British Foreign Policy, 2020, University of Plymouth, 17-19 June 2020 p1-61
24. https://dokumen.pub/the-willow-wand-some-cricket-myths-explored-2nd-revised-1854107291.html
25. We will discuss the famous Body Line Series in Australia in more detail in further chapters.
26. Heyhoe-Flint, Rheinberg, op.cit.
27. ibid p.17
28. ibid p.17
29. ibid p21-22
30. ibid p18
31. Howitt, Mary opcit
32. https://blog.britishnewspaperarchive.co.uk/2019/07/16/july-2019-early-history-of-womens-cricket/
33. ibid
34. Heyhoe-Flint, Rheinberg, op.cit. p23-4
35. ibid, p24
36. ibid, p.24
37. https://www.lords.org/lords/news-stories/women-s-cricket-evolution/
38. Heyhoe-Flint, Rheinberg, op.cit. p 25
39. ibid, p26
40. ibid, p26/7
41. Nicholson, Rafaelle :Like a man trying to knit?: Women's Cricket in Britain, 1945-2000, PHD thesis, Queen Mary College, University of London, July 2015.
42. ibid
43. Thompson E.P., op. cit.
44. The Rights of Man proposed that popular, political revolution is permissible when a government does not safeguard the natural rights of its people. Paine called for the abolition of monarchical rule in favour of a parliamentary system elected on the basis of universal adult suffrage. He also advocated for social equity for all citizens through the introduction of a living wage for workers, subsided education for children and income support for the sick, unemployed and the aged. It's little wonder that The Rights of Man resonated, not only with the emerging industrial working class of Britain, but democratic

| | | | |
|---|---|---|---|
| | movements all over the world, including France and America. | 77 | Of course, one or two female felons found Australia to be a redemptive place. Esther Abrahams for example was sentenced to 7 years transportation to Australia for stealing lace. She turned her misfortune into a triumph when she met and married the New South Wales Lieutenant Governor George Johnson and died a wealthy landowner in 1846. Let's not forget the horse thief Mary Reibey who founded the Bank of New South Wales in her house. However most female convicts and free settlers were not so lucky. |
| 45 | Thompson E.P., op. cit., p,605 | | |
| 46 | Thompson E.P., op. cit. p 746-60 | | |
| 47 | Light, op. cit. | | |
| 48 | ibid | | |
| 49 | ibid | | |
| 50 | ibid | | |
| 51 | According to Light this commercial model later found expression in the development of league cricket in England; a semi-professional form of the game centred on local clubs mainly drawn from small to medium sized mill towns of the Midlands. It could also be argued that the Clarke's commercial model has re-emerged in the professional competition of the Indian Premier league (IPL) and various other professional cricket franchises such as the Australian Big Bash League and the recent British innovation the Hundred. All are proving to be enormously popular and lucrative throughout the cricketing world. | | |
| | | 78 | Wright, Clare, op. cit. p, 130/31 |
| | | 79 | https://www.chartistancestors.co.uk/chartism-in-australia/ |
| | | 80 | https://www.abc.net.au/news/2019-09-29/political-convicts-chartists-made-australian-democracy/11520622 |
| | | 81 | Zedda-Sampson Louise, Bowl the Maidens Over, LZS Press, 2019 p5/6 |
| | | 82 | ibid, p15 |
| | | 83 | ibid, p28 |
| | | 84 | Heyhoe- Flint, Rheinberg, op.cit. p, 90 |
| | | 85 | Zedda-Sampson Louise, op.cit. p,32/3 |
| | | 86 | Ibid46 |
| | | 87 | ibid, p, 45. |
| 52 | Howitt, Mary op. cit, | 88 | ibid, p, 45 |
| 53 | Howitt, Mary op. cit, | 89 | ibid p, 61-63 |
| 54 | Hughes, Robert, The Fatal Shore, Collins Harvill, London , 1987 | 90 | Bolton, Fiona, Bonsor Matt Clearing the Boundaries, The rise of Australian women's cricket, Churchill Press, 2020 p, 12 |
| 55 | ibid p 174 | | |
| 56 | ibid p.24 | 91 | op.cit, p,12 |
| 57 | Howitt, Mary op.cit p. 123 | 92 | Heyhoe-Flint, Rheinberg, op.cit. p, 94 |
| 58 | Hughes, op.cit p. 29 | 93 | https://www.theguardian.com/world/2018/nov/11/women-first-world-war-taste-of-freedom |
| 59 | Thompson op.cit. p.65/6 | | |
| 60 | Hughes, op.cit. p73) | 94 | Nicholson, op.cit. p,19 . |
| 61 | Ibid, p24 | 95 | ibid, p16. |
| 62 | ibid, p25 | 96 | Stell, Marion Dr, The Bodyline Fix: How women saved cricket, University of Queensland Press (UQP) St Lucia Queensland, 2022 |
| 63 | Hughes, p163 | | |
| 64 | Ibid, p168 | | |
| 65 | Callil, Carmen Oh Happy Day, Those times and these times, Jonathan Cape, London, 2020, p137) | 97 | Nicholson, Raf, op.cit. p,13 |
| | | 98 | Haigh, op. cit. |
| | | 99 | In articles and books about Peggy she was referred to as the 'Girl Grimmett' in reference to the great Clarence Grimmett – the great Australian leg break and googly bowler credited with inventing the flipper. |
| 66 | https://trove.nla.gov.au/newspaper/article/163805900 | | |
| 67 | Boyce, James 1835, Black Inc. Melbourne, 2011, x111 | | |
| 68 | ibid as quoted in https://overland.org.au/2012/07/melbourne-from-the-falls/ | | |
| | | 100 | https://theconversation.com/revealed-how-women-cricketers-mended-australias-relationship-with-britain-after-bodyline-192601 |
| 69 | https://www.emelbourne.net.au/biogs/EM00029b.htm | | |
| 70 | Batchelder, Alf The First 50 Years of the MCC p,1 https://mcc.org.au/_/media/files/mcc/about-the-club/first-50-years-of-mcc.pdf | 101 | Haigh, op. cit. |
| | | 102 | Stell op.cit, p,11/12 |
| | | 103 | ibid, p,12 |
| 71 | https://amp.abc.net.au/article/100573218 | 104 | ibid, p14. |
| 72 | Golding, Barry, Six Peaks Speak, p,32 https://barrygoanna.com/category/contact-history/ | 105 | ibid, p,14 |
| | | 106 | ibid, p15 |
| 73 | Wright,Clare, The Forgotten Women of Eureka, Text Publishing, Melbourne, 2013, p X1 | 107 | ibid, p15 |
| | | 108 | ibid, p16 |
| 74 | Bradley, J op. cit. p, 60 | 109 | Nicholson, op.cit. quoting A. Davies Leisure, |
| 75 | Nicholson, op. cit. p,12 | | |
| 76 | https://ergo.slv.vic.gov.au/explore-history/colonial-melbourne/everyday-life/women-settlers | | |

|     |     |
| --- | --- |
|     | gender and poverty. Working-class culture in Salford and Manchester, 1900-1939 p 26 |
| 110 | Stell, op.cit, P11 |
| 111 | ibid, p11 |
| 112 | ibid, p,6 |
| 113 | ibid, p,6 |
| 114 | Haigh, op. cit. |
| 115 | ibid, |
| 116 | Richardson, Nick The Conversation February 4, 2022 |
| 117 | https://www.theguardian.com/sport/2023/feb/08/90-years-on-england-bodyline-tactics-retain-heat-australia-ashes-cricket |
| 118 | https://amp.theguardian.com/sport/2023/feb/08/90-years-on-england-bodyline-tactics-retain-heat-australia-ashes-cricket |
| 119 | Richardson, op.cit |
| 120 | ibid |
| 121 | Nicholson, op.cit. .p.10 |
| 122 | Stell op.cit, p,80 |
| 123 | Haigh, op.cit. |
| 124 | Stell op.cit p92 |
| 125 | ibid, p113 |
| 126 | Nicholson, op.cit. p,10 |
| 127 | Haigh, op.cit. |
| 128 | Stell op.cit, p,93 |
| 129 | Nicholson, op.cit. N. p,18 |
| 130 | Stell op.cit. p, 55 |
| 131 | Nicholson, op.cit. p,87 |
| 132 | Stell, pages 110-111 |
| 133 | ibid, p113 |
| 134 | ibid, p 93 |
| 135 | ibid, p99 |
| 136 | Haigh op.cit |
| 137 | ibid |
| 138 | ibid |
| 139 | ibid |
| 140 | ibid |
| 141 | ibid |
| 142 | Stell, op.cit p2/3 |
| 143 | ibid, 2/3 |
| 144 | ibid p100 |
| 145 | ibid, p,100 |
| 146 | Haigh, op.cit |
| 147 | ibid |
| 148 | ibid |
| 149 | ibid |
| 150 | ibid |
| 151 | Nicholson, op.cit |
| 152 | ibid |
| 153 | https://www.oldtreasurybuilding.org.au/work-for-victory/a-womens-world-in-post-war-victoria/ |
| 154 | ibid |
| 155 | Sir Robert Menzies, The Forgotten People's speech May 22, 1942 |
| 156 | This section based on: Harding, Leslie, Morgan Kendrah, Modern Love, The lives of John and Sunday Reed, The Miegunyah Press, 2015 p,70 |
| 157 | Heywood, Michael, The Ern Malley Affair. University of Queensland Press, 1994, p,10 |
| 158 | Harding, Morgan, op. cit. p, 84 |
| 159 | ibid, p,140 |
| 160 | Heywood, op.cit, p.xv |
| 161 | Maggie Nolan The Conversation in August 2024 |
| 162 | https://trove.nla.gov.au/newspaper/article/230578229 |
| 163 | ibid |
| 164 | ibid |
| 165 | https://www.womenaustralia.info/exhib/sg/wilson.html |
| 166 | ibid |
| 167 | ibid |
| 168 | Watling, Sarah Tomorrow Perhaps the Future, writers, rebels and the Spanish Civil War, Vintage 2024 |
| 169 | This section referenced from: Dominic Sandbrook the author of 'Never Had it So Good: A History of Britain from Suez to the Beatles' as quoted in: https://www.nationalarchives.gov.uk/education/resources/fifties-britain/ |
| 170 | Nicholson, Raf Women's cricket during the war, Wisden Almanac |
| 171 | Nicholson, Rafaelle : Like a man trying to knit?: Women's Cricket in Britain, 1945-2000, PHD thesis, Queen Mary College, University of London, July 2015. |
| 172 | ibid |
| 173 | ibid |
| 174 | ibid p 98 |
| 175 | ibid, p,99 |
| 176 | ibid |
| 177 | ibid p,84 |
| 178 | ibid, p.29 |
| 179 | ibid, p74 |
| 180 | ibid p,71 |
| 181 | ibid p, 82 |
| 182 | Nicholson, Raf, Like a man trying to knit p,143 |
| 183 | ibid, p,144 |
| 184 | ibid p142 |
| 185 | Bollen, Bonser op.cit P57 |
| 186 | Nicholson op.cit. p, 104 |
| 187 | https://www.talkinaboutwomenscricket.com/teams/australia/miriam-knee/ |
| 188 | a smokey is a horse racing term meaning under rated by the market |
| 189 | https://sirensport.com.au/cricket/history-makers-anne-gordon-that-76-tour-and-why-the-history-of-womens-cricket-matters/ |
| 190 | https://www.talkinaboutwomenscricket.com/teams/australia/miriam-knee/ |
| 191 | https://www.abs.gov.au/articles/changing-female-employment-over-time |
| 192 | https://www.cricket.com.au/news/3734341/patsy-fayne-womens-odi-cricket-world-cup-1973-nsw-noosa-history-reunion-ca-australia-aca |
| 193 | Nicholson, op.cit. p,144 |
| 194 | https://www.cricket.com.au/news/3734341/patsy-fayne-womens-odi-cricket-world-cup-1973-nsw-noosa-history-reunion-ca-australia-aca |

195 https://sirensport.com.au/cricket/history-makers-anne-gordon-that-76-tour-and-why-the-history-of-womens-cricket-matters/
196 ibid
197 ibid
198 ibid
199 Nicholson, p,146
200 Game details in this chapter were drawn from Bolton and Bonser –Clearing the Boundaries
201 https://www.talkinaboutwomenscricket.com/teams/australia/sharon-tredrea/
202 https://www.afr.com/policy/economy/aspirational-1990s-marked-the-start-of-australia-s-modern-prosperity-20220223-p59z43
203 NOTE: Then in 1997, the Bringing Them Home report by the Australian Human Rights Commission acknowledged and documented the forced removal of First Nations children by governments, these children were referred to as the Stolen Generations. Hundreds of thousands of Australians marched in the streets of major cities, calling for an apology from government and for compensation for the damage inflicted on removed Australians. Hope was palpable that things were about to get better for our First Australians. But then a conservative government was elected in 1997 and First Nations hope shrank to despair. Australia descended into a vicious culture war backed by mining interests and the Murdoch press, a war that still rages today.
204 Clark would eventually go on to score a career 919 Test runs at 45.90 and 4,844 ODI runs at 47.49. She was made captain of the international team at just 23 – and holds the record as Australian captain, leading the side 101 times at a winning ratio of 83 % including captaining Australia in the nations triumphant ICC Women's World Cup tournaments in 1997 and 2005.
205 https://www.cricket.com.au/news/3260852
206 Bollen, Bonser, p95
207 Ibid
208 Ibid, p,96
209 Nicholson, op.cit. p, 221
210 Ibid p, 232
211 Ibid p, 233
212 Ibid p,230
213 Ibid p,231
214 Ibid p,231
215 ibid p,237
216 ibid p,240
217 Bollen, Bonsor, op.cit p,124
218 ibid
219 Andrew Wu Healy ticking all the boxes except one, The Age March 8, 2025
220 The Age January 1, 2018
221 https://balancethegrind.co/daily-routines/ellyse-perry-daily-routine/
222 https://www.bbc.com/sport/cricket/articles/c04nepk34pdo#:-:text=Increased%20funding%20%3D%20increased%20success,to%20%22female%20friendly%22%20infrastructure
223 https://www.bbc.com/sport/cricket/articles/c04nepk34pdo
224 https://www.bbc.com/sport/cricket/articles/c04nepk34pdo
225 Nicholson, op.cit, p, 236
226 https://theicec.com/
227 https://theicec.com/
228 https://www.aljazeera.com/sports/2023/6/27/english-cricket-racism-sexism-elitism-widespread-icec-report
229 Britain entered into a secret pact with France in 1916 to share in a carved up of the Ottoman Empire's Middle-Eastern oil-rich territories at the end of World War Known as the Sykes-Picot Agreement, it resulted in Britain establishing mandates in Iraq, Jordan and parts of Palestine, while the French took modern –day Syria, Lebanon, and parts of northern Iraq as well as southern Turkey. It could be argued that the current refugee crisis in the Middle East and the misery on display in Beirut can be traced back to the 1916 Agreement. Perhaps the MCC's involvement in the Alsama program is also in someway an acknowledgement that Britain used cricket as an instrument of Empire to promote hegemonic notions of white, British supremacy and racial hierarchy that legitimised Britain's naked power grab of Middle Eastern oil states.
230 https://www.antlearning.co.uk/statevsprivateschoolsintheukcomparativeguide/#:-:text=What%20Are%20State%20Schools?,percent%20go%20to%20state%20schools.
231 https://www.abc.net.au/news/2022-01-20/is-english-crickets-class-problem-behind-their-ashes-defeat/100762798
232 Dr. Thomas Fletcher The making of English cricket cultures: Empire, globalisation and (post) colonialism Paper accepted by Sport in Society.
233 https://www.bbc.com/sport/cricket/66045095.amp
234 https://sport.vic.gov.au/resources/inquiry-into-women-and-girls-in-sport-and-active-recreation
235 ibid.
236 Today in Australia, the top 20 per cent of Australians control 50 per cent of the wealth and the bottom 20 per cent just 5 per cent. The reason for this is simple. Australia has abandoned its once lauded egalitarianism in favour of what I will call a neo-liberal, free market heroin. From the 1980s and beyond, Australia has enthusiastically turned its back on its' traditional Scandinavian style collectivism in favour of a seductive dream of weightless, individualised entitlement. Consequently, public services that once, as the name suggests, served the public have now been sold-off to serve the interests of shareholders, or other privileged members of society. The coun-

try's education system was one of them. https://povertyandinequality.acoss.org.au/news/new-data-shows-wealth-gap-widening/

237   A recent report by the Commonwealth Parliamentary Library revealed that on a real dollar, per student basis, combined recurrent funding from Commonwealth, state and territory governments to independent (elite) schools increased 34.04 per cent from 2012-2021, while spending increased 31.17 per cent to Catholic (private) schools. Additionally private schools have an ability to charge students unlimited tuition fees – elite independents charge Year 12 students upwards of $50,000 per year.  In contrast, during the same period, government schools received a funding increase of just 16.174 per cent. https://www.theguardian.com/australia-news/2022/feb/16/private-school-funding-has-increased-at-five-times-rate-of-public-schools-analysis-shows

238   ibid

239   ibid

240   It appears that players with either an independent or Catholic private school background are over represented in the current Australian women's squad. This is based on the percentage of students enrolled in schools across Australia where, approximately 19.9 per cent attend a Catholic school, 16.7 per cent attend an Independent college while 63.4 per cent are enrolled at a government funded secondary school.

241   https://dro.deakin.edu.au/articles/report/The_professionalisation_of_Australian_women_s_cricket_new_times_and_new_opportunities/20878087

242   ibid

243   https://www.sbs.com.au/news/article/alana-king-didnt-see-cricketers-like-her-growing-up-now-shes-an-australian-icon/qlx65gv2z

244   https://humanrights.gov.au/education/stats-facts/statistics-about-cultural-and-racial-diversity

245   The Northcote United Cricket Club recently changed its name to the Alphington United Cricket Club.

246   These were a people who fished Birrarung and the saltwater river, a people who nurtured and hunted on their lands that extended to Mounts Disappointment and Macedon in the north and across to Mount Baw Baw in the east. But by the time of Alphington's white settlement in 1840, the Wurundjeri -willum of the woiwurrung were fast disappearing. https://www.emelbourne.net.au/biogs/EM00029b.htm. Alphington Park exists by an act of dispossession and appropriation, a fact I know well. The park was once a part of my several great grandfather and great uncle's estate dating from 1840.

247   https://www.cricket.com.au/news/3645076/cricket-australia-records-big-uptick-in-female-participation#:-:text=Cricket%20Australia%20census%20numbers%202022%2D23&text=Registered%20participation%20in%20cricket%20clubs,to%2050%2C377%20(%2B26%25

248   There has also been a corresponding uptick in the participation of women from diverse back ground playing the women's game in parts of Britain. In Wales for example the percentage of cricket clubs with a women's team has grown from seven percent in 2018 to over 50 percent in 2024. https://connectsport.co.uk/research/equality-and-diversity-driving-cricket-wales-new-strategy#:-:text=The%20percentage%20of%20cricket%20clubs%20with%20a,of%20investment%20into%20this%20area%2C%E2%80%9D%20he%20says.

## *About the Author*

Craig Horne has worked as a public servant, speechwriter, archaeological surveyor and author. He has also pursued a successful parallel career as a musician and singer in the Melbourne scene over the last fifty years. His previous books include a historical work and a trio of music biographies. *Full Corset and Stockings: A history of women's cricket* will be Horne's fifth book with Melbourne Books.

**Previous titles (with Melbourne Books)**
*Daddy Who?: The inside story of the rise and demise of Australia's greatest rock band*
*Roots: How Melbourne became the live music capital of the world*
*I'll Be Gone: Mike Rudd, Spectrum, and how one song captured a generation*
*Line of Blood: The truth of Alfred Howitt*

*Craig Horne receiving his mother's cap at Cricket Victoria, 2025.*